JESUS SPRINGS

JESUS SPRINGS

EVANGELICAL CAPITALISM AND THE FATE OF AN AMERICAN CITY

WILLIAM J. SCHULTZ

The University of North Carolina Press
Chapel Hill

This book was published with the assistance of the
Anniversary Fund of the University of North Carolina Press.

© 2025 The University of North Carolina Press

All rights reserved

Designed by Jamison Cockerham
Set in Scala, Scala Sans, and Avenir Next
by codeMantra

Manufactured in the United States of America

Cover art: "Pew-Eye View of the United States Air Force Academy Cadet Chapel in Colorado Spring." Photograph by Carol Highsmith. Courtesy of the Library of Congress.

LIBRARY OF CONGRESS CATALOGING-IN-PUBLICATION DATA
Names: Schultz, William J. (William John), author.
Title: Jesus Springs : evangelical capitalism and the fate
of an American city / William J. Schultz.
Description: Chapel Hill : University of North Carolina Press,
[2025] | Includes bibliographical references and index.
Identifiers: LCCN 2025015182 | ISBN 9781469689364
(cloth ; alk. paper) | ISBN 9781469689371 (paperback ; alk. paper) |
ISBN 9781469689388 (epub) | ISBN 9781469689395 (pdf)
Subjects: LCSH: Evangelicalism—Colorado—Colorado Springs—History—20th century.
| Evangelicalism—Economic aspects—Colorado—Colorado Springs. | Evangelists—
Political activity—Colorado—Colorado Springs. | Cold War—Influence. | Nationalism—
Religious aspects—Christianity. | Colorado Springs (Colo.)—History—20th century. |
BISAC: RELIGION / Christian Ministry / Evangelism | HISTORY / United States / General
Classification: LCC BR1642.U6 S38 2025 | DDC 270.8/20978856—dc23/eng/20250429
LC record available at https://lccn.loc.gov/2025015182

For product safety concerns under the European Union's General Product Safety Regulation (EU GPSR), please contact gpsr@mare-nostrum.co.uk or write to the University of North Carolina Press and Mare Nostrum Group B.V., Mauritskade 21D, 1091 GC Amsterdam, The Netherlands.

For my mother and father

Contents

List of Illustrations ix

Acknowledgments xi

Introduction: The Garden of the Gods 1

1 THE MIRACLE PLACE 11

2 MAKING JESUS SPRINGS 35

3 A CIVIL WAR OF VALUES 59

4 UPWARD, CHRISTIAN SOLDIERS 91

5 THE INVISIBLE WAR 115

Conclusion: The Sanctuary 139

Notes 145

Bibliography 177

Index 199

Illustrations

Easter sunrise service at the Garden of the Gods   3

Dawson Trotman, Ruth Graham, and Billy Graham at Glen Eyrie   26

James Dobson   51

Protest against Amendment 2 at the Colorado state capitol   72

Gazette Telegraph cartoon about the Colorado boycott   74

United States Air Force Academy Cadet Chapel   97

Ted Haggard   128

New Life Church   137

Acknowledgments

Writing this book was an enormous pain. Painful as it was, however, it also gave me a chance to meet some wonderful people. I'm happy that I now have the opportunity to thank them in print.

All my life I've been blessed with great teachers. Betsy Newmark and Eric Grunden encouraged my love of learning in high school. At the University of North Carolina, John Kasson transformed my idea of what history was; Michael Lienesch introduced me to the fascinating subject of American religion; and the late Roger Lotchin, my thesis adviser, taught me the value of rigorous scholarship. Dan Rodgers, Julian Zelizer, and Judith Weisenfeld gave me much-needed guidance in my first years at Princeton, helping me transform vague enthusiasms into clear ideas. Margot Canaday and Bob Wuthnow, my dissertation readers, always made time for me—and, as I now know, time is the most valuable thing an academic can give. Just as important as the history department's faculty was its staff. Without Judy Hanson, Judie Miller, Kristy Novak, and Jackie Wasneski, I probably would never have finished my degree.

I came to Princeton specifically to work with Kevin Kruse. It was the best decision of my life. Kevin gave me direction, advice, and—most important—reassurance in moments when it was sorely needed. It's been an honor to work with him, and I only hope I can serve my students as well as he served me.

Some strokes of good luck allowed me to navigate the fraught passage between "graduate student" and "academic." As a fellow at the Andrea Mitchell Center for the Study of Democracy, I learned a great deal from Anthea Butler, Jeff Green, Jim Hrdlicka, Gabriel Raeburn, Heather Sharkey, Rogers Smith, and Ronit Stahl. Two years as a lecturer at Princeton gave me a chance to grow more comfortable in the classroom, thanks in particular to the guidance of Beth Lew-Williams. And when the coronavirus brought life to a halt, I was fortunate to find a position at the Charles Warren Center for Studies in American History. There, Kristen Beales, Melissa Borja, Catherine Brekus, Emily Conroy-Krutz, Heather Curtis, Curtis Evans, David Holland, Jim Kloppenberg, Monnikue McCall, Arthur Patton-Hock, and Dan Vaca created a warm, collegial environment that provided the perfect counterbalance to the confusion and uncertainty of the pandemic era. I'm delighted that the past years have given me a chance to meet many of these people outside of Zoom.

I am fortunate to work at an institution that retains its commitment to the scholarly study of religion even as religious studies programs around the country are being devalued. Conversations with colleagues, especially Clark Gilpin, Margy Mitchell, Rick Rosengarten, and Christian Wedemeyer, have been enormously helpful in completing this book. Matt Harris, Stephan Licha, Sarah Pierce Taylor, Anand Venkatkrishnan, and Erin Walsh provided much-needed support and friendship. Emily Crews has been a wonderful conversation partner and has given me the opportunity to try out ideas on the unsuspecting public. I am especially grateful to Curtis Evans, who has been a model colleague and a model scholar. Many thanks as well to the staff and leadership of the Divinity School: Tiffany Annett, Sara Bigger, Bill Geraci, Philip Guzman, Irema Halilovic, Russell Johnson, Jaime Jones, Kate LeBoeuf, Anita Lumpkin, Mimi Maduff, Madison McClendon, Nathelda McGee, Suzanne Riggle, and Jim Robinson.

Working with the students at the University of Chicago has been a privilege. Many of the ideas expressed here first found their articulation in the classroom or in office-hour conversations. There are too many names to thank, but I am particularly indebted to Tyler Ashman, Guillermo Flores Borda, Joel Brown, Greg Chatterley, Sam Gee, Maggie Goldberger, Hannah Ozmun, Erin Simmonds, and Nathan Tucker.

This book benefited enormously from the input of many scholars. Alice Echols, Paul Harvey, Jay Lockenour, and Chris Rein provided useful suggestions as I began exploring the history of Colorado Springs. Bob Loevy graciously shared his unparalleled knowledge of Colorado politics with me. Jen Meredith and Greg Atkins were always willing to discuss "Jesus Springs." For valuable comments and conversations over the years, I thank David Barak-Gorodetsky, Jim Block, Eli Cook, Rebecca Davis, Larry Eskridge, Sarah Barringer Gordon, Darren Grem, Jenn Holland, David Hollinger, Bob Orsi, Anthony Petro, Courtney Rabada, Jeff Scholes, Katherine Stewart, Matt Sutton, Eda Uca, Leah Davis Witherow, Molly Worthen, and Kyla Young, as well as all the participants of workshops at Princeton University, Northwestern University, and the University of Haifa. Special thanks go to Darren Dochuk, who has encouraged my work for years, and to Matt Lassiter and Jon Zimmerman, who provided thoughtful feedback on an early version of this manuscript. Leo Ribuffo, who also read and commented on that manuscript, is no longer with us, and the world is poorer for it. I know I have forgotten some names, and for that I apologize.

Research for this book involved spending the better part of a year living in Colorado Springs. I am grateful to the many residents of that city who shared their thoughts with me, including Angie Adams, Jody Alyn, Jack Beal, Wilson Brissett, Carolyn Cathey, Jeff Cooper, Margi Duncombe, Judy and Dave Finley, John Hazlehurst, Donna Johnson, Les Krohnfeldt, Bruce Loeffler, John Miller, Miles Reese, Nori Rost, Nolan Schriner, Will Stoller-Lee, Bill Sulzman, Deb Walker, and Chuck Zimkas. Jim White provided me with sparkling conversation, often conducted over excellent food and wine. Steve Rabey's knowledge of Colorado Springs and of religious history was a tremendous help. Richard Skorman generously shared his thoughts on local politics, and his restaurant/bookstore Poor Richard's made a wonderful place to take a research break. A long conversation with Patton Dodd helped me see Colorado Springs, and modern evangelicalism, in a new light. Mary Elizabeth Ruwell not only guided me through the special collections at the Air Force Academy but also (along with her family) opened her home to me on Thanksgiving, for which I will always be grateful.

Research, like most things, does not go far without money. A grant from the (sadly defunct) Institute for the Study of American Evangelicals let me spend a week browsing the collections at Wheaton College. Research trips to Colorado Springs were made possible by grants from the History Project at Harvard and the Charles Redd Center for Western Studies at Brigham Young, as well as by an Albert J. Beveridge Award from the American Historical Association. Princeton's Center for the Study of Religion provided me not only with funds but also with a valuable intellectual community. A Phil Zwickler Memorial Research Grant from Cornell University and a Donald J. Sterling Jr. Fellowship from the Oregon Historical Society allowed me to do research at important collections in Ithaca and Portland. Research funds from the University of Chicago Divinity School, in particular an Anthony C. Yu Junior Faculty Fellowship, made possible some eleventh-hour research that had a significant impact on the final version of this book.

Money only gets you to the archives. Once there, you put your faith in the archivists—and in my case that faith has always been rewarded. There are too many people to thank individually, but I need to praise the staff of the Special Collections of the Pikes Peak Public Library District, especially Erinn Barnes, Tim Blevins, Dennis Daily, Heather Jordan, Chris Nicholl, and Bill Thomas; the staff of the Christian and Missionary Alliance headquarters, especially Jen Rohde; the staff of the Western History Collection of the Denver Public Library; the staff of the Colorado State Archives in Denver; Susan Finley and Patrick Kochanasz at the Navigators Archives; Jessy Randall and the staff of the Special Collections at Tutt Library; Laura Fuller at the Pioneer Museum's Starsmore Center for Local History; Mary Rupp at the Special Collections of the University of Colorado at Colorado Springs; Teresa Hedgpeth at the United States Olympic Committee archives; Tonia Shaw and Clare Davis at the Young Life Archives; the staff of the Seeley G. Mudd Manuscript Library; the staff of the Stephen H. Hart Library and Research Center; the staff of the Billy Graham Center Archives, especially Bob Shuster; the staff of the Oregon Historical Society; the staff of Cornell University's Special Collections; and the staff of the Clark Special Collections Branch at the United States Air Force Academy, especially Mary Elizabeth Ruwell. Jean Truty of Every Home for Christ, Duane Birkey of Reach Beyond (formerly HCJB), and Donna Johnson of the Pikes Peak Justice and Peace Commission provided additional material. I am also greatly indebted to the many people connected with the Gay and Lesbian Archives of the Pacific Northwest, especially Pat Young. Thanks go to Alexander Callaway for conducting proxy research in the depths of the pandemic and to Maggie Kurkoski for her invaluable help in finding images.

The University of North Carolina Press has been a delight to work with. Every scholar should be so lucky to have the kind of support I received from Thomas Bedenbaugh, Julie Bush, Erin Granville, Tara Jordan, Elaine Maisner, Mark Simpson-Vos, Lindsay Starr, and the rest of the staff at UNCP.

Friendship has made life sweet even in the midst of challenges (this book included). Graduate school was so much more bearable when shared with friends like Vaughn Booker, Sarah Coleman, Dylan Gottlieb, Tikia Hamilton, Reut Harari, Molly Lester, Kathryn McGarr, Ingrid Ockert, Ronny Regev, Sean Vanatta, Marc Volovici, and David Walsh. Special thanks go to the "Nerd Night" crew of Flori Pierri, Alexis Siemon, Christina Welsch, and Bing Zheng, with whom I enjoyed many a terrible anime. Jan van Doren was a wonderful roommate for two years—one of them in the midst of a pandemic, where his company was more appreciated than ever. From Raleigh to Princeton to Chicago, there are so many other people who mean so much to me: Katie Allen, Rebecca Anderson, Naomi Barlaz, Stacie Feldman, Gill Frank, Breanna Fritz, Maxwell Fritz, Clare Halpine, Anastasia Klimchynskaya, Maggie Kurkoski, Paulina Gonzalez Latapi, No'a bat Miri, Emily Morrison, Kelsey Ockert, Henry and Gloria Rich, Jared Sagoff, and Victor Smith. Reading Shakespeare with Ben Edwards, Ashleigh Fata, Megan Force, and Hannah Rich and playing Dungeons & Dragons with Christina Alderman, Olivier Burtin, Wai Yee Chiong, Kay Duffy, Julia Lopez Fuentes, Elijah Greenstein, Julie Gualtieri, Sara Johnson, Emily Kern, Connor Luong, Timothy Nielsen, Alexis Siemon, Sam Spies, Jan van Doren, Bing Zheng and Andrew Zonderman have been sources of joy for many years.

Richard Anderson was an ideal roommate and remains a dear friend. He—along with Harold, Olive, and Virgil, all dearly missed—deserves a great deal of credit for the completion of this book (and for my general development as a human being). I have known Chris Florio since the first day of graduate school; for all that time, he has been a model of generosity, integrity, and wisdom. Cristina Florea is an international treasure. Her curiosity, creativity, humor, intelligence, good taste, and love of pugs are unrivaled. I am lucky to know her.

Completing this book would have been impossible without the encouragement of my family and loved ones. Theo and Houdini made for marvelous writing companions as I finished this book. Ellin Martens, my aunt, always offered me a welcome refuge from academia. My grandparents—Helen Schultz and the late Jack Schultz, Bill Martens, and Rosemary Martens—supported me not only during graduate school but for a lifetime before that. My brothers, Matt Schultz and Peter Schultz; Peter's wife, Rachel, and their newly arrived daughter, Harriet; and my sister, Kate Schultz, her husband, Alex Vetter, and their children, Joanna Vetter and Felix Vetter, have all made the journey of life worth taking. I am so fortunate to know and love Louise Lerner and through her to know and love Ken Lerner, Aida Novickas, and Elizabeth Novickas.

Everything I am I owe to my parents, John and Kathy Schultz. This book is for them.

JESUS SPRINGS

Introduction
THE GARDEN OF THE GODS

On April 12, 1943, the sun rose on an impressive sight in the Garden of the Gods. This park, located a few miles west of Colorado Springs, was always picturesque; its pinkish-red sandstone formations drew tens of thousands of visitors every year. But that April morning witnessed something unique: 25,000 people gathered at the park's Gateway Rocks to take part in an Easter sunrise service. The tradition of the sunrise service had been established decades earlier by a local pastor, Albert W. Luce. Luce had gone walking in the Garden of the Gods one morning, Bible in hand; when he sat down to read, he opened to a passage from the Gospel of John: "Now in the place where he was crucified, there was a garden—there they laid Jesus."[1] Reading this verse inspired Luce to organize the first sunrise service in the Garden of the Gods in 1921. The tradition grew with time. Originally sponsored by Luce's church, it was later taken over by the Colorado Springs Ministerial Alliance, which incorporated music and pageantry into the service.[2]

What set the 1943 service apart from previous ones was its scale. With 25,000 attendees, it was the largest event in the park's history. CBS broadcast the service via radio, allowing millions more to listen in. The cause of this massive expansion was simple: World War II. Before the war, Colorado Springs had been a resort community that catered to the rich.[3] But the Great Depression and the looming threat of war had undermined the tourism that sustained the local economy, forcing the community's boosters to search for other forms of capital. They found salvation in defense spending. The federal government placed a US Army camp and an airfield in Colorado Springs, bringing tens of thousands of soldiers to the region. That April morning, the crowd swelled as thousands of soldiers came from nearby Camp Carson, while a military orchestra and choir provided music.[4] The sermon, delivered by Reverend Gerald Berneking of the First Christian Church of Colorado Springs, used the language of war: "Victory is always the goal of battle," he told attendees. Berneking shared the stage with Col. Wilfred Blunt, an officer from Camp Carson, who explicitly linked piety with military success. Blunt denounced the Germans ("Hitler has been placed before God") and the Japanese (an "idolatrous people") and reminded listeners that "in fighting to preserve the American way of life we are also fighting to preserve our own religious freedom." The Easter sunrise service was no longer just a celebration of Christianity. It celebrated America as well.[5]

Almost half a century later, on March 31, 1991, another crowd gathered in the Garden of the Gods Park to welcome the Easter sunrise. But the tenor of this celebration was different. Now, it had a distinctly evangelical tone. The opening prayer was delivered by Jim Powell, president of the International Bible Society, which had recently relocated to the Springs from New Jersey. In contrast to Gerald Berneking's First Christian Church, located in downtown Colorado Springs, the International Bible Society's new headquarters was in the city's sprawling suburbs. The sermon was delivered by another newcomer, Dick Eastman of Every Home for Christ. Eastman was an advocate of intense, even violent prayer, a man who spoke often of the ongoing "invisible war" between the forces of good and evil.[6] Speaking to the people assembled in the Garden of the Gods, Eastman celebrated the migration of evangelical organizations—including his own—to Colorado Springs. He hailed the city as "one of Christ's key centers" for reaching the world. And when he asked the crowd, "Is Jesus alive in Colorado Springs?," they responded with a resounding "Amen!"[7]

The transformation of the Easter sunrise service resulted from broader changes in the city's religious demographics. The Colorado Springs

An Easter sunrise service at Garden of the Gods Park, west of Colorado Springs.
Photo courtesy of the Colorado Springs Pioneers Museum. Catalog no. A71-299-2.

Ministerial Alliance, dominated by ecumenical Protestant institutions like the First Christian Church, sponsored the Garden of the Gods service for several decades, while the Colorado Springs Association of Evangelicals sponsored a separate Easter service in the smaller and less picturesque Memorial Park.[8] By the 1980s, however, the Ministerial Alliance had fallen on hard times. The cash-strapped organization dissolved itself and, as one of its last acts, willed the Garden of the Gods service to the city's evangelical churches.[9]

Jesus Springs uses the difference between those two Easter sunrises to illuminate the religious history of the modern United States. Colorado Springs is the ideal place to study one of the most important aspects of this history, namely, the growth of a social movement called "evangelicalism." Dozens of evangelical organizations called the city home: denominational headquarters, radio stations, publishing companies, missionary organizations, and more. They ranged from multimillion-dollar enterprises to one-person operations run out of a basement. The Springs was also home to multiple megachurches, including New Life, which one journalist called "America's most influential megachurch."[10] The evangelization of the Springs began in the 1940s, when the city's businesspeople and pastors began courting Christian institutions with promises of cheap property and a welcoming community. The process unfolded gradually over the following decades. Not until the 1990s did this transformation receive widespread public attention, when a series of high-profile political conflicts led people to nickname the city "Jesus Springs" and the "Evangelical Vatican."

The religious transformation of Colorado Springs overlaps with the Cold War era, and herein lies my argument: The early Cold War was the pivotal moment in the emergence of modern American evangelicalism.[11] Between the 1930s and the 1950s, a rising generation of conservative Protestants undertook a sustained effort to "Christianize" the United States, carrying forward an impulse that had motivated many American Protestants throughout the nineteenth and early twentieth centuries.[12] These men (almost all were men) believed that the Protestant mission to create a Christian nation had been vitiated by infighting within and among Protestant communities. To reassert Protestant Christian dominance in American life, they needed to bring order out of chaos. They did so by encouraging theologically diverse but generally conservative Protestants to think of themselves as "evangelical," an identity that fused Protestantism with American nationalism.

Scholars have debated the precise meaning of "evangelical" and "evangelicalism" ever since.[13] One of the most common definitions, a four-part typology proposed by the historian David W. Bebbington, defines evangelicals as Protestants who believe in the importance of conversion, the inerrancy of the Bible, the centrality of the crucifixion, and the need to evangelize. In recent years, however, many scholars have challenged this definition as too restrictive, too vague, or both.[14] A new wave of scholarship de-emphasizes theology and instead stresses some combination of white supremacy, conservative politics, and consumer capitalism as the essence of American evangelicalism.[15] Neither approach is wholly satisfactory. Critics of Bebbington's quadrilateral are correct to point out its frustrating ambiguities. The new scholarship also has its flaws, however. Most notably, it treats relatively common attitudes as distinctly evangelical. Evangelicals may have embraced white supremacy, conservative politics, and consumer capitalism, but so did most white Americans in the twentieth century.[16]

In *Jesus Springs*, I seek to harmonize these approaches by emphasizing how historical context has shaped both religious belief and practice. I define evangelicalism as a twentieth-century social movement that developed out of nineteenth-century Protestant revivalism and that sought to Christianize the United States by converting as many people as possible and by securing recognition of Christianity as the dominant force in American culture. The core attributes of this movement have remained relatively unchanged since it emerged in the late nineteenth century.[17] It was a flexible, pragmatic, market-driven faith that sought to make its message as appealing as possible. It emphasized the need for personal transformation, for making a "new heart" by accepting the sovereignty of Jesus and the power of the Holy Spirit. And it was led by charismatic preachers who eschewed existing churches and built their own empires.[18]

What changed is not evangelicalism itself but its context. It is with these changes that *Jesus Springs* is concerned. The historian Matthew Sutton has noted the pivotal role that World War II and its aftermath played in the development of modern evangelicalism, writing that "post–World War II evangelicalism is best defined as a white, patriarchal, nationalist religious movement made up of Christians who seek power to transform American culture through conservative-leaning politics and free-market economics." His assessment, while (in my opinion) accurate, raises the question of why this particular era marked a turning point in American religious history. *Jesus Springs* answers this question by demonstrating how the political economy of war intersected with American evangelicalism to create a new religious geography in the United States.[19]

To understand the war's impact on evangelicalism, it is first necessary to understand the structure of the movement. American evangelicalism was dominated by parachurch ministries: voluntary Christian organizations dedicated to a specific end. Some had distinct goals, like translating Bibles; others targeted distinct constituencies, like high school students or the military. Their emphasis on technique and results rather than on doctrine enabled ministry leaders to work together across denominational boundaries, blurring the lines that had long divided conservative Protestants.[20] Many parachurch ministries were products of World War II or the immediate postwar era: Youth for Christ, World Vision, Compassion International, and the Fellowship of Christian Athletes, for example. Because these organizations served a national audience rather than a local congregation, they were not tethered to a specific place and could move wherever they chose. Many chose the archipelago of Southern and Western cities blessed by military spending during World War II and the Cold War.[21] Colorado Springs was not the only military-dependent city to nurture a cluster of evangelical institutions. Virginia Beach was a hub for both the US Navy and Pat Robertson's broadcasting empire; San Diego was home to multiple military bases and to evangelical institution-builder Tim LaHaye; Houston's aerospace-fueled growth made possible the simultaneous growth of a network of parachurch ministries.[22] But none of them could compare to Colorado Springs. Evangelical Christians around the United States listened to radio programs, read books, and even said prayers produced in the Springs. The city's history thus reveals the political economy of American evangelicalism, those material factors that made evangelicalism a cultural force.[23]

The Cold War had an ideological as well as a material impact on American evangelicalism. This was an era when patriotism was a prerequisite for entering the American mainstream, and evangelical Christians were not immune to this pressure. Indeed, most yielded to it gladly, eager to reclaim the cultural prestige they had lost in the preceding decades. Evangelical leaders bound their religious vision to the values of the Cold War–era United States, insisting that to be a good Christian was to be a good American.[24] In *Jesus Springs*, I argue that many ideas that seem distinctive to post–World War II evangelicalism—specifically, that the United States is divided by a "culture war," that good Christians make good soldiers, and that invisible forces are working to subvert American society—are best understood as inheritances of the Cold War. The case of Colorado Springs, a center of both military *and* evangelical power, demonstrates this point. The notion of a "culture war," that the country is divided by an irreconcilable split between religious and secular people, developed from the idea of a "battle for the mind" in the early Cold War. At the Springs-based United States Air Force Academy, military leaders loudly proclaimed that good soldiers were good Christians and vice versa, a claim later taken up by evangelicals.[25] Finally, the demonology embraced by many Colorado Springs evangelicals resembled nothing so much as the anti-communism of the Cold War era.[26]

Uniting these ideas was a vision of the United States as a Christian nation. It was beset by anti-Christian dangers from within and without, but it was Christian nonetheless, and its Christianity had to be vigorously defended. *Jesus Springs* thus offers insight into a key term in the contemporary study of religion: "Christian nationalism." Andrew Whitehead and Samuel Perry's *Taking America Back for God* (2020), one of the earliest, most important, and most influential analyses of the term, defined Christian nationalism as an "ideology that idealizes and advocates a fusion of American civic life with a particular type of Christian identity and culture." According to Whitehead and Perry, Christian nationalists conflate Christianity with whiteness, heterosexuality, and conservatism.[27] Most of the current literature on Christian nationalism adopts Whitehead and Perry's definition.[28] Recently, however, some scholars have pointed out various shortcomings in this literature, most notably its failure to delimit the boundaries of "Christian nationalism."[29] *Jesus Springs* adds specificity by adding history. If we want to understand Christian nationalism, we have to understand where it came from, which means recognizing that this ideology did not originate with evangelicals. Americans who express Christian nationalist beliefs often lament the declining political power and cultural prestige of Christianity in the United States. The phrase "taking America *back* for God" expresses this feeling. Importantly, this lament contains a kernel of truth. There *was* an era when the US government and American culture embraced religion—World War II and the early Cold War.[30] In this era, Christian nationalism was not an ideology but a fact of life.[31]

Jesus Springs argues that Christian nationalism as it currently exists is not a form of idolatry or America's "original sin" but the preservation of a Cold War ideology by the institutions of evangelical Christianity. These institutions were founded at a time when Christianity and American nationalism were seen as one and the same. With some exceptions, the founders of those institutions and the men who succeeded them never questioned this conflation of Christianity and patriotism. Indeed, many loudly reaffirmed this idea as a way of distinguishing themselves from their ecumenical Protestant rivals, most of whom had begun emphasizing America's religious pluralism rather than its Christianity.[32] In Colorado Springs, we see how evangelicals came to understand themselves as stewards and defenders of a Christian heritage against a rising tide of secularism.

This book begins in World War II. As the first chapter demonstrates, wartime growth created the economic conditions necessary for the arrival of Christian organizations in Colorado Springs. But this change did not signal a radical rupture with the past. From the moment of its founding, the city was marked by a fusion of religious piety, corporate power, and military values. William Jackson Palmer, founder of the Springs, embodied this fusion. Born into a family of prominent Philadelphia Quakers in 1836, Palmer served in the Union army during the Civil War, rising to the rank of brigadier general by the war's end. Like many young, ambitious Americans, Palmer struck out westward after the war. After undertaking a land survey for the Kansas Pacific Railway, he began planning his own railroad, the Denver & Rio Grande, which would run along the Front Range of the Rocky Mountains. Palmer envisioned a town that could both anchor this railroad and serve as an oasis of culture in the West.[33] The first stake for the new town was driven in July 1871; it was incorporated as Colorado Springs in September of that year, its name a reference to the nearby sulfur springs.[34] The new settlement was open to anyone "of good moral character and sober habits" who could afford to purchase a lot.[35] "Sober" was not a figure of speech; Colorado Springs began its life as a dry town. Its first inhabitants were quick to establish other markers of culture. The local Presbyterian church, for instance, dedicated its new house of worship in January 1873, only a few months after the town was incorporated.[36] Palmer also collaborated with the Congregational Church to establish Colorado College, a liberal arts school modeled on Oberlin.[37] This veneer of high culture, combined with the number of tourists who arrived from England, earned the city the first of its many nicknames: Little London.

Future leaders followed the path that Palmer blazed. They too combined a stern morality (or, at least, the desire for others to abide by such a morality) with a shrewd business sense. These factors were interrelated, as Colorado Springs boosters used the town's reputation for righteousness, symbolized by its churches and temperance laws, to attract capital.[38] For the most part they succeeded in their goal of drawing the "right" people. When gold was discovered in nearby Cripple Creek, the Springs became home to many of those who made their fortunes operating the mines (the miners themselves were less welcome). Foremost among these mining millionaires was Spencer Penrose, who became the community's most important booster in the first decades of the twentieth century. Penrose, scion of a wealthy Philadelphia family, sunk much of his money into projects that would lure tourists to his adopted hometown. His greatest achievement was the Broadmoor Hotel, whose luxury attracted famous guests like business tycoon John D. Rockefeller Jr. and boxer Jack Dempsey.[39] Many of the tourists who stayed at the Broadmoor and other local hotels came to the region to marvel at its dramatic landscape. Another category of visitors was tuberculosis patients; they stayed at one of the town's many sanatoriums in hopes that the dry climate and altitude would alleviate their disease.

The Springs welcomed tourists and health seekers, but it treated other groups less warmly. Local boosters were virulently anti-union, none more so than Penrose.[40] They also responded coldly to the resurgent Ku Klux Klan in the 1920s, less for the Klan's racism than for the threat it posed to law and order. Though the Klan dominated politics in the rest of the state, it never gained a foothold in the Springs.[41] This was the political culture of the Springs on the eve of World War II: a community dominated by a paternalistic booster class whose members took upon themselves the duty of bringing in capital while keeping out those who might disturb local unity and their own authority.

Wartime growth built on this foundation, creating a modern city that maintained the spirit and values of a small town. The first chapter of *Jesus Springs* describes how this combination of economic growth and moral traditionalism attracted evangelical organizations, which began relocating to the Springs in the 1940s and 1950s. The greatest influx came in the 1980s and 1990s, when local boosters, in an effort to rebuild the economy in the wake of a real estate crash, stepped up their recruitment of evangelical organizations. Chapter 2 discusses how the arrival of dozens of Christian ministries in these decades cemented the city's reputation as an "Evangelical Vatican." That reputation did not always match reality. Events in the 1990s and the following decade revealed that evangelical influence in Colorado Springs was always provisional, limited not only by progressive opposition but also by moderating forces like courts, bureaucracies, and local businesses. In chapter 3, I use these conflicts to expose the limitations of the "culture war" model of American politics.

Chapter 4 focuses on a particular institution within Colorado Springs: the United States Air Force Academy. Its history recapitulates my argument in miniature. The academy was founded in the midst of the Cold War religious revival and reflected the concerns of that era. Its curriculum and architecture celebrated the fusion of patriotism and Christianity. By the 1970s, that heritage had passed into the hands of evangelical Christians, who took it on themselves to uphold the idea that being a good soldier meant being a good Christian. Chapter 5 returns to the city's broader evangelical milieu to discuss the rise of spiritual warfare, the practice of using intense prayer to combat demons. Colorado Springs was the center of the spiritual warfare movement in the 1990s and the following decade, thanks to the efforts of megachurch pastor Ted Haggard and author and educator C. Peter Wagner. This chapter argues that spiritual warfare reveals the influence that both Pentecostalism and Cold War ideology had on American evangelicalism. The language of battle, struggle, and conquest, which evangelicals would carry with them into the twenty-first century, was the inheritance of a religion reborn in the shadow of global war.

1
THE MIRACLE PLACE

Jim Rayburn's daughter shook him awake at 4:15 in the morning. Light was streaming through the windows, and she thought it was sunrise. Rayburn immediately realized something was wrong. Moments later, one of his coworkers burst in to deliver the news that a raging forest fire was bearing down on them. For the second time in less than two years, Rayburn faced the possible destruction of all his dreams. Rayburn's Young Life ministry had purchased Star Ranch, a property near Colorado Springs, in 1946 for use as a summer camp. In April 1948, a forest fire raced down the mountainside and encircled the property; only a last-second change in the wind saved it.[1] Now—January 17, 1950—disaster loomed again. This fire dwarfed the earlier one. Rayburn described how he and other Young Life staff struggled desperately to save their property (and their lives): "The flames leaped and roared, taking on fantastic shapes as they were driven. The gusts tore at us from every direction. I have never experienced such violence."[2]

Amazingly, Star Ranch was spared once again. The blaze destroyed some small buildings, but most of the property remained intact. Rayburn saw God's hand at work: "The desire of all of our hearts as we have thanked and praised the Lord together in prayer since the fire is that we may more devotedly serve Him and more effectively use this beautiful place as a perennial token of our love and gratitude to God for His miraculous work in saving us in the midst of this disaster."[3]

Star Ranch's survival was remarkable, whether or not one attributes it to providence. And Young Life knew just how remarkable it was. The proof: It took the organization less than a month to turn the story into a fundraising appeal. Rayburn's gripping account of the fire was sent to potential donors, accompanied by a letter stating, "I believe all of us who love to see young people won to Jesus Christ and who love Young Life work because God is using it for just that, should pitch in together and make a real thank offering to the Lord for His great deliverance."[4] This letter illuminates the nexus between miracles and fundraising that was so crucial to the evangelical movement. To succeed in the competitive world of evangelicalism, with many organizations competing for a limited audience, one had to develop personal relationships that could yield a steady stream of income. This explains the weight that Young Life and other evangelical organizations placed on "winsomeness." Being winsome meant making friends; making friends meant making money; and making money gave one confidence that one's work was blessed by God. Miraculous stories like that of the Star Ranch fire played an important role in this dynamic, persuading potential donors that they would be giving to a cause favored by God.

Place was a key factor in mediating the relationship between evangelical organizations and their donors. Property gave donors tangible proof that their money was being well spent. It also yielded new stories—like that of the Star Ranch fire—that could further develop those all-important social and financial relationships. Evangelical organizations that wanted to expand thus needed to be on the lookout for property. When they looked, many of them saw Colorado Springs. The Springs was one of many military-dependent communities that blossomed across the American West as the warfare state poured billions into the region.[5] Many industries saw these communities as potential new homes, places where they could find low taxes, cheap property, and nonunion labor.[6] The "industry" of evangelicalism was no different. The institutions that anchored post–World War II evangelicalism in the United States were clustered in Northeastern and Midwestern cities like New York, Boston, Philadelphia, and Chicago.[7] By the 1930s and 1940s, many of these organizations were looking westward. There, they could afford to buy or build enormous campuses, sprawling headquarters, and huge summer camps, places where they could train young people and send them back into the world to win it for Christ. Colorado Springs, with its abundance of cheap, scenic property, was an ideal place to realize this vision.

Colorado Springs welcomed these newcomers. The city's leaders recognized that members of the new evangelical movement shared their values; both groups embraced economic growth, moral traditionalism, and American power. A counterexample demonstrates this point: the case of the Freedom School, a libertarian institution headquartered near Colorado Springs in the 1950s and 1960s. Though conservative on most matters, the leadership of the Freedom School challenged the militarism of the Cold War era. The Colorado Springs booster class, unwilling to accept this heresy, drove the Freedom School out of the community. These boosters worried that a reputation for extremism would harm their ability to attract capital. They had no such concerns about Young Life and similar organizations, an indication of evangelical success at entering the American mainstream in the postwar era.

The Neo-Evangelical Milieu

In the 1930s and 1940s, a loosely affiliated group of people and institutions sought to smooth the rough edges of fundamentalism to create a more palatable faith that they called "neo-evangelicalism."[8] Neo-evangelicalism was not bound to any denomination or church. Rather, its banner was carried by parachurch ministries: nonprofit, nondenominational organizations dedicated to specific ends, like distributing Bibles or evangelizing college students.[9] The most influential neo-evangelical ministry of the 1940s was Youth for Christ (YFC), whose open-air worship services attracted young people by the tens of thousands. YFC catapulted the young revivalist Billy Graham to fame; other YFC members founded influential organizations like World Vision, Overseas Crusades, and Greater Europe Mission.[10] YFC's approach to evangelism, which borrowed freely from popular culture in order to attract young people, was carried forward by other important ministries like Campus Crusade for Christ and the Fellowship of Christian Athletes. Schools like Fuller Theological Seminary and periodicals like *Christianity Today* promoted and sustained neo-evangelical ministries in their efforts to "Christianize" the United States.[11] Even the sunniest neo-evangelicals retained some of the brooding apocalypticism of the fundamentalist movement. Billy Graham, for instance, warned of the "internal decadence that is causing [America] to rush faster than any civilization before us toward destruction and hell."[12] But this sense of doom was tempered by a confidence that they could win the world for Christ in a single generation, thanks to a combination of American power and new technology.

Neo-evangelicals believed God was on their side, but they had good reason to think that American society was with them as well. American culture "got religion" in the 1940s and 1950s, as growing numbers of Americans watched religious movies and television shows, read religious books, and attended religious services.[13] The federal government gave its imprimatur to this revival, with Harry Truman establishing the National Day of Prayer and Dwight Eisenhower calling on Americans to join the "Day of Prayer for Peace."[14] Many American politicians and military leaders explained the nation's Cold War struggle with the Soviet Union in religious, even apocalyptic terms.[15] Senator Edward Martin (R-PA) spoke for many when he declared, "America must move forward with the atomic bomb in one hand and the cross in the other."[16] Such declarations did not go unnoticed by neo-evangelicals, who eagerly seized upon them as an endorsement of their worldview. When Bill Bright, founder of Campus Crusade for Christ, evangelized to young people, he "began with a description of the Cold War 'crisis hour' and cited prominent authority figures such as [Gen. Douglas] MacArthur and Eisenhower on the need for a spiritual awakening."[17] Men like Bright eagerly touted the contribution their version of Christianity could make to the American cause in the Cold War.

Conversion was their most important goal—indeed, many neo-evangelicals believed it was the *only* goal—and so they considered it essential to reach as many people as possible, as quickly as they could. Evangelical organizations adopted a variety of strategies in the pursuit of efficient proselytization. One was to broadcast their message as widely as possible, in the belief that its infallible truth would be enough to convert anyone who heard it. Clarence Jones, founder of the missionary radio station HCJB, explained it this way: "A radio preacher or missionary never knows who is listening, or when the message will go 'home' to the heart; but he is thrown entirely upon the Holy Spirit's operation.... He must trust implicitly the fact that 'faith comes by hearing.'"[18] Other organizations took a more targeted approach, aiming their messages at specific audiences—part of the era's trend toward market segmentation, as corporations targeted ever more precise categories of consumers.[19] The desire to capture a specific market, in this case young people, explains why neo-evangelical organizations like Campus Crusade focused on the most popular students when they evangelized high schools and colleges. They believed that popular converts could deliver large numbers of their classmates, speeding up the process of Christianization.[20] Not everyone was comfortable with this approach. A member of Inter-Varsity Christian Fellowship lamented "[how] often today a Christian group chooses its leader primarily because of personality, prowess as an athlete, popularity, effectiveness in public speaking, or genius for organization" rather than for that person's piety.[21] But these complaints of shallowness and opportunism had little impact. Most neo-evangelicals, acutely aware of their faith's marginal status in American culture, trumpeted the conversion of campus celebrities.

Young Life and the Navigators emerged from the neo-evangelical milieu and reflected its worldview. The two organizations had much in common: Both were products of the Sunbelt (one from Texas, the other from California); both were founded by charismatic evangelists who drove themselves and their followers relentlessly; and most importantly, both preached a message of fellowship, though they envisioned two very different kinds of fellowship—one clubby and friendly, the other defined by an almost militaristic camaraderie. Young Life was founded by Jim Rayburn, the son of a Texas minister, who, after a brief dalliance with engineering, returned to his father's business. While enrolled at Dallas Theological Seminary in the late 1930s, Rayburn began evangelizing to high school students in the nearby city of Gainesville. At first, he did so under the auspices of the Miracle Book Club, a nationwide Protestant organization. Eventually Rayburn split with the club (taking along many of its chapters) and created his own organization, the Young Life Campaign, which he incorporated in 1941.[22] What Rayburn was to Young Life, Dawson Trotman was to the Navigators. Trotman was born to evangelical parents in Southern California; his mother was a devotee of the media-savvy Pentecostal preacher Aimee Semple McPherson.[23] After some youthful carousing, Trotman rededicated himself to Christianity and became an evangelist, founding an organization—first called the "Fishermen Four," then "The Minute Men," and finally incorporating as "The Navigators" in 1943—to evangelize servicemen at Southern California's military bases.

Rayburn spoke constantly about the need for Christians to be "winsome." The organization's goal was to make "the presentation of the Gospel" in "the most attractive and winsome way possible," a message in keeping with the neo-evangelical emphasis on effective persuasion. Accordingly, Young Life's meetings jettisoned the trappings of church and Sunday school in favor of activities like "singing [and] comedy skits."[24] The organization also focused its efforts on the most popular students. Rayburn believed this was the most efficient means of evangelism. As he put it, Young Life wanted to win the "top-notch—the athletes, the officers, the leaders," because it was those people who "are the ones who sway the mass."[25] Critics faulted Young Life for putting "winsomeness" ahead of Christianity. The most comprehensive attack on this point came from Wallace Chappell, an employee of the United Methodist Church's Youth Department, who prepared a ten-page memo assailing Young Life's methods. Chappell contrasted Young Life's focus on popular high school students with Jesus's ministry to "the lost and the least." He also charged Young Life with shallowness: "The whole Campaign is based on fellowship, recreation, personal contact, and the gospel meetings in which one 'sits, sings, and listens,'" he wrote. "It is a religion of talk, friendship, and conversion, not service and fruits."[26] Young Life took these charges seriously enough to produce a point-by-point rebuttal. The reply rejected Chappell's charges of shallowness, gimmickry, and emotionalism. As to his point about ministering only to the popular students: "The 'major emphasis on . . . athletes and leaders' is a matter of strategy. These young people are the key to any high school, but that does not mean that all others are 'second class.'"[27] Protests aside, Young Life undeniably tailored its methods to the youth culture of the day.

The Navigators also conformed to contemporary American culture, but to the culture of the military barracks rather than of the high school. Like generations of American Christians before him, Trotman believed the best way to make Christianity winsome was to make it masculine.[28] As Trotman's most perceptive biographer noted, his fondness for motorcycles and leather jackets reflected his desire to "squelch the impression of sissiness that some associated with evangelical witness." For Trotman, the ideal Christian was not only tough but also supremely self-disciplined. One of his friends remarked, "His discipline was basic to everything." Trotman made a habit of rising early to memorize Bible passages and encouraged his fellow Navigators to do the same, exhorting them to "shake from every fiber of our being each tendency to be lazy." The Navigators also prized efficiency, with Trotman promulgating various techniques to help people memorize Bible passages as quickly as possible. As with Rayburn, Trotman occasionally faced criticism that he was putting method ahead of evangelism. These critics accused him of valuing efficiency as an end in itself rather than as a means to conversion. Trotman fended off these charges by claiming (according to biographer Betty Lee Skinner) that he "was merely packaging a product for which there was both need and demand."[29]

In their early years of existence, the Navigators focused on selling this product to members of the US military, especially to the sailors stationed at naval bases in Southern California.[30] As the United States drew closer to intervening in World War II, the Navigators increasingly touted its good relations with the military. Uniformed Navigators proved a major draw at revivals. One New York businessman who supported the Navigators advised Trotman, "[Wherever] possible have a uniformed Navigator with you. . . . A uniform is a very popular thing today and we must do everything we can to make our witness attractive."[31] Young Life recruited star athletes in order to be winsome; the Navigators recruited soldiers for the same reason.

Young Life and the Navigators held one important belief in common: that the United States could and should be a force for world-transforming Christian evangelism. This was a belief they shared with much of the neo-evangelical movement. In the fundamentalist-modernist conflicts of earlier decades, modernists had accused their fundamentalist foes of being insufficiently patriotic because of their unwillingness to support American involvement in World War I.[32] The neo-evangelicals, successors to the fundamentalists, would not leave themselves open to similar accusations. They did not celebrate the United States uncritically. Following a long tradition, neo-evangelicals lamented what they perceived as the moral decay of the United States. Rising divorce rates, the popularity of jazz music and titillating films, the sale of liquor—all of these things seemed to invite God's wrath. But their lamentations were intermingled with a confidence that the United States, if recalled to God by revival, could transform the world.[33] And so, while they may have condemned the United States for failing to live up to its status as God's chosen nation, few neo-evangelicals questioned that it *was* chosen by God. It is telling that Jim Rayburn conducted his very first evangelizing campaign beneath a banner that read "God Bless America."[34] And it is equally telling that Dawson Trotman, writing for the fundamentalist publication *The King's Business* in the closing months of World War II, celebrated America as "the richest of all nations and the most enlightened," a country that "has the best in science, education, transportation, production, and unlimited resources." He called on Christians to put those tremendous resources into the service of evangelism, to spread "the Gospel of Jesus Christ" throughout the world.[35] Indeed, it was patriotism that first brought Young Life and the Navigators together. Young Life sponsored a series of mass meetings during World War II to promote the twinned causes of Christianity and national defense, with Trotman serving as the featured speaker.[36] Young Life, the Navigators, and other neo-evangelical organizations did not hesitate to conflate their cause with that of the United States, first in World War II and then during the Cold War.

Neo-evangelicals emphasized being winsome—recruiting star athletes, showcasing their members in uniform, and touting their patriotism—because winning friends was how they raised the money needed to carry out their evangelism. The movement's literature overflowed with advice on "making friends," with the strong implication that every new friend was also a potential new donor. The invocation of friendship signaled a quiet but important shift in how conservative Protestants thought about money, away from what was called "faith financing" and toward a more routinized approach. Faith financing was a product of the nineteenth century; most neo-evangelicals associated the idea with the German-born English evangelist George Müller and the English missionary Hudson Taylor. As described by one neo-evangelical author, practitioners of faith financing "do not solicit funds or pursue popular methods of raising money, but look to the Lord in faith and prayer for the supply of the means to carry on their work."[37] One did not ask for funds but waited for funds to arrive, accepting whatever came as God's blessing. Many neo-evangelical organizations, as part of their move away from fundamentalism, sought to harmonize faith financing with a more professional approach to fundraising. The concept of friendship eased this transformation. Asking for money was still frowned upon, but one *could* "make needs known" to a circle of friends. Making needs known could involve a personal conversation or more impersonal forms of persuasion like direct mail. Charles and Grace Fuller, hosts of the enormously popular *Old Fashioned Revival Hour* radio program, perfected this art. Grace Fuller took time during every show to read aloud letters from their far-flung audience—and many letters involved stories of people making deep financial sacrifices to donate to the program. Grace Fuller made it clear that she hoped other listeners would follow these examples. "These letters are a real inspiration," she said on one broadcast, "and I wish I could read every one over the air. I feel more confident than ever that, with this spirit of sacrifice, we are going to be able to keep our Hour which is so expensive."[38] Neo-evangelical fundraising was dominated by such appeals: exhortations to "friends" to give beyond what seemed possible.

The Navigators and Young Life exhorted potential donors the same way the Fullers did. Young Life literature spoke incessantly about making friends. "The future of our work depends on many small gifts from many friends," said one staff bulletin. "That's why this matter of finding new friends is so important."[39] Every new friend was a potential donor, and so to make friends—to be winsome, as Rayburn so often put it—was a way to raise money while respecting the principle of faith financing. As the ministry's constitution said, though Young Life would "look to God alone for the supply of all temporal needs," the "needs of the Campaign may be made known to Christian friends."[40] These friends included a national network of Christian businesspeople, anchored by Chicago businessman Herbert J. Taylor. Taylor's Christian Workers Foundation provided essential funds to numerous neo-evangelical institutions, including Fuller Theological Seminary and the National Association of Evangelicals.[41] Young Life's board of directors included other business leaders like lumber executive C. Davis Weyerhaeuser and manufacturing company CEO John Mitchell.[42] It was all these men could do to keep Young Life afloat. The organization was in a constant state of financial crisis, often running months behind on paying employees. Mitchell discovered that "the girls in the office here in Dallas had reached such financial straits, unknown to us, that they were not even getting enough to eat."[43] Mitchell, Taylor, and their allies repeatedly wrote personal checks to staffers to cover the organization's chronic budgetary shortfalls.[44] In letters to one another, these men complained of Rayburn's unwillingness to make Young Life's unstable financial state known to potential donors. "I know there are those who feel that this represents a departure from the faith basis," Weyerhaeuser wrote in a letter to Taylor, "but I disagree with this attitude because I believe it presumptuous to pray for financial help and then be unwilling to do anything about it."[45]

The Navigators also shifted—albeit in a slow and unsteady way—from faith-based financing to a more routinized approach. Early in his career as an evangelist, Trotman vowed to "follow the example of George Müller and Hudson Taylor, trusting God to supply through prayer." Trotman's biography is filled with stories of money miraculously coming through just when the Navigators needed it most. In his diary, Trotman wrote, "I am convinced, as each day goes by that as each need arises, God will supply in one way or another, mostly in another. He so often does it in the way least expected. This is a great delight to the soul."[46] Only gradually did Trotman and the Navigators take steps to organize their finances. As with Young Life, the Navigators smoothed this transition by framing it as a matter of making needs known to friends.[47] One reason both Young Life and the Navigators were so reluctant to give up the principle of faith financing was because they understood it as a spiritual discipline. Betty Lee Skinner, Trotman's biographer, wrote that Trotman believed "repeated exercise of faith as the evidence of things not seen" could "reinforce a habit that could lead to larger ventures of faith."[48] Relying on God alone for funds toughened one's soul and strengthened one's faith.

What was this money used for? To acquire the property that Young Life and the Navigators needed to fulfill their visions. Young Life did much of its work at sleepaway camps, which Young Life's leaders believed would serve as crucibles for personal transformation. There, young people could be separated from secular influences, transformed by exposure to a purely Christian atmosphere, and sent back into the world to win it for Christ. At first, the ministry used (in the words of Jim Rayburn) "any old kind [of camp] we could get for this purpose."[49] By the middle of the 1940s, however, Young Life had begun seeking a single camp that could serve young people from across the entire United States. Rayburn wanted this camp to be as grand as possible: "Who started the idea that Christians . . . ought to have camps in tents?" he asked. "We're gonna get the classiest camps in the country!"[50] A "classy" camp would make Christianity winsome by associating it with prosperity rather than poverty.

Just as Young Life needed property to provide the right kind of Christian atmosphere for young people, the Navigators needed property to carry out its mission of person-to-person evangelization. The group's work had expanded significantly as of the early 1950s thanks to its association with Billy Graham, the country's most famous evangelist. Graham's enthusiastic delivery of a simplified Christian message proved hugely popular in the 1940s and 1950s.[51] Essential to Graham's success were his crusades, multiday revivals held in major cities. Every service of every crusade ended with Graham calling on attendees to approach the altar and accept Christ; over the course of his long career, many hundreds of thousands responded. Graham worried that these commitments would not last outside the emotionally charged atmosphere of the revival. Accordingly, his Billy Graham Evangelistic Association asked

Trotman and the Navigators to provide "follow-up work" at his crusades. Navigators met with converts at the end of each service, collected their personal information, and referred them to local pastors for further spiritual development.[52] Graham and Trotman dreamed of acquiring property and using it to transform the Navigators' methods into a permanent institution. Graham spoke of his desire for a "place where a 12-month indoctrination course can be offered" in the work done by the Navigators.[53] The Navigators, for its part, was desperate for space. The organization had outgrown one Southern California headquarters after another. One building, expected to last at least five years, proved too small after only eighteen months.[54] Frustrated, Trotman now sought a property large enough to accommodate any amount of future growth. He wanted something that could provide space for "not only the present staff... but with the potential of housing twice that many in the not too distant future."[55] And he had a place in mind: Colorado Springs.

Looking West

The economic and social transformation of Colorado Springs in the 1940s paved the way for the arrival of evangelical organizations at the end of the decade. The Colorado Springs Chamber of Commerce shepherded the community through these momentous changes. The chamber had long followed the simple principle that all the community's problems could be solved by ever-increasing economic growth. The military mobilization that took place prior to American entry into World War II offered new opportunities for growth, and the chamber was quick to seize them. Months before the United States entered the war, businesspeople from Colorado Springs were already canvassing politicians in Washington, talking up the Springs as an ideal site for military bases.[56] These efforts paid off: In January 1942, the War Department announced it would build an Army base, Camp Carson, a few miles east of Colorado Springs. The new installation dwarfed the town in both its size and economic value.[57] The end of World War II and the beginning of the Cold War accelerated this transformation. When the newly independent United States Air Force began seeking a location for a service academy, something equivalent to the Military Academy at West Point and the Naval Academy at Annapolis, the same boosters who fought for Camp Carson sprang back into action. They courted the Air Force by presenting their city as a military-friendly community that would welcome the academy.[58] The boosters succeeded once again; the Air Force ultimately placed the new academy just north of the city. A front-page article in the local *Gazette Telegraph* credited God for this success, thanking the deity for "endowing us with our climate, scenery, and beautiful countryside." But the newspaper made sure to thank someone else: the Colorado Springs Chamber of Commerce.[59] Regardless of how one divided the credit, the result was the same. No longer a health resort for Eastern socialites, the Springs was now a thriving military metropolis at the foot of Pikes Peak.

For Colorado Springs—or at least for its boosterish business leaders—the future seemed bright. The population of El Paso County, home to the Springs, almost doubled between 1940 and 1954. And while military bases drove much of the growth, these government jobs were supplemented by an expanding manufacturing sector and a vibrant tourism industry. An economic survey of the Pikes Peak region conducted in 1954 concluded that the area's future "can be viewed only in terms of expansion and growth." The survey noted that the Springs was especially successful at attracting businesses that, "for lack of a better name, might be termed 'placeless' industries." Such industries (the report cited publishing houses, insurance companies, and magazines as examples) moved to the Springs not for access to raw materials but because of the city's pleasant climate, low cost of living, and central geographic location.[60] These factors proved enticing to another placeless industry: evangelical organizations.

Young Life was the first to make the move. Jim Rayburn had visited Colorado Springs in his boyhood, when his family, like so many others, spent their vacation in the Pikes Peak region.[61] Decades later, he returned to evangelize at Colorado Springs High School. Visiting the Springs, he was struck by the region's beauty. "I do not know what to say as to the future of our work in Denver and Colorado Springs," he wrote to his staff, "but those of us who were there feel that there are more wide-open opportunities there for us now than any place we know of."[62] A Young Life staff conference held at Manitou Springs, a small town located a few miles west of Colorado Springs, stoked Rayburn's enthusiasm. He was impressed not only by the region's scenery but by its impact on staffers, enthusing that the "mountain atmosphere" had "contributed greatly to the strengthening of our bodies in preparation for the intensive months ahead."[63] The aura of toughness so dear to Rayburn, and to many neo-evangelicals of this era, found its reflection in the rugged landscape surrounding Colorado Springs. Young Life, in turn, introduced the Navigators to the Pikes Peak region. Navigators staff attended Young Life's Manitou Springs conference; Trotman himself attended other Young Life conferences in the region and "went away singing [its] praises."[64] For the first time, but certainly not the last, personal connections paved the way for an evangelical migration to Colorado Springs.

Young Life wanted a "classy" camp, and the Navigators wanted space for an educational institution. Guss Hill, a Colorado Springs real estate agent and devout Christian, provided both organizations with the answer to their prayers. Hill, who would earn the nickname "God's real estate agent" for his work with Christian organizations, introduced Rayburn to Star Ranch, a property south of Colorado Springs. Rayburn described the ranch to Young Life staffers as "one of the most beautiful places I have ever seen." "I have taken young businessmen from the Colorado Springs Chamber of Commerce out there," he wrote, "and they have just about gasped for breath."[65] Hill provided the Navigators with an equally impressive property: Glen Eyrie. Like Colorado Springs itself, Glen Eyrie was the creation of railroad magnate William Jackson Palmer. Palmer envisioned Glen Eyrie as a mansion in the English Tudor style, going so far as to import its roof from an old English church to give the house an air of antiquity. Following Palmer's death in 1909, his mansion was purchased by a New York rug manufacturer, after which it passed into the hands of a Houston oil tycoon.[66] By the time the Navigators began eyeing Glen Eyrie, it had long since fallen into disrepair. Yet the allure of the mansion and its surrounding landscape was undeniable. Rayburn and Trotman had both found properties that would make their cause "winsome" by lending it an air of majesty.

Young Life and the Navigators relied on a network of personal connections to purchase these properties. Young Life turned to one of its "Christian friends," Chicago businessman Herbert Taylor, for help buying Star Ranch. Taylor purchased the ranch with $50,000 of his own money and transferred its ownership to the nonprofit Christian Camps Foundation of Colorado, which then leased the property to Young Life for an annual fee of one dollar.[67] To secure Glen Eyrie, Trotman and the Navigators relied on their friendship with Billy Graham. Graham became a salesman for the project, pitching the idea to an audience of "75 Colorado Springs ministers and business leaders" in May 1953.[68] Graham was eventually pressured to drop out of the Glen Eyrie project by associates who feared he was spreading himself too thin, but he encouraged the Navigators to forge ahead with the project and lent his name to the cause.⁶⁹ Various Graham allies, including the Texas oilman Earl Hankamer and the machine gun manufacturer Russell Maguire, also lent their support to the cause, an indication of how valuable Graham's name was within the neo-evangelical milieu.⁷⁰

Young Life and the Navigators wrapped these social relations in the language of providence. "Providence" at once recognized God's sovereignty and left space for individual action. The success or failure of projects could be explained as evidence that one was either following or straying from the path God had ordained. Providential thinking was omnipresent in neo-evangelicalism; the historian Joel Carpenter, assessing several memoirs written by key figures in the movement, noted their repeated references to "remarkable Providences" in which "by odd twists of events, the authors met the right people in unexpected circumstances, saw urgent needs met in surprising ways, and had insurmountable obstacles suddenly cleared away."⁷¹ One of these books, a memoir by Clarence Jones, founder of the HCJB radio station, contained a succinct statement of providential thinking: "Nothing is coincidental in God's plans. Things that look like the fruit of a moment's decision were planted and nurtured by Him long ago just for this moment."⁷² Tellingly, Jones made this comment regarding an effort to raise money (in this case, to buy a new transmitter). Money, and the want of it, was often the topic of providential speculation. Many neo-evangelicals looked on fundraising as a divine test, in which one sought to read God's intentions in the amount of money raised. An account of Charles Fuller's *Old Fashioned Revival Hour* noted that "the testings have been many and severe. Some weeks, Mr. Fuller has come up to Thursday and, on one or two occasions even to Friday morning, with almost nothing in the treasury for the coming Sunday broadcast. . . . But in answer to prayer, time after time, God has undertaken and the money has come in miraculously."⁷³ As that statement shows, talk of providence was inextricable from talk of miracles. Miracles were providence in action, a sign that one's actions were in keeping with God's plan. They were, moreover, signs one could show to the unbelieving world. A manual published by Youth for Christ—in a chapter with the title "Let's Keep It on a Miracle Basis"—enthused, "We want everyone to know that God's hand is on this movement. We want folks to see that this is too big and too great for any man or group of men to accomplish by themselves. We want folks to say, 'GOD DID IT!'"⁷⁴ That phrase, "God did it," recurs throughout neo-evangelical literature, a testimony to the evangelical belief that human actions echoed a divine plan.

Young Life and the Navigators were quick to assert that "God did it" when explaining their move to Colorado Springs. Young Life narrated the acquisition of Star Ranch as the action of divine providence and the property itself as something chosen by God. One Young Life staffer described how Jim Rayburn, Herbert Taylor, and several other men visited a potential property in Colorado, only to find the property "engulfed in a dense cloud" when they arrived.[75] This mysterious stumbling block directed Young Life toward Star Ranch—one of those "odd twists of events" that signaled the working of providence. Jim Rayburn put the matter more simply. "If you don't think you're in a miracle place, I do! I was there when it happened!" he told an audience gathered at Star Ranch.[76]

The Navigators, too, cast its efforts to purchase Glen Eyrie in providential terms, interpreting it as a divine test. After Billy Graham withdrew from the project, Trotman wrote to his staff that "[Graham's withdrawal] means that if it is God's will for us to have the property . . . we must raise the money for the purchase."[77] On another occasion, he asserted, "I believe God has given us Glen Eyrie—but we must possess the land, and this is going to take every sacrificial penny and every sacrificial prayer we can give."[78] Meeting the divine test required great financial sacrifice. Other Navigators felt the same way. At a staff meeting held a few days after Graham's announcement, one member declared, "God is forcing us into Glen Eyrie." Others cited passages from Exodus, Chronicles, and Jeremiah to suggest that God wanted them to have the mansion.[79]

As the Navigators scrambled to raise money, members scrutinized the donations they received, searching them for further providential signs. The amount of money was important, of course, but Trotman and the Navigators were also interested in the stories attached to each donation. Some stories involved the conversion of valued goods into cash—beginning with Trotman himself, who sold his car and donated the resulting $2,000 to the Glen Eyrie campaign.[80] When people donated cash, they often included an explanation of what they had originally planned to do with the money. One fundraising report, for instance, described how "one of the staff girls gave the $100 she had been saving for her wedding."[81] We know these stories because the Navigators publicized them in reports with titles like "How God

Dawson Trotman, Ruth Graham, and Billy Graham at Glen Eyrie, the property that Billy Graham helped Trotman acquire for the Navigators. Courtesy of Regional History and Genealogy, Pikes Peak Library District, 001-2265.

Gave Us Glen Eyrie," braiding individual stories into a narrative of sacrifice and triumph. This narrative had multiple audiences. One was the Navigators members themselves, for whom the stories demonstrated the significance of their work. Another audience was the secular world. In a letter to Navigators staff, Trotman warned that "the eyes of the unsaved world are watching to see what will happen.... We must not fail. We cannot afford to fail."[82] For Trotman and the Navigators, Glen Eyrie became a stage upon which they performed their faith before a skeptical audience. And when they raised the money they needed, the result was predictable: On hearing the news, Billy Graham exclaimed, "The Lord did it!"[83]

Star Ranch and Glen Eyrie became symbols of evangelical success. Young Life staffers had high hopes about what they could do with their new property. A spokesperson enthused, "This is the greatest opportunity for Young Life Campaign and for our Christian friends throughout the nation that we have ever had."[84] Indeed, Young Life's leaders were so enthusiastic about the Pikes Peak region that in 1947 they decided to relocate their headquarters from Dallas to Colorado Springs. Rayburn's letter to staff announcing the move captured his excitement while also suggesting the continued importance of "winsomeness" to Young Life's mission: "God has honored us and blessed us in an unusual way in giving us a National Headquarters which will catch the fancy of every youngster with whom we come in contact." The letter also demonstrated that Rayburn understood the story of Star Ranch in providential terms: "I am bowled over by the succession of events and impressions in the hearts and lives of many of God's men that all point to His sovereign leading in the matter of preparing this place for us and preparing us for this place."[85] Star Ranch did indeed transform Young Life. An insider account of the movement observed, "It was as if, overnight, Young Life was in a whole new league. Jim had something tangible to show people, a window through which the methods of Young Life could be seen."[86] Importantly, Young Life now had something tangible to show *donors*. When, for instance, Herbert Taylor arranged for Rayburn to meet with a group of Chicago businessmen, Rayburn brought along colored slides of Star Ranch to show them.[87] Star Ranch also provided the ministry with another source of revenue: the many "graduates" of camps held at the ranch. One Young Life staff bulletin discussed plans to "develop another good potential source of income which we are not realizing on now—the kids who have graduated from Young Life."[88] The ranch thus became a place where Young Life could carry on its work of evangelical fellowship—fellowship that could be transformed into a steady income stream. Glen Eyrie played a similar role for the Navigators, strengthening the group's relationship with other evangelical organizations by allowing it to play the generous host. Glen Eyrie hosted conference after evangelical conference; by 1963, less than a decade after the Navigators purchased the property, 5,000 people had attended conferences there.[89]

Acquiring these properties also created valuable relationships outside the neo-evangelical milieu, with local business leaders welcoming Young Life and the Navigators to the community. Rayburn celebrated the warm welcome his organization had received from "bankers, grocers, butchers, produce men, cold storage men, [and] Chamber of Commerce leaders." Guss Hill, the real estate agent who had guided Young Life to the Springs, also set up the Star Ranch Committee, a group of Western businessmen who raised money on Young Life's behalf.[90] Similarly, the acquisition of Glen Eyrie enmeshed the Navigators in a network of Colorado Springs elites. One local bank president, Jasper Ackerman, extended the Navigators $10,000 worth of credit to help the organization make its payments on Glen Eyrie—a gesture the Navigators recognized as "very unorthodox." Ackerman convinced two other Springs banks to extend similar loans.[91] Not surprisingly, Ackerman attended the dedication of Glen Eyrie in July 1963, as did Young Life's Rayburn and numerous local pastors. The event included the ceremonial burning of the Glen Eyrie mortgage, a demonstration that the Navigators finally "possessed the land" the group had desired for so long.[92]

Occasionally, the welcome was not quite so warm. A minister in Pueblo, Colorado, reportedly warned a Young Life representative against holding a meeting in his city: "If you do you'll be in jail before night as communists, involved in subversive activities with the high school crowd."[93] Such suspicions explain why Young Life was so quick to tout its closeness with Federal Bureau of Investigation director J. Edgar Hoover.[94] But this was nothing compared with the hostility aroused by the Freedom School. Its libertarian politics, especially its criticism of public education and military spending, led many locals to denounce the school as "un-American." At stake in this conflict was the public image of Colorado Springs. Would the community be known as a good place to do business, or would it be associated with extremism?

The Boundaries of Americanism

The Freedom School was the brainchild of Robert LeFevre, a prolific writer and devout libertarian. LeFevre first attracted national attention for his involvement with the Mighty I AM movement, one of the most controversial of the alternative religious movements that flourished in the United States in the 1930s.[95] The I AM movement preached that people could achieve health, happiness, and prosperity by embracing positive thoughts and chanting positive affirmations. Tens of thousands of people packed into auditoriums to join the movement's leaders, the married couple Guy and Edna Ballard, in shouting demands at cosmic entities called "Ascended Masters," demanding health and wealth for themselves and annihilation for their enemies. LeFevre worked as a propagandist for the I AM movement, cowriting a book that detailed the miraculous doings of the Ascended Masters.[96] I AM generated a tremendous amount of enthusiasm—and an equal amount of anxiety. These anxieties intensified as the Ballards became more authoritarian in their leadership and right-wing in their politics.[97] Guy Ballard's death in December 1939 plunged the movement into crisis; a few months later, in July 1940, a federal grand jury indicted Edna Ballard, her son Donald, and twenty-two other I AM leaders on charges of mail fraud. Among those twenty-two others was Robert LeFevre. The charges against the Ballards led to years of trials, but most of the other indictments were dropped, including the one against LeFevre.[98] After leaving I AM and spending several years in the US Army during World War II, LeFevre joined the Falcon Lair Foundation, a Los Angeles–based organization that sought to forestall World War III by encouraging people to pray for peace three times each day.[99]

Though LeFevre claimed to oppose any kind of "ism," he was an inveterate joiner, promoter, and organizer of right-wing causes. In 1950, having left the Falcon Lair Foundation, he ran (unsuccessfully) for Congress on a platform of "complete Americanism."[100] Next, he spent time working as a television commentator in Florida. From there he moved to New York to serve as executive director of the Congress of Freedom, an anti–United Nations organization.[101] LeFevre's work with the Congress of Freedom brought him into contact with some of the more extreme figures on the American right. When the organization elected LeFevre as its executive director, it chose as its secretary Willis Carto, who would go on to become one of the nation's most influential antisemitic propagandists.[102] LeFevre won his own small share of notoriety during this period by attacking the Girl Scouts of America. He charged that the Girl Scouts handbook contained subversive themes, such as its "unqualified endorsement" of the United Nations.[103]

LeFevre was living in Colorado Springs at the time of his campaign against the Girl Scouts, having moved there to assume leadership of yet another right-wing group, the United States Day Committee. LeFevre found a perfect ally in his new home: R. C. Hoiles, owner of the local *Gazette Telegraph*. Hoiles was a doctrinaire libertarian whose chain of "Freedom Newspapers" assailed "public schools, libraries, majority rule, paper money, collective bargaining, social welfare laws, [and] most taxes."[104] The paper's editorial pages featured conservative columnists like anti-union crusader Westbrook Pegler; they also featured Hoiles himself, who used his daily column to attack enemies ranging from Joseph Stalin to Franklin D. Roosevelt to Robert Taft (whom Hoiles dismissed as a "collectivist").[105] Hoiles, recognizing LeFevre as a kindred spirit, hired him to write editorials for the *Gazette Telegraph*.

LeFevre's ambitions went beyond writing editorials, however. With financial support from Hoiles, LeFevre sought to realize his long-held dream of founding a school that would teach libertarian principles. He incorporated the "Freedom School" in February 1956; the filing papers were signed by LeFevre, his wife, Lois, and a retired steel executive named Robert Donner.[106] Donner's involvement signaled another link between LeFevre and the far right: Donner had spent years campaigning against the supposed leftist takeover of American education, often invoking antisemitic conspiracies while doing so.[107] Construction of the Freedom School began in the fall of 1956, as volunteers tore down dilapidated cabins at an old campsite to make room for the school. The first students arrived at the Freedom School in the summer of 1957.[108]

These students were instructed in a curriculum stamped with LeFevre's version of libertarianism. He described his philosophy as "autarchy," which he took care to distinguish from anarchy.[109] Autarchy, unlike anarchy, made room for the profit motive. It also drew a sharp distinction between the individual and the government, categories LeFevre considered mutually exclusive. Government had only one legitimate function: protecting individuals from people who might be "physically a criminal, mentally unbalanced, or morally degenerated." That function was best handled by "small and local constabularies." National governments, by contrast, punished not criminals but "law-abiding citizens" who ran afoul of state regimentation and so were illegitimate.[110] LeFevre thus rejected essentially all forms of taxation and regulation. Though these views placed him well to the right on the American political spectrum, they were not idiosyncratic; Barry Goldwater sounded some of the same themes in his 1964 campaign for the presidency. What distinguished LeFevre from many other conservatives was his ambivalent view of the national security state. He granted the need for some form of national defense but warned that governments "tend to engender fear. They end by believing their own engenderings."[111] Fears about foreign enemies might be used to justify the expansion of government—and the restriction of freedom—at home.

Not surprisingly, almost everyone involved in the Freedom School had ties to other right-wing organizations. While LeFevre managed to convince some of the country's most influential libertarians, including future Nobel laureate Friedrich Hayek, to serve as "academic advisers" to the Freedom School, these luminaries taught classes only on rare occasions. The bulk of the teaching was handled by a cadre of conservative activists, many of whom had close ties to the business world. Several faculty members made their living busting unions when not teaching at the school.[112] The Freedom School had a particularly close association with the John Birch Society, the era's most controversial right-wing group. The John Birch Society was notorious for its secretive nature, intense anti-communism, and proclivity for conspiracy theories.[113] Conservative politicians sought to distance themselves from the group's extremism even as they courted its members. Robert LeFevre had no such qualms and embraced the society without hesitation. Wichita businessman Robert D. Love was both a member of the National Council of the John Birch Society and a trustee of the Freedom School. Love introduced fellow Kansan—and fellow John Birch Society member—Charles Koch to LeFevre. Koch, who would become one of the most important financial backers of American conservatism, would eventually serve as the Freedom School's vice president.[114]

Love and Koch were both part of a network of right-wing donors that funded the Freedom School. A good deal of this money came from R. C. Hoiles, who gave about $25,000 to the school in 1964.[115] The most generous donor was Roger Milliken, a South Carolina textile manufacturing executive and John Birch Society member.[116] Milliken was so enthusiastic about the "Freedom Philosophy" that he hired LeFevre to lead classes at his company's headquarters. After one such class, Milliken wrote a letter to LeFevre pledging $100,000 to his school as "evidence of our appreciation."[117] Numerous other corporate executives and corporate-affiliated foundations poured money into the Freedom School.[118] Though the largest donors came from outside Colorado Springs, more than a few residents of the city contributed money. Local donors included H. Chase Stone, a banker who had played a major role in bringing Fort Carson and the Air Force Academy to the Springs.[119]

The Freedom School may not have been a Christian organization, but its mission resembled those of Young Life and the Navigators. It too promised a refuge, not from moral decay but from creeping socialism. Like the Christian ministries, the school emphasized the secluded and idyllic nature of its campus. "The noise and confusion of urban centers vanish as if by magic," boasted one brochure.[120] And just as Young Life targeted young people and the Navigators targeted servicemen, the Freedom School also targeted a specific constituency. It sought to reach "businessmen, executives, branch managers, department heads and others who carry the burden of free enterprise."[121] Teenagers would leave Young Life camps prepared to spread the gospel of Jesus Christ; managers and executives would leave the Freedom School prepared to spread the gospel of free enterprise.

The first class of students arrived at the Freedom School in the summer of 1957; by the mid-1960s, the school had graduated over 700 students from its two-week summer courses.[122] These students came from across the United States and represented a variety of occupations, from housewives to nuclear physicists.[123] Despite LeFevre's ambivalence toward the military, quite a few students were affiliated with the armed forces. The recipients of Freedom School scholarships in 1963 included a captain at Fort Carson and a cadet at the Air Force Academy.[124]

Not every student was welcome, however. Though LeFevre claimed the Freedom School did not discriminate, as of 1965 every single student was white. And, as LeFevre blithely noted in an interview, "some of his students [were] segregationists," meaning any Black students would need to find separate accommodations.[125] Nor, ironically, did all students attend the Freedom School of their own free will. The school's association with newspaper publisher R. C. Hoiles provided a steady supply of captive students, as Hoiles sent his employees to the school to prevent any ideological "backsliding."[126] Some of those who did attend were disturbed by what they learned. When four teachers from Rockford, Illinois, returned from a summer session at the Freedom School, they wrote an angry letter to their town's chamber of commerce—which had paid for their classes—saying, "We do not believe the Rockford Chamber of Commerce wants us to teach what we were taught [at] this seminar." They noted that the school taught there should be no government whatsoever, "not even national defense supported by taxation." They also accused the school of teaching that "all religion is a myth" and criticized it for failing to fly an American flag.[127] These disgruntled students regarded the Freedom School as an offender against the political and religious norms of the era.

These and similar accusations proved a stumbling block to LeFevre's dream of expanding the Freedom School into a four-year liberal arts college. LeFevre worked hard to win local support for this dream, gathering dozens of Colorado Springs businessmen at the city's Antlers Hotel in February 1963 to pitch them on "Rampart College." "The Pikes Peak Region," he promised them, "can become one of the nation's leading educational and cultural centers."[128] His efforts bore fruit. The executive committee of the Colorado Springs Chamber of Commerce drafted a letter welcoming Rampart College to the region, stating that it marked "another step forward in the economic development of the Pikes Peak area."[129] Not everyone in Colorado Springs shared the chamber's enthusiasm, however. The Freedom School had always been controversial in the Springs, thanks to its association with the *Gazette Telegraph*. That newspaper's relentless attacks on local government had earned it many enemies. William C. Henderson, mayor of Colorado Springs from 1959 to 1963, hated the paper so much that he barred it from his home and office.[130] Rampart College aroused similar feelings. One local television commentator warned that a "gathering of extremists" in the Pikes Peak area would hurt the region's ability to attract business.[131] Criticism also came from within the local business community. After the chamber's executive committee extended its welcome to Rampart College, one member of the committee protested the decision, saying, "I can think of many enterprises which would bring additional dollars to the community . . . yet which would be no more wanted by the Chamber members than is a skunk welcomed at a family picnic."[132]

The strongest opposition came from the *Free Press*, the city's morning newspaper. The *Free Press* was a fierce rival of the *Gazette Telegraph*; indeed, it had been created explicitly to oppose R. C. Hoiles and his libertarian philosophy. When Hoiles purchased the *Gazette Telegraph* in 1946, its unionized printers broke with the paper to establish the *Free Press*.[133] The *Free Press*'s unrelenting hostility to the *Gazette Telegraph* extended to Robert LeFevre, the Freedom School, and Rampart College. The paper launched countless attacks on the Freedom School, often in hyperbolic language. One *Free Press* editorial charged that libertarianism was an atheistic philosophy because the "extreme freedom advocated by the libertarians was incompatible with the notion of Divine omniscience"—a grave charge to make in an era of religious revival.[134] In the midst of the debate over Rampart College, the *Free Press* published a twenty-page pamphlet assailing the proposed school. "This newspaper has declared war," the pamphlet's introduction said. "We are not waging this war for personal gain; we are in it because we love our country, our state, our community, our friends." This pamphlet attacked the *Gazette Telegraph* and its affiliates from every angle, but it emphasized the threat the "Freedom Philosophy" posed to the local economy. It complained that the *Gazette Telegraph* sought "to tear down, not to build" and that the Freedom

Philosophy "would cripple the economy of the Pikes Peak region." And beneath photographs of the Air Force Academy and Fort Carson, a headline blared, "TAXES PAID FOR THESE BUILDINGS AND INSTITUTIONS—COULD WE GET ALONG WITHOUT THEM?"[135] In the Pikes Peak region, contests over ideology were inseparable from debates over economic development.

Multiple factors killed LeFevre's dream of a libertarian college. Fierce opposition from the *Free Press* and other Colorado Springs organizations certainly contributed. So too did the scope of his ambition. The Freedom School had successfully raised tens of thousands of dollars, but Rampart College would require millions to simply get off the ground. This was difficult to pull off, especially when there were other, better-established programs preaching the virtues of free-market capitalism and the evils of communism.[136] Natural disasters compounded these problems. A series of storms and floods struck the Pikes Peak region in the summer of 1965, burying part of the Freedom School in mud.[137] Late in 1968, LeFevre decamped for Santa Ana, California, taking with him the remnants of the Freedom School. He explained the move in quintessentially libertarian terms: "It became apparent that we had to get out of the woods and into the market place in order to attract students."[138] LeFevre would continue teaching and writing in Southern California until his death in 1986.

The Freedom School had failed to find a place within the "American way of life" envisioned by the boosters of Colorado Springs. Evangelical organizations like Young Life and the Navigators proved a better fit. A combination of ideology and self-interest bound these ministries to the city's business leadership. The city's reputation as a place where Christianity and commerce worked together drew other ministries to the Springs in the years ahead, most notably the Christian Booksellers Association, which relocated from Chicago to the Springs in 1970; International Students Inc., which moved from Washington, DC, in 1972; and Compassion International, which moved from Chicago in 1980. But this was only the start. In the 1980s, changes in the political economy of American religion turned what was already a steady stream of ministries into a deluge that threatened to overwhelm the city.

2
MAKING JESUS SPRINGS

The dedication of Focus on the Family's new headquarters in Colorado Springs was a day to remember. The ceremony, held Saturday, September 25, 1993, began with the Air Force Chorale performing "Battle Hymn of the Republic." Next onstage was James Dobson himself, president of Focus, the man whose stern child-rearing advice had made him a hero to millions of Americans. Focus's new $30 million headquarters, sprawling over forty-seven acres, testified to his influence, as did the crowd of 15,000. But Dobson insisted that the headquarters was "not a monument to me. This is a gift from you, our friends, to help us stand up for the family in these critical times." After Dobson came speeches from prominent evangelicals, concluding with one by Prison Fellowship Ministries founder (and convicted Watergate felon) Charles Colson. Where Dobson was folksy, Colson was fiery: "There is a battle going on for the soul of America. . . . When there's a battle going on you want to be on the front lines, and this is the front line." Yet the ceremony was not solely a religious affair. Robert Isaac, mayor of Colorado Springs, and Bill Armstrong, former US senator from Colorado, shared the stage with Dobson and Colson. Former president George H. W. Bush sent a congratulatory telegram that was read from the stage. And the crowning moment came when the Wings of Blue, the skydiving team from the nearby Air Force Academy, parachuted onto the site and handed Dobson the key to the building.[1]

Some later recalled that the skydivers gave Dobson not the key to his new headquarters but the key to the city.[2] An understandable mistake, for the ceremony seemed to herald the start of an evangelical age in Colorado Springs. Focus on the Family was only one of more than fifty evangelical Christian ministries to move to the city between 1980 and 1995. Little wonder that observers began to give the city nicknames like the "Evangelical Vatican" and "Jesus Springs."

Why did these organizations relocate to Colorado Springs? Answering this question reveals an important truth: Evangelical institutions are businesses. They may be other things as well, but they are as concerned with their bottom line as any for-profit corporation.[3] It was this concern for the bottom line that brought them to Colorado Springs. They were drawn by changes to Colorado's tax code: Between the 1940s and 1980s, the state gradually expanded the tax exemptions available to religious institutions, to the point where almost any property owned by a religious organization was considered tax-exempt. And they were also drawn by the blandishments of the Colorado Springs Chamber of Commerce. The chamber, seeking to revive a local economy devastated by cutbacks in defense spending and a real estate crash, plied evangelical organizations with promises of cheap land and cheap labor. This proved an irresistible combination. Evangelical organizations relocated to the Springs by the dozens, growing and strengthening the community established decades earlier by the arrival of Young Life and the Navigators.

Neither the evangelicals who came to the Springs nor the boosters who recruited them intended to turn the city into a battleground. Like previous generations of business and religious leaders, they prized consensus, unity, and cooperation.[4] But the volume of this evangelical migration to the city, which far outweighed the previous ones, proved more destabilizing than they anticipated. Then, too, the Colorado Springs of the 1990s looked very different from that of the 1940s, when the first ministries arrived. Growth had brought increasing diversity to the city: diversity not only of religion but also of race, ethnicity, ideology, and sexuality. Many non-evangelicals began to worry that their city might be the target of an evangelical takeover. And here is this chapter's second key claim: Though evangelical organizations were businesses, they were not *only* businesses. Decisions made for economic reasons, like the decision to relocate to Colorado Springs, had significant impacts in the world of culture and politics.

No Particular Creed

Colorado's courts struggled to define both the rationale for and the extent of tax exemptions for religious institutions. From the passage of the Revenue Act of 1894 onward, federal legislation exempted religious institutions from the federal income tax; most states, including Colorado, provided similar exemptions. Congress and state legislatures alike studiously avoided defining the term "religious institution," giving judges significant leeway to interpret what did or did not count as religious.[5] Judges in Colorado tended to define the term expansively, leading the state tax commission to complain about the revenue lost as a result of these generous interpretations.[6] One such case, *Kemp v. Pillar of Fire*, decided by the Colorado Supreme Court in 1933, dealt with 200 acres of land owned by a Bible institute. The school used the land to grow fruits and vegetables for its students. Did this count as a religious (and hence tax-exempt) purpose? The court held that it did, because "[to] confine the exemption to the building and the campus would seriously cripple the institution in carrying out its laudable purpose."[7] This decision suggested that anything that contributed to a religious purpose, even if it was not in itself obviously religious, merited an exemption. The court reaffirmed this point in *McGlone v. First Baptist Church* (1935). Denver's First Baptist Church owned property on which it planned to build a new worship space; when the Great Depression devastated the church's finances, it was left with a vacant lot on its hands. The court ruled that, because this vacant lot was intended for religious use, it ought to be tax-exempt. This was going too far for some justices. One dissenting judge grumbled that the *McGlone* decision "announces in effect that doctrine that all real estate owned by a religious corporation is exempt from taxation."[8] With *First Congregational Church of Fort Collins v. Wright* (1942), the Colorado Supreme Court marked the outer limit of what it counted as "religious purposes." The First Congregational Church leased one of its buildings to an "Academy of Fine Arts," which in turn occasionally subleased the property to other organizations. Here, the Colorado Supreme Court drew the line: "We think under the facts disclosed by the record that this building was not used 'exclusively for religious worship' but on the contrary was employed primarily for commercial and business purposes, and hence taxable."[9] Thus, when Young Life and the Navigators arrived, Colorado provided generous tax exemptions for religious property. But its generosity was not unlimited; some things were not "religious" enough to deserve an exemption.

Soon after moving to Colorado Springs, Young Life found itself embroiled in this ongoing debate over the meaning of religion. The struggle hinged on the question of whether the organization used its Colorado properties for religious purposes. The commissioners of Chaffee County, Colorado, home to a property that Young Life purchased a few years after buying Star Ranch, argued that the camp was not used for worship and thus should not be exempt from property taxes. Young Life protested that, while it might use these camps for activities like fishing and horseback riding, such things were simply "incidental yet necessary" to its primary purpose of bringing young people to Christ.[10] Far from draining the state's finances, the camps actually performed a valuable social service by teaching young people that "the Bible and the Christian faith is important to American democracy and to their personal way of life."[11] Young Life's brief also invoked the rhetoric of the Cold War: "In America," its brief asserted, "God fearing and democracy loving citizens have joined in charitable enterprise to relieve our government of the burden of . . . training our youth to resist the evils of Communism and to fight for the survival of Christian democracy."[12] Lawyers for Chaffee County dismissed these claims, arguing that Young Life could hardly be considered an authentic religious organization, as it had "no particular creed." When the case reached the Colorado Supreme Court in 1956, the court ruled against Young Life, determining that, because the organization was not incorporated in Colorado and did much of its work outside the state, it did not merit an exemption. An exemption, the court held, was earned by providing a social benefit to the people of Colorado—something the justices believed Young Life failed to do.[13]

Over the following decades, however, a series of legal changes undermined that ruling by shifting the meaning of religion. The changes began in 1967, when a bipartisan group of state legislators expanded property tax exemptions to include "property, real and personal, that is owned and used solely and exclusively for religious worship and not for private and corporate profit."[14] Religious institutions took this as an invitation to renew their demands for broad tax exemptions. The General Conference of the Church of God (Seventh Day) sought an exemption on a publishing house it owned and operated, arguing that members of its denomination could not engage in religious worship without the material it produced. In an echo of the arguments against Young Life, attorneys for the state tax assessor argued that the material produced by the publishing house was not truly religious: "None of the exhibits in the court's records were hymnals, prayer books, or other materials commonly used in a worship service." This argument did not carry the weight it once had, however. The state supreme court, in *General Conference of the Church of God v. Carper* (1976), cited the new Colorado law in siding with the denomination.[15] For the purposes of taxation, "religion" in Colorado now included practices that took place outside houses of worship.

Even this broad definition of "religion" had limits, which the Colorado Supreme Court marked out in *West-Brandt Foundation, Inc. v. Carper* (1982). Like the *Young Life* case, *West-Brandt* concerned a ranch: the "Singin' River Ranch" owned and operated by the Louisiana-based West-Brandt Foundation. The foundation claimed that the ranch merited a religious exemption because it was made available "to schools and church groups on a nondenominational basis."[16] This was not enough to convince the Colorado courts. The Colorado Court of Appeals noted that, while the ranch might be used by religious organizations, it was also used by "ski groups" as well as by "a family reunion, a wedding rehearsal dinner, [and] a retirement dinner."[17] Noting that "the presumption is against tax exemption and the right to an exemption must be clearly established by the claimant," the court declined to grant a property tax exemption to the Singin' River Ranch, a decision upheld by the Colorado Supreme Court. Though the West-Brandt Foundation lost the case, an amicus brief filed on the foundation's behalf would play an important role in future changes to Colorado's tax laws. This brief, written by attorneys for Christian Camping International, argued that *any* activity carried out by a religious organization was inherently charitable and thus deserved an exemption on charitable grounds.[18] This view, if accepted by the courts, would make it far more difficult for a government agency to challenge a religious organization's claim to a tax exemption—indeed, it would make it difficult to challenge an organization's claim to be *religious*, period.[19]

Young Life continued to seek tax exemptions during the 1980s, with mixed success; its ambiguous form, evidently religious but not obviously a church, proved puzzling to many judges. One case began in California,

Making Jesus Springs

where Young Life sought exemption from the state's unemployment tax. California's Unemployment Insurance Appeals Board determined that Young Life was not exempt because it was not a church. For decades, Young Life had avoided the label "church" as part of its effort to appeal to young people; now, it seemed as if that strategy might come back to bite it. But the decision in *Young Life Campaign v. Patino* (1981), handed down by a California Court of Appeals, overruled the appeals board and decided that Young Life was a religious institution after all: "[As] regards their purposes, their use of the Bible, promulgation of a creed or doctrine and the conduct of worship, [Young Life] performed 'church functions.'"[20] The organization might have denied the label of "church," but it was church-like enough to earn a tax exemption.

As this case worked its way through the California courts, a similar case arose in Colorado. There, too, Young Life sought exemption from the state unemployment tax. As in California, the case turned on how one defined a church. Colorado's Division of Employment, in denying Young Life's request for an exemption, argued that the organization lacked the essential characteristics of a church: "a local congregation, a denominational organization, and a local house of worship." Indeed, the division claimed that Young Life had "no membership at all," as its "participants could be different every week." Colorado's supreme court agreed; its decision determined that Young Life was neither a "religious denomination" nor a distinct "mode of worship" and was thus ineligible for exemption from the unemployment tax.[21] Parachurch organizations like Young Life failed to fit the conception of "church" held by state bureaucracies, at least in Colorado.

Less than a decade later, however, Young Life finally succeeded in its decades-long struggle to define its Colorado camps as religious property. In the wake of the *General Conference of the Church of God* decision, the ministry once again filed for a property tax exemption on its Colorado ranches. Yet again, the case came down to definitions. An investigator for the state's property tax division reported that, when she visited the ranches, she "did not see any buildings that appeared to be set aside for religious reflection."[22] Young Life's attorneys sought to rebut this argument by putting forward an expansive definition of religion—a change from the group's legal strategy in the 1950s, when it had sought an exemption on the basis of the social benefit the organization supposedly provided to Colorado's citizens. "The only reason that Young Life owns its properties," the ministry's brief asserted, was to fulfill its mission to "bring kids into a personal relationship with

Christ."[23] Young Life's attorneys also challenged the qualifications of a government employee to determine what was and was not religious, providing testimony from pastors as counterevidence. William Frey, Episcopal bishop of Colorado, claimed that Young Life's ranches, far from being secular, embodied the spirit of biblical Christianity: "The Christian Faith was begun in the setting of mountaintops, lakesides, rivers, and streams.... There were no formal Christian church buildings in those days."[24] Young Life pointed to this evidence as proof that its camps were religious. This time, the Colorado Supreme Court agreed. The court's decision in *Maurer v. Young Life* (1989) declared that protecting religious freedom required a broad definition of religion and equally broad tax exemptions for religious property.[25]

In 1989, the same year the Colorado Supreme Court handed down its decision in *Maurer v. Young Life*, the Colorado legislature passed a law that—like the court's opinion—conflated religious freedom with freedom from taxation. State senator Terry Considine, an evangelical Republican representing a suburban Denver district, introduced a bill that allowed religious bodies, rather than the state tax assessor, to define "religious worship." This change would give religious organizations greater leeway in claiming exemptions.[26] Considine called a diverse group of religious figures to testify on the bill's behalf, including several evangelical pastors; an attorney for the Catholic Archdiocese of Denver; and William Frey, the Episcopal bishop who had testified in Young Life's favor during its struggle against the tax assessor. These witnesses all argued for Considine's bill on the grounds of religious freedom, but several added an economic element to their claims. Frey noted that, because religious organizations often provide social services, lifting their tax burden would encourage the growth of "those institutions that get society's work done at the least possible cost to society."[27] Mary Anne Maurer, Colorado's property tax assessor, pushed back against such claims. She warned that Considine's bill would motivate organizations to claim "religious" status solely to escape taxation. To prove this point, Maurer prepared a memo listing organizations that would be tax-exempt under the new law. Her memo was a collection of horror stories; first on the list was the "Spiral of Friends," a commune whose members had been indicted for child abuse and possession of child pornography.[28] But Maurer's protest was overwhelmed by the ecumenical support for Considine's bill, which was passed by the Colorado legislature and signed into law by Governor Roy Romer in May 1989.[29]

This law, combined with the *Maurer* decision, made Colorado one of the most generous states in the country in terms of granting tax exemptions to religious organizations. Considine recognized that this might work to Colorado's advantage in the quest for economic growth. He said as much during the debate over his bill: "Colorado Springs has become one of three places in the country where national organizations with religious focus have made their headquarters," he said, arguing that easing the tax burden might entice still more organizations to relocate.[30] The evidence suggests he was right. A 1995 survey found that almost a quarter of the state's religious property tax exemptions had been filed since 1989, the date of both the court case and the new law. In El Paso County, home of Colorado Springs, the proportion of post-1989 exemption filings was greater than a quarter.[31] Legal changes made Colorado a religious tax haven.

Aerospace Capital, Foreclosure Capital, Evangelical Capital

The transformation of Colorado's legal landscape coincided with significant changes in the economy of Colorado Springs. Despite their successes in World War II and the early Cold War, business leaders in the Springs knew their city could not rely on military spending alone. They tried to diversify the local economy by enticing high-tech companies with offers of cheap land and low-wage labor. The strategy seemed to work: Kaman Science arrived in the city in 1957, followed in succeeding decades by Hewlett-Packard, Texas Instruments, NCR, and the Digital Equipment Corporation.[32] Successful business recruitment and a vigorous real estate market yielded a boom economy for the Springs as of the early 1980s. The value of nonresidential construction in the city almost tripled between 1982 and 1984; during the same period, its annual population rose almost 4 percent, making it one of the nation's fastest-growing cities.[33] Forecasters, looking at this increase, saw something more than a bubble. They predicted a period of sustained growth that would continue into the far future. No matter what one thought of the future, however, the facts of the present were undeniable—and they bore out the declaration of one real estate developer that in 1984 "Colorado Springs experienced its most spectacular year ever!"[34]

Yet not even a boom of this size could free Colorado Springs from its dependence on the military. As of 1980, the Department of Defense and defense-dependent activities accounted for more than 90,000 jobs and over a billion dollars in payroll in the city.[35] The military's presence was poised to grow further in the 1980s, as billions of dollars in aerospace-related funding flowed into the Springs. In 1979, the Department of Defense awarded the city the Consolidated Space Operations Center, which would coordinate all military-related activity in space.[36] The Springs also won the National Test Facility, where supercomputers would run simulations to model combat in space. Per one estimate, the National Test Facility would be worth as much as $1 billion to the city.[37]

Business leaders believed this federal money would transform Colorado Springs into a great city, the "Aerospace Capital of the Free World." Real estate developers, foreseeing a boom, bought up huge tracts of land adjacent to the Consolidated Space Operations Center site. One developer, Martin List, purchased 3,000 acres and announced plans to turn it into an "Aerospace Center" that would include a "List Institute for the Strategic Exploration of Space."[38] When talking to the press, developers used hyperbole as big as their properties. List, for instance, foresaw a new "industrial revolution" in the making, while another developer said that "Colorado stands at the leading edge of a new Renaissance."[39] These exaggerations seemed almost plausible in light of soaring land values. Property once valued at $2,000 an acre now sold for six times that amount. An 800-acre ranch near the site of the future Consolidated Space Operations Center sold for $5.6 million.[40] Boosters looked on with glee as defense contractors like Martin Marietta began placing offices in the Springs. As one observer noted, "It's the same thing they did in Houston. They come in and take 2,000 square feet, and then they come in with manufacturing space."[41] The comparison to Houston was telling, as many observers predicted the military space program would transform Colorado Springs in the same way NASA had transformed Houston in the early days of the space race.[42]

But within a few years, these dreams gave way to a harsh reality. Far from becoming the "Aerospace Capital of the Free World," the city instead became the "Foreclosure Capital of America." Military money proved less of a sure thing than the boosters assumed. In the mid-1980s, Congress began to make cuts in the defense budget, cuts that drew blood in Colorado Springs. The first victim was the Shuttle Operations Planning Complex, a $500 million project that evaporated when Congress cut its funding in 1987.[43] Further reductions came in 1988 when Congress slashed Ronald Reagan's request for Strategic Defense Initiative funding from $4.9 billion to $4 billion.[44]

These cutbacks coincided with instability in the city's high-tech industry. As high-tech manufacturers began to feel the squeeze of foreign competition, particularly from Japan, they fled the city in search of cheaper labor, repeating the process that had brought them to the Springs in the first place.[45] Microelectronic manufacturing plant closures eliminated almost 2,000 jobs in El Paso County between 1985 and 1988.[46] These blows crushed the overbuilt real estate market and plunged the local economy into a recession.[47] Throughout the latter half of the 1980s, Colorado Springs' *Gazette Telegraph* reported a seemingly endless stream of foreclosures, announcing dozens each month.

The Colorado Springs Chamber of Commerce sought a magic bullet to solve these problems, leading it to embrace ideas that seem absurd in hindsight. One was "Liberty Park," a theme park dedicated to the US Constitution. Both the chamber and the city's mayor endorsed the park, even though its founder could never explain where its funding would come from. Fantastic claims about a Disneyland-sized park that would feature "a monthlong outdoor pageant of patriotic drama" eventually yielded to reality. By 1992, even people who had once boosted the park admitted it would remain a dream.[48] Still, Liberty Park was harmless whimsy compared with Aries Properties, the biggest, boldest, and most toxic attempt to revitalize the local economy. Frank Aries made a fortune developing land around Tucson in the 1970s. He turned his attention to Colorado Springs in the 1980s, using a $225 million loan from Phoenix's Western Savings and Loan to buy 22,000 acres of land near the city. This land, he declared, would become a thriving suburban community, an "American Dream" made real. City council members, browbeaten by Aries and blinded by their hopes of rejuvenating the economy, took the unusual step of annexing the entire 22,000-acre tract in one swoop. No one thought Aries's scheme might fail—yet it did. Western Savings and Loan collapsed, followed soon after by Aries Properties. Aries fled Colorado to live on his Miami yacht, leaving behind nothing but empty scrubland populated by those few people who were unlucky enough to get in on the ground floor of his scheme.[49]

It seemed like these dire circumstances might shatter the nostrums that had guided the city's development for decades, namely, that attracting outside capital was the path to growth, and that the best way to attract capital was with offers of cheap property and low taxes. The chamber of commerce commissioned the Fantus Company, a Chicago-based consulting firm, to study the local economy and develop a plan of action. Between September 1987 and May 1988, Fantus consultants interviewed dozens of local politicians and businesspeople and scrutinized reams of economic data. Their conclusions were grim. They noted that while Colorado Springs was growing, it lagged far behind "megatrend" cities like Phoenix, Austin, and Orlando.[50] These cities all possessed greater amounts of available capital, superior educational facilities, and highly diversified economies.[51] The only solution, Fantus suggested, was for the chamber to merge with the municipal government, creating a public-private partnership to encourage business development. The chamber considered this proposal and promptly rejected it. Council members' fiscal conservatism revolted at the thought of working with local government.[52] Instead, the boosters returned to their well-worn strategy of attracting outside capital with promises of cheap land and labor. To lead this crusade for capital, they created an organization called the Economic Development Corporation (EDC). Though the EDC had the power to set its own policy and hire its own staff, it was funded entirely by business donations.[53]

Because the EDC was dependent on outside money, its mission could be shaped by whatever organization was willing to put up the necessary funds. The El Pomar Foundation quickly stepped into the role of the EDC's benefactor. El Pomar was a Springs-based philanthropy established in 1937 by mining millionaire Spencer Penrose for two purposes: promoting culture and avoiding taxes. For the first few decades of its existence, it did much more of the latter than the former. But the Tax Reform Act of 1969, which required foundations to spend a substantial portion of their endowments, prodded El Pomar to expand its philanthropy.[54] The foundation directed much of its effort and resources toward recruiting nonprofit organizations to Colorado Springs, with the goal of making the city a "mecca" for nonprofits. Throughout the 1970s and 1980s, El Pomar enjoyed particular success at attracting sports-related associations; it lured the United States Olympic Committee from New York City in 1977 with a $1 million grant and the promise of cheap land (land that had once served as a military base, an indication of how the military continued to shape the local economy).[55] Other nonprofits that El Pomar recruited to the Springs meshed well with the city's conservative culture; these included the US Space Foundation, which promoted the commercialization of space, and Junior Achievement, which taught students the virtues of free enterprise.[56] Bill Hybl, El Pomar's CEO, explained these efforts as a matter of economic necessity. Nonprofits, he argued, diversified the economy while also fulfilling "services that cannot be filled by government or private enterprise." But Hybl also praised the cultural impact of nonprofits: They provided "a sense of where this community could go."[57] Nonprofits could steer the community in (what El Pomar perceived as) the right direction.

El Pomar provided some of its money directly to nonprofits, but it also channeled hundreds of thousands of dollars through the chamber of commerce and the EDC. Robert "Rocky" Scott, director of the EDC, acknowledged the foundation's influence: "When El Pomar is ready to write a check, it usually becomes the dominant force behind a deal."[58] Scott further recognized that the EDC, given its straitened circumstances, needed to be selective about which sort of businesses it pursued. It could target only companies that were likely to accept the EDC's offer. El Pomar's money meant the EDC could include nonprofits in that category.[59] The task of recruiting nonprofits fell primarily to an EDC employee named Alice Worrell.

Alice Neddo Worrell made an ideal person to balance the worlds of Christianity and commerce. She graduated from Bethel College, an Indiana school affiliated with the Missionary Church, an evangelical denomination with Mennonite roots.[60] After a decade working for the chamber of commerce in South Bend, Indiana, Worrell moved to Colorado Springs in 1984 to take a job as vice president of the Economic Development Group (which would become the EDC). There, she had the all-important job of recruiting businesses to the Springs. Worrell targeted companies ranging from plastic manufacturers to computer programmers, but in addition to these more traditional concerns she also courted evangelical Christian organizations. Here, she had an advantage, for—as she put it—she could speak their language. She was the daughter of evangelical missionaries and was herself a devout evangelical Christian. And she knew what her target audience wanted: "Most people I talk to," she said, "are trying to escape liberalism."[61]

"Liberalism" meant more than a political persuasion. It referred to a whole host of social ills, most of them associated with big cities. One element of "liberalism" that evangelical institutions wanted to escape was the high cost of living in major metropolitan areas like New York, Chicago, and Southern California. Many of these organizations were cash-strapped to begin with. Talk of a "financial crisis in the churches" ran rampant in the late 1980s and early 1990s, with numerous studies finding that churches and ministries were struggling to make ends meet.[62] Ministries, unlike congregations, were rarely tied to a specific place, and so many responded to these economic challenges by relocating. Many moved south. SIM (formerly Sudan Interior Mission), a missionary ministry, moved from New Jersey, to Charlotte, North Carolina, in 1986, choosing that city over Atlanta and Tampa.63 Trans World Radio moved from New Jersey to Cary, North Carolina, in 1991. It was one of several Christian ministries to move there, leading the Raleigh *News & Observer* to dub Cary a "Christian mecca."64 Other institutions looked west: The leaders of Youth for Christ, the old flagship of the neo-evangelical movement, considered relocating their suburban Chicago headquarters to Dallas, Indianapolis, or Orlando before ultimately deciding on Denver.65 But while these cities attracted some evangelical ministries, Colorado Springs was the most popular destination, thanks in no small part to Alice Worrell's efforts.

Worrell used every option at her disposal to sell Colorado Springs, starting with the strong evangelical community already present in the city. She recognized that personal testimony would go a long way within the tightly knit world of evangelical organizations. Her pursuit of the Christian and Missionary Alliance was typical in this regard. Founded by Presbyterian minister A. B. Simpson in New York City in 1887, the alliance was a Holiness-influenced denomination that emphasized personal sanctification and divine healing.66 The rising cost of living drove the alliance's headquarters from New York City to Nyack, New York, in 1974, but within a decade the denomination found that Nyack's high housing costs made it impossible to hire new staff.67 Its leaders began to look for a new headquarters—and here Worrell intervened. She not only lobbied the alliance herself but also enlisted the aid of evangelical ministries already located in the Springs. In November 1987, as the alliance's relocation committee deliberated between the Springs and three other sites, committee members received a letter from Lorne Sanny, president of the Navigators. Sanny extolled the city's virtues, writing, "I believe you would discover Colorado Springs to have a warm supportive evangelical community." A similar letter from Compassion International, which had relocated to the Springs in 1980, praised the city as the "Little Wheaton of the West," a reference to the Illinois town that was home to Wheaton College and numerous other important evangelical institutions.68 When the alliance's relocation committee visited Colorado Springs in January 1988, Worrell made sure its members met representatives from the city's evangelical community, including the Navigators, Young Life, and the

International Bible Society.[69] The denomination's board of directors, swayed by these efforts, selected the Springs as the site for the new headquarters.

More tangible considerations supplemented the bonds of evangelical community. Cheap land and cheap labor had always been the city's chief selling points, and, thanks to the lingering effects of the real estate crash, Worrell could promise plenty of both. The Christian and Missionary Alliance's relocation committee made sure to note that "COLORADO SPRINGS IS AN ECONOMIC PLACE TO HIRE HELP."[70] Cheap labor helped the Springs win another large ministry, OC International. Founded as "Formosa Crusades" in Pasadena in 1951, OC International was one of the many evangelical organizations to emerge from the Youth for Christ movement. The ministry moved its headquarters from place to place in search of an affordable home, ending up in the San Jose metropolitan area in the late 1980s. The high cost of labor and housing there led the ministry to look eastward to Colorado Springs. The ministry's relocation committee noted, "Currently, there is under-employment in the area, with a large labor pool and labor rates [that] are significantly less than the Milpitas area and less than the Sacramento area."[71] The vast expanses of office space left vacant by the real estate crash proved equally alluring. As was the case with so many evangelical organizations—and so many nonprofits in general—the only significant asset OC International possessed was its property, namely, its California headquarters. Any move was contingent on finding property cheaper than that building.[72] Of all the cities the committee considered, a list that included Dallas, San Antonio, and Phoenix, Colorado Springs was the only one that "offered . . . possible deals for a new headquarters building, including a proposed trade."[73] One possible deal was the city's Union Pointe building. Built in 1984 at the height of the real estate boom, it struggled to find tenants after the crash. OC International eventually spent $750,000 to purchase Union Pointe.[74] From foreclosed property to evangelical property: this was Colorado Springs in microcosm.

Even with its low-wage labor, cheap property, and generous tax exemptions, Colorado Springs sometimes lost out in the struggle for ministries. Such was the case with Campus Crusade for Christ, one of the largest and most influential organizations to come out of the neo-evangelical milieu that also produced Young Life and the Navigators. Campus Crusade had enjoyed success in evangelizing college students since its founding in 1951, but it had never succeeded in achieving financial stability.[75] Late in the 1980s, the ministry sought to put its finances in order by moving its headquarters out of San Bernardino, California. Campus Crusade president Bill Bright announced that his ministry would choose its new home from among Atlanta, Dallas–Fort Worth, Charlotte, and Colorado's Front Range. Representatives from Colorado Springs quickly pressed their case. Alice Worrell, accompanied by several business and religious leaders, traveled to Campus Crusade's headquarters early in March 1989 and promised to provide the ministry with cheap property and financial contributions from local businesses. She made a persuasive case: Campus Crusade signed a "letter of intent" in late July to purchase a Springs mall left vacant by the real estate crash.[76] But the deal ultimately fell through. Campus Crusade wanted its new property to be a blank slate, and to move into a mall would force it to tailor its operations to fit the existing architecture. When a Florida real estate developer offered Campus Crusade 275 acres of land for free, the ministry tore up the letter of intent and announced it would move to Orlando.[77] Campus Crusade's example suggests that the same desire that motivated evangelicals in the 1940s remained important in the 1980s: the desire for a headquarters whose size and splendor would match their globe-spanning ambitions.

Though it failed to win Campus Crusade, Colorado Springs soon secured an even greater prize: Focus on the Family, perhaps the most powerful evangelical organization in the United States in the 1980s and 1990s. James Dobson, founder and president of Focus, built his media empire on a simple argument: "Permissive parenting" had destroyed the traditional family and now threatened to destroy the United States itself. Dobson set out to reverse the decline of family and nation by preaching discipline—which, for Dobson, meant reasserting the power that parents wielded over their children, up to and including the right to use physical violence against them. His book *Dare to Discipline* became a surprise bestseller; Dobson followed up this success by creating a seminar series called "Focus on the Family," which developed into a radio series of the same name in 1978.[78] Focus grew rapidly, and by 1990 it boasted over 700 staff members and an annual budget of almost $50 million. In a single month, the ministry received tens of thousands of phone calls and hundreds of thousands of letters from people seeking family advice.[79] Focus also produced huge quantities of media, including magazines, newsletters, radio programs, television shows, and books.[80] Even as it grew, Focus never strayed far from Dobson's original message: What the United States needed was a renewed respect for authority, in both family life and politics.

Focus eventually outgrew the space available in Southern California, where Dobson had begun his career.[81] Because it conducted most of its work via telephone, radio, and mail, the ministry was unbound by geographic constraints and could pick almost anywhere in the United States as its new home. It considered Seattle, Minneapolis, and the Raleigh-Durham area, but Colorado Springs could offer economic incentives that these other cities could not.[82] The recent changes to Colorado tax law would save the ministry almost a million dollars per year. The cheap property and low-wage labor available in the Springs would save several million more.[83] Still, savings alone were not enough. Focus was also looking for direct financial support—which is where the El Pomar Foundation stepped in. In Focus on the Family, the foundation saw a way to advance its dream of making Colorado Springs a mecca for nonprofits. El Pomar decided, as its CEO put it, that "it was in the community's best interests" to recruit Focus, a phrase that captures the foundation's paternalistic approach to economic development.[84] El Pomar offered Focus a $4 million grant to help finance its move to the Springs, an offer the ministry gladly accepted.[85] Focus used the money to purchase forty-seven acres in Briargate, a planned community north of Colorado Springs that had been devastated by the real estate crash. Then, the ministry began to build. After Focus outgrew its previous two headquarters, its leaders wanted the Colorado campus to meet the ministry's needs for the foreseeable future. Judging from the scale of the headquarters, they foresaw a future of tremendous growth. The new complex featured a "215,000-square-foot administration building and a 150,000-square-foot computerized distribution center," as well as a studio where Dobson could record his radio show while visitors watched.[86] Such a sprawling campus could not have been built in California or even in downtown Colorado Springs. Focus could realize its expansive vision only on the exurban frontier.

Focus was not simply attempting to escape the high cost of living in California. It was fleeing the racialized specter of urban decay, of which the cost of living was only a part. Dobson, who grew up in the small towns of the American South and Southwest, never reconciled himself to life in Los Angeles. He would later cite the Watts riots of 1965, which took place when he was a graduate student at the University of Southern California, as the event that sparked his political awakening.[87] Dobson also complained about the "unsafe neighborhoods" and "substandard housing" of Southern California.[88] Boosters in Colorado Springs knew how to address these fears.

James Dobson, founder of Focus on the Family, at the organization's Colorado Springs headquarters. Photo by Mark Reis / Colorado Springs *Gazette* / MCT / Sipa USA.

They had long advertised their community as an alternative to big cities, especially to those in California.[89] Focus on the Family and Colorado Springs thus made a perfect match for each other. Dobson celebrated the "calming influence" of the mountain environment on "those who are used to bumper-to-bumper traffic and high-rise living." Many Focus employees felt the same way. One explained why he was excited to move to Colorado: "I don't necessarily want to raise my children in southern California." Another enthused that in Colorado Springs one could go for an evening stroll without fear of being mugged. The Springs offered these people a refuge from the seeming chaos of urban life.[90]

Focus on the Family's arrival in Colorado Springs sealed the city's reputation as *the* capital of American evangelicalism. This was due partly to Focus itself and partly to the numerous evangelical organizations that followed in Focus's wake. Focus announced its move at the end of 1990. Over the next five years, at least twenty more evangelical organizations relocated to the Springs, including Every Home for Christ, which distributed evangelical literature; the Association of Christian Schools International, which provided curricula and other resources to evangelical schools; and Global Mapping

International, which did mapmaking work for missionary organizations. Most came from Southern California or suburban Chicago, traditional strongholds of evangelicalism, though Kansas, Texas, Florida, and Oklahoma were also represented in the migration. Ministry leaders often singled out Alice Worrell in explaining their decision to move to Colorado Springs. Dick Eastman, leader of Every Home for Christ, praised Worrell for understanding "the spiritual needs that are part of a relocation move like this."[91] Equally important was the presence of other evangelical organizations. Many newcomers relied on information provided by ministries already in the Springs when making their decision to relocate.[92] Some organizations, like Global Mapping International and Every Home for Christ, already had working relationships with Christian ministries in the city. This steady migration continued until it was checked in the mid-1990s by rising real estate prices.[93]

The sheer number of evangelical organizations that moved to Colorado Springs in this period makes it hard to generalize about them, but it should be emphasized that most of them focused on missionary or educational work. A few examples will suffice. HCJB, which moved to Colorado Springs from Miami in 1991, operated missionary radio stations throughout the world. Missionary Training International arrived from Farmington, Michigan, in 1991; like HCJB, its work was mission-oriented, in this case helping train missionaries for "effective intercultural service." Friendship International, which relocated to Colorado Springs from Haviland, Kansas, in 1993, supported evangelism in Eastern Europe and the former Soviet Union. Publishing companies formed another major part of the evangelical migration. The International Bible Society, which arrived from East Brunswick, New Jersey, in 1988, produced different editions of the Bible, including the best-selling New International Version. David C. Cook, which moved to the Springs from Elgin, Illinois, in 1994, was a titan of the Christian publishing world; of all the evangelical organizations which moved to Colorado Springs, it was second only to Focus on the Family in size. Smaller publishing companies included Master Books, which relocated from San Diego in 1993 and published books, videos, and school curricula promoting creationism. Though not a scientific sampling, this list suggests that most of the organizations that relocated to Colorado Springs were cultural producers whose audience lay outside the city.[94]

As more and more evangelical organizations clustered in Colorado Springs, they formed a business community bound by ties of faith, personal connection, and shared mission. Employees moved easily between ministries. Indeed, sometimes they moved a little too easily; a Young Life executive complained to a journalist about losing employees to other ministries: "We would have just as soon kept them."[95] Still, ministry executives worked hard to cultivate friendly relationships among themselves. The Navigators hosted regular meet-and-greet events at Glen Eyrie to introduce newcomers to the heads of other Christian agencies in the city.[96] Employees of larger ministries sometimes founded their own organizations, creating new nodes within the city's evangelical network. The Navigators produced the publishing company Helmers & Howard; Every Home for Christ produced Path Levelers, a ministry that instructed men on how to "perform their God-ordained responsibilities"; the longtime president of International Studies Inc., on retiring, formed a new Springs-based ministry called International Ministries Fellowship.[97] Springs boosters had once touted their city as "Silicon Mountain" in hopes of re-creating the success of California's Silicon Valley in nurturing high-tech industries. Now, that dream was fulfilled, albeit for a different industry. The Springs had become an incubator for evangelical entrepreneurship and innovation.

The Evangelical Vatican

By the mid-1990s, Colorado Springs had firmly established its reputation as the "Wheaton of the West." Some people even began to use a grander nickname: the "Evangelical Vatican." There were thirty-three ministries employing 2,200 people as of November 1991, fifty-three ministries employing 2,400 people as of December 1992, and more than sixty ministries as of February 1994.[98] These numbers were tabulated by Steve Rabey, a journalist who helped popularize the city's image as the capital of American evangelicalism. Rabey surveyed the city's evangelical community in 1991, sending every ministry a questionnaire and a letter that began: "Is Colorado Springs the Wheaton of the West? Or is Wheaton now the Colorado Springs of the Midwest? That's what our readers—and the readers of *Christianity Today*—want to know." The questionnaire asked the ministries about, among other things, their mission, their annual income, and the number of people they employed. Rabey turned the results into a front-page *Gazette Telegraph* story that declared, "The map of the Christian world is being revised in Colorado Springs, literally and figuratively."[99] A version of Rabey's story also appeared in *Christianity Today*, the evangelical movement's flagship journal. Both stories invoked Wheaton, but they also made loftier comparisons. The *Christianity Today* article described the Springs as a "'mecca' of American evangelicalism," and the *Gazette Telegraph* story referred to the city as a "virtual Vatican of American evangelicalism." When Rabey surveyed the ministries again in 1992, he affirmed that the city had "cemented [its] reputation as the Vatican of the American evangelical movement."[100] Colorado Springs now carried the "Evangelical Vatican" nickname that would define its image in the 1990s.

Yet the Evangelical Vatican label requires qualification. Though the migration of ministries was impressive, it was more a movement of institutions than of people, meaning it did little to change the local religious demographics. One reason ministries moved to the city in the first place was because its low-wage labor pool allowed them to hire new employees. Focus on the Family, for instance, hired 400 employees from the community after its arrival, doubling its workforce.[101] And so, while these ministries employed thousands of people, they did not simply uproot thousands of evangelicals and plant them in Colorado; many of their employees were longtime residents of the Pikes Peak region. Even at the height of the evangelical migration, Catholicism remained the single largest denomination in El Paso County (as it was for the state of Colorado as a whole). More striking is that, according to one survey, over half the county's population claimed no religious affiliation as of 1990. That number barely changed by 2000.[102] Reports of dozens of ministries moving to the city also require further explanation. Most of these organizations were small. Focus on the Family, with over a thousand employees, was an outlier. More typical were the Art of Family Living, a family counseling ministry, which employed four people; the Dave Dravecky Foundation, which worked with amputees and cancer patients and which employed two people; and the Foundation for Israel, a producer of prophecy literature that employed exactly one person.[103] The religious landscape of Colorado Springs was defined by a few large ministries surrounded by dozens of smaller ones.

Colorado Springs boosters, despite their efforts to attract these evangelical ministries, did not seem to attach much significance to their arrival. The chamber of commerce recognized that ministries could provide only a few hundred jobs, hardly enough to help the city escape its economic slump. For all the work the chamber put into recruiting religious organizations, it put far more effort into courting other, much larger concerns. Even Alice

Worrell did not focus solely on religious organizations; she spent most of her time recruiting manufacturers.[104] In 1991, the same year that Focus on the Family began its move to Colorado Springs, there were two other relocations whose economic significance far outstripped that of Focus. On March 20, Apple announced it would build a manufacturing facility in the nearby town of Fountain that would employ 1,000 people. A week later, MCI announced it would consolidate its engineering division in Colorado Springs, bringing another 1,700 jobs.[105] When the *Colorado Springs Business Journal* celebrated the city's economic resurgence at the end of 1991, it lavished attention on MCI and Apple but did not mention Focus on the Family at all.[106]

Statistics drive home the point that evangelical organizations did not dominate the local economy. Data collected by the US Census Bureau show that in 1993, near the end of the evangelical great migration, "religious organizations" (a term that included churches as well as ministries) employed 6,747 people in El Paso County out of a workforce of 146,463. This 4.6 percent figure was higher than that of any other Colorado county, but it nonetheless indicates that even the "Evangelical Vatican" did not depend entirely on evangelicalism.[107] Employment figures for individual firms tell the same story. Of El Paso County's twenty-four largest private employers in 1991, not one was an evangelical organization.[108] Private employers were dwarfed in turn by the county's public employers, especially the military. Fort Carson employed 20,541 people as of 1991, meaning that if one took the total employment of all the ministries in Colorado Springs that year and tripled it, it would still be smaller than the fort's workforce.[109] It is not surprising, then, that the booster class did not expect the evangelical newcomers to change much about their city.

Yet statistics do not tell the whole story. The arrival of so many ministries changed perceptions, creating a new self-consciousness among the city's evangelicals while arousing fears within the city's liberal community. Ted Haggard, pastor of New Life, an evangelical church with thousands of members, celebrated the arrival of these ministries: "I think God is sovereignly moving them here," he said, echoing the providential language used decades earlier by Young Life and the Navigators. Other people worried over this development. A local activist feared that "if [evangelicals] got in any positions of power—on school boards or in local government—they might come down on others and begin imposing their views."[110] The political and cultural conflicts that dominated local politics for the next few years were filtered through the belief that the city was an "Evangelical Vatican."

Some people in Colorado Springs used the newly arrived ministries as cover to conduct a campaign of harassment. Therapist Greg Snyder, founder of the Colorado Springs Men's Council, received a phone call telling him that his work was leading men to the devil. The owner of a clothing store received three harassing phone calls over the course of three months.[111] In each case, the callers claimed to be affiliated with Focus on the Family. This was almost certainly untrue, but it reflected the name recognition that Focus had in the community—and the willingness of some to exploit that recognition. There were also reports that someone claiming to work for Focus was calling local schools and asking for lists of (depending on the teller of the tale) either single or homosexual teachers. These stories were never verified, and the superintendents of the city's two largest school districts stated that no such thing had happened, but these reports stoked panic among local progressives.[112]

These incidents coincided with several pressure campaigns targeting "un-Christian" elements in local public schools, fanning fears of a right-wing takeover. Complaints from parents led one school district to drop gay and pagan participants from a planned diversity symposium and caused an elementary school to restrict access to a book series intended to teach self-esteem.[113] However, the biggest battle over religion in the public schools concerned not Jesus but Zeus. It began when David Skipworth, pastor of the Cowboy Church of the Rockies, attacked a course on mythology taught at Woodland Park High School. "This material is a misleading way to get kids' eyes on gods other than the almighty God," said Skipworth. "They aren't teaching about God, and Satan is filling the void with other paganistic religions, and these pagan gods are misleading children."[114] Skipworth and two other parents withdrew their children from the course, which the school accepted. But Skipworth and the other parents then demanded that the school do away with the course entirely. When that failed, they filed a lawsuit against Colorado's commissioner of education, demanding that the lesson include Bible passages as well as Greco-Roman myths. Skipworth argued that his lawsuit was about fairness: It was not fair that Greek and Roman mythology received more time than biblical teachings.[115] But the text of his lawsuit quickly slipped from the fairness argument into a demand to restore Christianity to the classroom. The plaintiff's brief argued, "Since 1962, when religion was effectively banned from public schools, morality has been perceived as a religious issue, and also prohibited in public schools. . . . The result has been an abandonment of the moral principals [sic] upon which our free society's existence depends."[116] The judge, unpersuaded, dismissed the case as frivolous.[117]

What would have otherwise been treated as a relatively minor dispute was refracted through the image of the Evangelical Vatican. When Skipworth announced his challenge, he clearly believed that local Christian organizations would rally to his cause: "I'm going to contact every Christian organization, and all the churches, and we're going to rally the troops." The largest of those organizations politely declined to get involved. A spokesperson for Focus on the Family told the press, "Mythology is an important part of Greek and Roman culture, which is an important part of Western civilization, so teaching about that is appropriate. . . . If someone in Woodland Park starts a cult and begins worshipping Thor, call me again." But though Skipworth received no outside support, progressive activists warned that his suit was part of a broader right-wing assault on public education. A representative of People for the American Way commented on the case by saying, "This is part of a systematic effort by right-wing groups to control and narrow the public school curriculum in this country."[118] Both sides saw the conflict as something more than just the efforts of one small group of parents.

Skipworth's lawsuit had one significant long-term consequence: the formation of the Citizens Project, an organization that would become the leading opponent of right-wing activism in Colorado Springs. Billing itself as the "voice of opposition" to conservative Christians, the Citizens Project was the brainchild of Amy Divine and Doug Triggs, a Colorado Springs couple. Its leadership included several prominent members of the community, among them the chair of the Department of Behavioral Sciences at the Air Force Academy and a professor of geology at Colorado College.[119] The Citizens Project positioned itself at the center of the political spectrum. *Freedom Watch*, the group's newsletter, declared, "We are dedicated to maintaining the traditional American values of separation of church and state, freedom of religion and speech, pluralism, individuality, and tolerance and compassion for others." In practice, this meant keeping an eye on local right-wing activists, especially those associated with evangelical Christianity. Citizens Project tried to dispel some of the rumors racing around the community. It noted, for instance, that Focus on the Family probably had nothing to do with the harassing phone calls to businesses and schools.[120] Still, Citizens

Project warned its members to stay vigilant. It feared that conservative evangelicals would run stealth candidates to win local office, as they had done in San Diego (a city whose example became paradigmatic for opponents of the Christian right).[121]

Many people affiliated with evangelical organizations disavowed any connection with the Christian right. An executive with Compassion International, whose focus was on sponsoring children in impoverished countries, stated, "We're a very apolitical organization, and there's much going on in the political arena that is none of our business."[122] But some evangelicals in Colorado Springs, emboldened by their newfound sense of cultural power, took the opportunity to go on the offensive against the creeping liberalism they saw in their community. Their first target: the city's incipient movement for gay rights.

3
A CIVIL WAR OF VALUES

Conservative Christians meeting in a secluded castle to plot an antigay agenda sounds like a progressive fever dream. But it was real, and it happened in Colorado Springs. Representatives from major evangelical organizations gathered at Glen Eyrie, the mansion owned by the Navigators, in May 1994 to discuss plans for a national campaign against gay rights. Talk of war was in the air. One presenter after another spoke of the ongoing struggle between good and evil, light and darkness, God and Satan. "The truth is," said one, "that although we lead normal human lives, the battle we are fighting is on a spiritual level." Said another, "What we're looking at is a contest between good and evil, between the right way to do things and the wrong way to do things." "I would not say this as frankly as I will now in other contexts," admitted a third speaker, but "the gay agenda has all the elements of that which is truly evil."[1] The men and women gathered at Glen Eyrie believed they were combatants in a culture war, a war in which defeat meant the end of the United States.

Cultural conflict is a given in the United States, but the notion of a "culture war" must be historicized. Talk of a culture war exploded in the 1990s because of changes in American evangelicalism. The founders of evangelical Christianity wanted a faith that was in step with American culture; they believed that to be a good Christian was to be a good American, and vice versa. By the 1990s, many evangelicals had begun to question that assumption. They no longer felt at home in an American culture that had grown more diverse—and more secular—since the early days of the Cold War.[2] A coalition of conservative religious and political leaders, recognizing that this discontent could provide the foundation for a powerful social movement, called on evangelicals to take back "their" country and culture. These political entrepreneurs invoked a "culture war" as part of their effort to mobilize evangelical Christians on behalf of the Republican Party.[3] Far from an accurate description of reality, the reference to a culture war was a political strategy. It was, moreover, a strategy that—like modern evangelicalism—had its roots in the Cold War. Declarations that the United States was hopelessly divided between the forces of religion and secularism, tradition and modernity, Christianity and humanism, drew upon (and indeed grew out of) older claims about the cultural threat posed by communism.

Colorado Springs demonstrates both the successes and limitations of this strategy. Institutions headquartered in the city, most notably Summit Ministries, Focus on the Family, and Colorado for Family Values (CFV), warned American evangelicals that religion in the United States was under attack by "secular humanism."[4] They emphasized the threat posed by gay rights, arguing that homosexuality was a radical political movement that sought to overthrow Christianity and traditional American culture. Summit, Focus, and CFV provided conservative activists across the United States with resources for rolling back gay rights, including a powerful slogan ("No Special Rights") and a host of experts who could provide putatively scientific arguments against homosexuality. The strategy worked, for a time. Colorado was the site of its greatest victory: Amendment 2, approved by Colorado voters in November 1992. The amendment, which originated in Colorado Springs and was promoted by the Springs-based CFV, overturned all gay rights laws in the state and prohibited the passage of new ones. It was, one historian later wrote, the most "broadly exclusionary [act] since the slavery era."[5]

Yet Colorado Springs also demonstrates the flaws of the culture war model. Progressives pursued a different strategy. They did not attack conservatives from the left but rejected the culture war framing entirely, instead emphasizing moderation, consensus, and cooperation. This strategy succeeded at preventing a repeat of Amendment 2. The amendment's success in Colorado was due to factors unique to that state: the presence of powerful Christian organizations like Focus on the Family; the endorsement of local elites; and laws that made it relatively easy to place constitutional amendments on the ballot. Without these advantages, almost every Amendment 2 clone failed. Ultimately, the judicial system proved the greatest obstacle to the culture war strategy. CFV and its allies had designed the amendment to sway voters; it was less effective at swaying judges.

Moderation trumped polarization. The conservative Christians who led the fight for Amendment 2 watched their support melt away as they became more strident in their evangelicalism. Coloradans were less willing to endorse a "culture war" when it seemed the war was not between "normal" Americans and LGBTQ people but between evangelicals and everyone else. Yet while progressives triumphed in this case, they did not secure a lasting victory for their ideology. Colorado Springs remained a deeply conservative community. On the national level, these setbacks only reinforced the sense of frustration that launched the culture war strategy in the first place. The architects of Amendment 2 recognized that, if they wanted to win this "war," they had to win the courts.[6]

The Battle for the Mind

A little over a decade after Young Life and the Navigators relocated to Colorado Springs, they were joined there by another Christian organization: Summit Ministries, a school that provided teenagers with an education in conservative Christianity. Summit was the creation of Billy James Hargis, one of America's leading anti-communist preachers, and of Hargis's right-hand man, David Noebel. Hargis and Noebel both emerged from the same fundamentalist milieu that produced the neo-evangelical movement. Hargis recalled growing up listening to Charles Fuller's *Old Fashioned Revival Hour* and proudly claimed membership in "the independent, fundamental, Bible-believing Christian churches."[7] Noebel, after attending Milwaukee Bible College and Hope College, pastored a nondenominational, fundamentalist church in Madison, Wisconsin.[8] Unlike the leaders of the neo-evangelical movement, however, who tried to be at least somewhat circumspect in their conservatism, Hargis and Noebel were quite explicit in their support for right-wing politics. Hargis and his Christian Crusade ministry barnstormed the country delivering broadsides against communism, liberalism, and ecumenism; these crusades featured not only Protestant preachers but also conservative politicians like Joseph McCarthy and activists like John Birch Society founder Robert Welch.[9] Hargis explicitly instructed his audience, "In the South you've got to elect conservative Democrats and in the North conservative Republicans."[10] Before he joined Hargis, Noebel ran for Congress as a self-declared "Goldwater Republican."[11] Hargis and Noebel saw their mission as one of political education. Specifically, they sought to educate Americans about the urgency of confronting communist subversion.

Colorado Springs became the site of their most ambitious program of education. The Christian Crusade's ties to the Pikes Peak region dated back to the 1950s, when Hargis, sensitive about his lack of formal education, sought a degree from Burton College in the town of Manitou Springs. Though the college had a reputation as a degree mill, its promise to provide courses for "busy pastors and Christian leaders" with "a minimum amount of residence work" appealed to Hargis.[12] Burton still required Hargis to attend at least a few courses in person, and so the evangelist spent one summer conducting Christian Crusade rallies in the area.[13] There, he would likely have become familiar with the Grand View Hotel, an elegant but slightly run-down establishment in Manitou Springs that served as Burton College's headquarters. In 1962, the Christian Crusade purchased the Grand View, renamed it "The Summit," and made it the headquarters for its new educational venture, the Christian Anti-Communism Summer College.[14] Its two-week programs would help Christian students defend themselves against the Marxist "brainwashing" taught in high schools and colleges. The Summit prioritized politics over theological specifics; its stated doctrine was "the Scriptural foundation which C. S. Lewis described as 'Mere Christianity.'"[15] Just as neo-evangelicals saw theological controversy as an obstacle to evangelism, Hargis and Noebel saw it as an obstacle to right-wing unity.

Hargis envisioned the Summit as part of a larger educational and media empire. As the school in Manitou Springs expanded, Hargis also made plans for an "American Christian College" based in his home city of Tulsa.[16] But these plans collapsed when, in November 1974, Hargis abruptly resigned from both the Christian Crusade and American Christian College and retreated to his farm in the Ozarks, citing poor health and overwork.[17] Hargis did not stay on the farm for long; he returned to Tulsa the following year to resume his political activism. It was only then that the truth came out regarding his sudden retirement. *Time* magazine reported that Hargis had resigned when five students at American Christian College—four men and one woman—alleged that Hargis had had sexual relations with them. The students brought these allegations to Noebel, who confronted Hargis. The evangelist admitted the truth of the charges and promised to resign (he would later claim that the allegations were false).[18] Hargis's downfall left Noebel in complete control of Summit Ministries. Over the following decades, Noebel would use Summit to advance his crusade against "secular humanism" in the United States.[19]

Noebel understood his mission, and the mission of the Summit, as the defense of American culture against communist subversion. He gained notoriety for his claim that communists were encoding dangerous political and psychological messages in popular music. He considered the Beatles public enemy number one, denouncing the group as "four mop-headed anti-Christ beatniks" out to "destroy our children's emotional and mental stability and ultimately destroy our nation."[20] But he certainly did not limit his concerns to music. In *Slaughter of the Innocent*, published shortly after the Supreme Court's decision in *Roe v. Wade*, Noebel explained why he cared about abortion: "Abortion . . . is merely another indication of misused freedom in a permissive society. . . . Since most civilizations have declined morally before being crumbled militarily, every American has a stake in the issue of abortion."[21] Noebel filtered every issue through his vision of the Cold War as a struggle over American culture.

Throughout the 1970s and into the 1980s, Noebel increasingly saw gay rights as the key battleground in this struggle. His *Homosexual Revolution* (1977) suggested that homosexuality, like pop music, posed an existential threat to the United States: "No nation that allows its young to be enticed into such abominable behavior can survive. For one thing, God will not allow that nation to survive. He destroyed cities and nations in the past for such behavior!"[22] Noebel's book joined a burgeoning antigay rights literature that depicted homosexuality not as an identity but as a political movement seeking to destroy Christianity and remake American culture.[23] In 1982, a Catholic priest and Cuban exile named Enrique Rueda published *The Homosexual Network*, a 700-page tome that became a reference text for antigay activism across the country. Rueda saw an irreconcilable divide between the "homosexual movement" and those who treasured "traditional American values and culture." The homosexual movement included not only gay people but those among the elite who accepted and even encouraged homosexuality. If Rueda did not yet have the phrase "culture war" at hand, he clearly imagined something similar.[24] The AIDS pandemic gave these authors an opportunity to escalate their attacks on homosexuality. Noebel's pamphlet *AIDS*, cowritten with Summit teacher Wayne C. Lutton and antigay social scientist Paul Cameron, linked AIDS and homosexuality to the struggle against secular humanism. "The battle against AIDS," they wrote, "is not just a battle against a plague. It is a battle against a philosophy—a philosophy that embraces homosexuality as an integral part of its ethic."[25] For people like Noebel, the battle over gay rights was simply one front (albeit an important one) in a larger struggle between America's secular elite and its Christian majority.

Focus on the Family's James Dobson introduced this worldview to his audience of millions. He embraced the idea that the United States was riven by a conflict between Christianity and secular humanism. *Children at Risk* (1990), coauthored with conservative activist Gary Bauer, captured Dobson's vision. The book opened with a sobering declaration: "Nothing short of a great Civil War of Values rages today throughout North America. One side believes in God; the other does not."[26] Dobson, of course, assumed his readers belonged to the former camp. Like Noebel and Hargis, Dobson believed it was his duty to alert Christians to the existence of this struggle. "Unfortunately," he wrote "so many people who share traditionalist views appear not to know a war is going on—a conflict that will have profound implications for future generations. By contrast, our opponents are highly motivated, well-funded, deeply committed and armed to the teeth."[27] This was a common claim among culture warriors, who sought to portray themselves (and their audience) as unwilling combatants in a war declared by their opponents. Some of Dobson's coreligionists objected to this grim vision. The church historian John D. Woodbridge wrote a long essay for *Christianity Today* titled "Culture War Casualties," lamenting the pervasiveness of war discourse among evangelicals.[28] Dobson's rebuttal, published with the title "Why I Use 'Fighting Words,'" proudly embraced talk of war. Conflicts over abortion and gay rights were "a continuation of the age-old struggle between the principles of righteousness and the kingdom of darkness." For Dobson, cultural warfare was spiritual warfare. No quarter was possible.[29]

It was an academic who finally found a name for this worldview. James Davison Hunter received his PhD in sociology from Rutgers, where he studied with the neo-Weberian sociologist Peter Berger.[30] His first book, *American Evangelicalism: Conservative Religion and the Quandary of Modernity* (1983), argued that religious groups have only a few options in the modern world. They can withdraw from the world entirely, they can accommodate the forces of modernity, or they can fight back. Hunter dedicated the rest of his career to exploring the dynamics of that last option. He had a front-row seat to this conflict in his role as an expert witness in *Smith v. Board of School Commissioners of Mobile County*, the "Alabama textbook case." *Smith* involved a group of Christian parents who claimed that textbooks used in the local public schools taught the "religion" of secular humanism and thus violated the Establishment Clause. The National Legal Foundation, an organization affiliated with the conservative televangelist Pat Robertson, provided the parents with financial and legal support.[31] Hunter, hired to serve as an expert witness on behalf of the parents, testified that secular humanism was indeed a religion and that this religion had infiltrated the textbooks in Mobile County. These books were "anti-religious," he testified, so much so that their use amounted to "censorship" of "traditional theism." He struggled to defend some of these claims on cross-examination, admitting that he had found "no passages in those social studies textbooks that were consistent with secular humanism."[32] Nonetheless, Judge William Brevard Hand relied heavily on Hunter's testimony when he ruled in favor of the parents.[33]

Hunter's ideas reached full flower in *Culture Wars: The Struggle to Define America* (1991). Its thesis was straightforward: "[What] seems to be a myriad of self-contained cultural disputes actually amounts to a fairly comprehensive and momentous struggle to define the meaning of America."[34] It was, Hunter argued, a *cultural* struggle rather than a political one, which meant no compromise between the parties was possible. He identified the competing factions as the progressive and the orthodox. The former (according to Hunter) located moral authority within the individual; the latter found it in transcendent authorities outside the individual—for example, in the Bible. Hunter strove for a tone of neutrality throughout this book. He insisted that the two sides were morally equivalent: "The Left is the Right and the Right is the Left."[35] However, the argument of the book conveyed a strong sympathy for the orthodox cause, a sympathy that grew stronger as the pages went by. Hunter's insistence that the only solution to the culture war was to find a new "public philosophy" that could unite Americans—that is, to find a new form of external authority—essentially restated the orthodox claim. By the end of the book, Hunter was arguing that the progressive impulse would legitimize rape and murder, quoting the Marquis de Sade as his source.[36] Many critics reacted to the book with skepticism.[37] But the phrase "culture war" proved too memorable to fail.

Ground Zero

The "culture war" did not come to Colorado all at once. Rather, it unfolded over the course of decades. Home rule, which decentralized Colorado politics by granting most lawmaking authority to cities, enabled the piecemeal advance of gay rights in the state. Beginning in the 1970s, several Colorado cities used their home rule privileges to protect gay rights. These efforts often met fierce resistance. Voters in Boulder rejected a gay rights ordinance in 1974; a second attempt was approved by a margin of only a few hundred votes in 1987.[38] The conflict over gay rights next came to Denver, where in October 1990 the city council approved an antidiscrimination ordinance that included sexual orientation among the protected categories.[39] Within days of the council's vote, conservative evangelicals in Denver organized to repeal the ordinance. After a bruising campaign, the city's voters affirmed the ordinance by a margin of 55 percent to 45 percent.[40] Gay rights was a contested issue even in the state's more liberal communities.

David Noebel regarded the advance of gay rights in his state, no matter how slow and piecemeal, as an imminent threat. In his pamphlet on AIDS, he had condemned antidiscrimination laws as part of the homosexual assault on traditional values.[41] Now those laws were coming to Colorado. Noebel was particularly alarmed by HB1059, proposed legislation that would have expanded the state's "Ethnic Intimidation Law" to include sexual orientation. Put forward by state representative Wilma Webb, HB1059 responded to growing awareness of hate crimes in Colorado and around the nation.[42] Noebel worked with Tony Marco, an evangelical Christian copywriter from Colorado Springs, to prepare a case against HB1059.[43] Marco testified against the bill before a subcommittee of the Colorado legislature, arguing that it would give the state's blessing to all manner of deviant sexual behaviors: "Should we let necrophiliacs also demand open admission to our funeral parlors to exercise their sexual preference?" he asked. Testimony from Marco and other conservatives helped kill HB1059.⁴⁴ But Tony Marco's war against gay rights had just begun. Only a few months later, in May 1991, the Colorado Springs City Council debated an antidiscrimination ordinance that would have included sexual orientation among the protected categories. Noebel and Marco sprang back into action, organizing a pressure campaign that convinced the council to reject the ordinance.⁴⁵ For the moment, Noebel seemed to be winning the culture war against gay rights.

Noebel, Marco, and their allies built on these successes to establish Colorado for Family Values, with the goal of going on the offensive against gay rights. Its secular name notwithstanding, CFV emerged from the evangelical churches and ministries of Colorado Springs, Summit Ministries in particular. Tony Marco worked as a grant writer for evangelical ministries, and so he and his wife went where the ministries were: first Charlotte, then Virginia Beach, and finally Colorado Springs.⁴⁶ Will Perkins, a car dealership owner who served as CFV's spokesperson, had close ties to several of the city's ministries, including Young Life and the Navigators.⁴⁷ Marco, Perkins, and a number of CFV members worshipped at Village Seven Presbyterian, one of the city's largest and most conservative churches.⁴⁸ Noebel attended the first meetings of CFV, as did Summit's vice president, Jay Butler. Another Noebel associate, Kevin Tebedo, would eventually become executive director of CFV.⁴⁹ The city's evangelical milieu provided the new organization with the resources and personal connections necessary to translate its local struggle into a statewide campaign.

Colorado's tradition of home rule had allowed gay rights advocates to slowly advance their cause; the state's tradition of direct democracy allowed voters to roll back these advances in one stroke. Coloradans gained the power to amend their state's constitution by popular vote in 1910.⁵⁰ Activists often used this option to circumvent the state legislature and submit their ideas directly to the electorate. Conservative activists enjoyed particular success in doing so throughout the 1980s and early 1990s, using the initiative process to restrict abortion access, make English the official state language, and impose term limits on elected officials.⁵¹ CFV, inspired by these past successes and by an ongoing antigay rights campaign in Oregon, decided to create its own statewide initiative. Noebel seems to have been the one who first proposed the idea.⁵² The task of writing the initiative fell to Tony Marco, who drew upon his extensive contacts in the evangelical world while crafting the amendment. Marco exchanged several drafts with Brian McCormick, an attorney with Pat Robertson's National Legal Foundation. Early drafts contained a prohibition on same-sex marriage, but McCormick warned that this might generate sympathy for homosexuals. For the same reason, he cautioned Marco against explicitly prohibiting "special privileges" for homosexuals, as it would "allow homosexuals to argue that they are not asking for special privileges, just those granted to everyone else." McCormick nonetheless recognized the value of "No Special Privileges" as a slogan, and so he suggested that CFV leave the phrase out of the amendment itself while still making it the centerpiece of its campaign.[53] Marco's final draft barred all government bodies in Colorado from enacting laws that allowed homosexuals to "claim any minority status, quota preferences, protected status or claim of discrimination." In practice, this would overturn all gay rights laws in the state, including those in Boulder and Denver, while prohibiting the passage of new ones. CFV now had to gather the approximately 49,000 signatures needed to put the amendment on the November 1992 ballot.

High-profile endorsements gave CFV's campaign legitimacy, while a network of grassroots volunteers gave it muscle. Former US senator Bill Armstrong, long an ally of the Christian right, wrote a fundraising letter on CFV's behalf that implored donors to help stop "militant homosexuals and lesbian activists" in their drive to "force you and me to condone . . . aberrant homosexual behavior and lifestyles."[54] University of Colorado football coach Bill McCartney allowed CFV to use his name and title on its letterhead; when some complained that McCartney was abusing his position as a state employee, he called a press conference in which he not only defended his support for CFV but also denounced homosexuality as an "abomination." The angry backlash nearly cost McCartney his job, but CFV considered it a victory: It brought them free publicity.[55] James Dobson of Focus on the Family, though still a newcomer to Colorado, saw the issue as important enough to justify a foray into local politics. This was, after all, part of the "Civil War of Values" that he believed would decide the fate of the United States. He dedicated an hour-long episode of his radio show to CFV's campaign, affording the group yet more free publicity.[56] But these endorsements would have counted for little without the organizational strength to capitalize on them. That strength came from the state's evangelical churches, which provided CFV with hundreds of volunteers to collect signatures. Conservative organizations like the Eagle Forum, Concerned Women for America, and the Christian Coalition also lent their support. With these factors working in its favor, CFV gathered over 80,000 signatures, far more than the 49,000 it needed. Its initiative became "Amendment 2" on the November 1992 ballot.[57]

Amendment 2 marked the crest of a wave of antigay rights activism in the United States early in the 1990s. These campaigns clustered in the West, where relatively open ballot access laws enabled conservative activists to put gay rights to a vote, city by city and state by state. CFV had analogues in other Western states, most notably California's Traditional Values Coalition and the Oregon Citizens Alliance (OCA). The Anaheim-based Traditional Values Coalition repealed antidiscrimination ordinances in several Southern California cities, while the OCA overturned an executive order from Oregon's governor that protected homosexuals from discrimination.[58] The OCA was also pushing for a statewide antigay rights measure in 1992, albeit one much harsher than Amendment 2. The OCA's Measure 9 compared homosexuality to pedophilia and required the state government to "discourage" such "deviant behaviors." These organizations, like CFV, claimed to be secular but were clearly evangelical. The Traditional Values Coalition was led by a former Presbyterian minister, while the OCA was founded by a Baptist minister. All these organizations drew their arguments from the same cadre of "experts" who gave a scientific gloss to antigay claims. No expert was as prolific, ubiquitous, or controversial as Paul Cameron, a psychologist who peddled antigay agitprop in campaigns and court cases across the country. CFV, the Traditional Values Coalition, and the OCA freely used Cameron's statistics in their campaign literature.[59] Cameron also coined a phrase that both CFV and the OCA used in their campaigns: "No Special Rights."[60]

"No Special Rights" allowed CFV to claim the moral high ground even while titillating audiences with tales of homosexual depravity. Spokespeople like Tony Marco, Will Perkins, and Kevin Tebedo insisted that their only concern was fairness. They wanted to keep gays from claiming the "special rights" that only "true" minorities like African Americans deserved. CFV sought to prove this point by foregrounding African American support for Amendment 2.[61] This was less about winning African American votes than about swaying whites, however. CFV granted after the election, "Minority support is not only crucial because of their numbers, it's also crucial as a bellwether signal to swing voters about which side truly represents 'fairness.'"[62] African American support signaled to whites that voting for Amendment 2 did not make them bigots. And CFV had to work hard not to appear bigoted, given the venom it poured onto homosexuals. CFV spokespeople argued that voters had to know the details of the "gay lifestyle" to make an informed judgment about whether homosexuals deserved "special rights," and so—drawing heavily on the work of Paul Cameron—they depicted gays as promiscuous, violent, and disease-ridden.[63]

Assailing gay rights as "special rights" fit neatly within the landscape of national politics in 1992. George Bush and the Republican Party, hoping to overcome a weak economy, pushed cultural issues to the forefront of their campaign. The Bush campaign gave a primetime speaking slot at the Republican National Convention to conservative ideologue Pat Buchanan, who used the spotlight to broadcast the language of "culture war" to a national audience: "There is a religious war going on in this country. It is a cultural war, as critical to the kind of nation we shall be as was the Cold War itself, for this is a war for the soul of America."[64] Fighting this "cultural war" usually meant attacking gay rights, as when Bush declared that he opposed antidiscrimination laws protecting homosexuals.[65] Though Bush's Democratic opponent, Bill Clinton, was friendlier toward gay rights, he nonetheless edged toward the center on cultural issues, praising family values and emphasizing his religious faith. Indeed, the manifesto of the Democratic Leadership Conference, a centrist organization that boosted Clinton early in his career, called on Democrats to recommit themselves to the credo of "equal opportunity for all and special privileges for none."[66] Lamenting the excessive focus on "rights" was a bipartisan exercise in this era.

Amendment 2's opponents landed hits on CFV but had a harder time attacking the amendment itself. They denounced CFV as religious extremists; when CFV leader Kevin Tebedo was caught on tape declaring, "We can say we should have the separation of church and state, but you see, Jesus Christ is the King of Kings and the Lord of Lords," opponents publicized it as proof of CFV's religious agenda.[67] These charges stuck: A focus group conducted in April 1992 found that voters familiar with CFV "characterized the group as an ultraconservative organization, with a strong fundamentalist orientation." But Amendment 2 proved a harder target. Its opaque language made it seem more confusing than threatening. The same focus group that characterized CFV as "fundamentalist" had "great difficulty in understanding what [the amendment] was intended to do," even after a moderator read it aloud to them.[68] By contrast, opponents of Oregon's Measure 9 did not need to explain the initiative. Its description of homosexuality as "deviant" was crystal clear. Progressive activists in Oregon had another advantage over their counterparts in Colorado. The OCA had run several statewide campaigns prior to Measure 9, giving progressives the opportunity to build a political infrastructure. Equality Colorado, which spearheaded the campaign against Amendment 2, had to start from nothing. Still, the organization held a significant edge over CFV in fundraising. And polls consistently showed Amendment 2 losing, often by a wide margin.[69]

On the evening of November 3, 1992, progressives gathered at a Colorado Springs community center to watch the election returns. The party's organizers, confident in the polls, "arranged for red, white and blue balloons" to drop when Amendment 2's defeat was announced.[70] But the balloons never fell. The crowd watched in shock as Amendment 2 won with 53 percent of the vote.[71] In percentage terms, the amendment won its biggest victories in rural counties in eastern Colorado. It also carried El Paso County, home of Colorado Springs, by an almost 2-to-1 margin. But the key to the amendment's victory lay in the suburban Denver counties of Arapahoe, Jefferson, Weld, and Adams, as well as Larimer County, home of Fort Collins. For comparison, George Bush lost Larimer and Adams, while Republican senatorial candidate Terry Considine lost Larimer, Adams, Arapahoe, Jefferson, and Weld.[72] Clearly, some voters had split their tickets, voting for both the amendment and the two Democratic candidates. Pundits were blindsided. A *Denver Post* columnist confessed, "We should have known better than to believe the polls.... Did you see a yard sign saying 'Vote Yes on 2'? I didn't."[73]

As the immediate shock of the election faded, observers tried to make sense of the result. Many people blamed Colorado Springs and its evangelical population for imposing its morality on the rest of the state.[74] Yet this explanation ignored the fact that, while the Springs may have produced the amendment, the entire state had voted for it. Others blamed Equality Colorado. Frustrations repressed during the campaign burst into the open after the election. Some activists complained that the Denver-based organization had ignored the rest of the state. Black and Hispanic activists charged Equality Colorado with sidelining them during the campaign. Others accused the organization of running a "closeted" campaign that de-emphasized homosexuality.[75] Colorado soon became an anti-model for the national gay rights movement, a lesson in how not to run a campaign.[76]

Polls and interviews revealed that the likeliest explanation for the amendment's victory was also the simplest: Voters accepted the "No Special Rights" argument. A survey taken in January 1993 found that 54 percent of

Protesters gather at the Colorado state capitol in Denver to oppose Amendment 2, which sharply curtailed gay rights in the state. Courtesy of the Denver Public Library, Western History Collection, WH2129.

respondents agreed with the statement "When homosexuals talk about gay rights, what they are really saying is they want special treatment." A poll taken the next month found a similar result: 56 percent of respondents agreed that "gay rights" meant special treatment.[77] CFV had convinced voters that homosexuals sought not equal rights but special rights. Its success was even more striking given that, according to these polls, most voters rejected the rest of CFV's ideology. The January poll found that 81 percent of those surveyed agreed that "except for their choice of sexual partners, homosexuals are not really different from everyone else." A plurality of respondents rejected the idea that homosexuality was morally wrong. These results intimated what future events made clear: Coloradans may have approved Amendment 2, but that did not mean they accepted CFV's broader agenda.

For the moment, however, CFV seemed a formidable force, its influence magnified by the reporters who flocked to Colorado Springs in the wake of Amendment 2's victory. Less than three weeks after the election, the Religion News Service filed a story on the Springs—"Evangelical Influx Splits Colorado City"—which was reprinted in multiple newspapers. *Newsweek*,

Businessweek, the *National Catholic Reporter*, and the *Los Angeles Times* all wrote about Colorado Springs before the end of 1992. In 1993, PBS aired an hour-long special on the Springs with the telling title *The New Holy War*. That same year, stories about the city appeared in *Christianity Today*, *Mother Jones*, the *Village Voice*, *Esquire*, and *Newsweek*. In 1994, *The Economist* and the *Washington Post* profiled Colorado Springs; *The Nation* did the same a year later in a cover story titled "God and Man in Colorado Springs." On the opposite end of the political spectrum, the conservative journal *First Things* hailed the city as America's "Spiritual NORAD," a reference to the military base located near the Springs. The journalist Michael Lewis, on the campaign trail for the 1996 presidential election, filed a dispatch from the city for the *New Republic*.[78] Given this attention and the negative tone that most of these stories carried, Fred Brown of the *Denver Post* was not far from the truth when he wrote, "Amendment 2 may be the biggest public-relations disaster ever to hit Colorado."[79]

Brown reached this grim conclusion after surveying the growing Boycott Colorado movement. Less than a week after the election, author Armistead Maupin canceled an appearance in Denver, saying, "Colorado has become the South Africa of the U.S. for the gays."[80] The boycott movement quickly gained momentum. Progressive activists had learned the value of boycotts the previous decade, when a nationwide boycott of Arizona led that state's voters to rescind their prior rejection of Martin Luther King Jr. Day as a state holiday.[81] Boycotts simplified and clarified abstract issues by giving prejudice a place. As Arizona became a symbol of racism, so Colorado became a symbol of homophobia. Advocacy groups like the National Gay and Lesbian Task Force, the Gay and Lesbian Alliance Against Defamation, and the American Civil Liberties Union called for boycotts of Colorado, as did some gay rights organizations in Colorado, including the Springs-based Ground Zero. Numerous organizations canceled conventions in the state, while New York, Atlanta, and other cities prohibited employees from traveling to Colorado on city business.[82] More than a few boycott announcements reflected the continuing economic competition between Colorado and other states. When Edward Rendell, mayor of Philadelphia, declared that he would not attend a meeting of the US Conference of Mayors held in Colorado Springs, he quickly added, "As a statement of denouncing bigotry and affirming civil rights, I will personally request that the conference be moved to Philadelphia, the birthplace of civil rights."[83] Colorado's loss could be Pennsylvania's gain.

Chuck Asay, cartoonist for the Colorado Springs *Gazette*, was one of many conservatives angered by boycotts of Colorado following Amendment 2's passage. Illustration by Chuck Asay; courtesy of Regional History and Genealogy, Pikes Peak Library District, 448–25.

The state's business community was jarred into action by these threats. Businesses in Colorado had never been enthusiastic about Amendment 2. US West and Apple Computer, two of the state's largest employers, had opposed the amendment, as had the Denver Chamber of Commerce.[84] But most of the business community had been too concerned with opposing Amendment 1, which sharply cut taxes, to pay much attention to Amendment 2. Economic fallout from the boycott changed that. As the estimated impact of the boycott mounted by the millions, Colorado business leaders fought against the impression that Colorado was the "hate state."[85]

That task was especially urgent for businesses in Colorado Springs, where the end of the Cold War and the looming threat of military cutbacks made economic recruitment more important than ever.[86] Even before Amendment 2, boosters in the Springs struggled to counter their city's image as isolated, intolerant, and hostile to diversity. Ironically, the themes promoted by previous generations of boosters—homogeneity, patriotism, social conservatism—were now liabilities. Minority leaders in the Springs had even threatened to organize a national economic boycott of the city to protest what they called a "pervasive climate of racism."[87] Now, the charge of homophobia was added to that of racism. One Colorado Springs businessperson fretted, "For us to be painted the way we're being painted because Amendment 2 came out of Colorado Springs, we're in a heap of trouble. If we don't do something about it, Colorado Springs may be destined to become a backwater in the global economy."[88] The local chamber of commerce responded by distributing thousands of bumper stickers with the slogan "There's room for everyone in Colorado Springs."[89] But local business leaders recognized that bumper stickers alone were not enough, and so they eagerly pursued anything that looked like a solution to their city's image problem.

Opponents of Amendment 2 sought to use this business awakening in their efforts to undermine the amendment. A Colorado Springs attorney (and evangelical Christian) named Greg Walta proposed a compromise that would repeal the amendment and replace it with one that prohibited both "special rights" for homosexuals and discrimination on the basis of sexual orientation. Walta worked ceaselessly to recruit supporters for this compromise, pursuing business leaders with special vigor: "In Colorado Springs," he noted, "if the business community doesn't want to do it, you might as well forget it." Tellingly, he disavowed the cause of gay rights. His compromise was not about protecting the rights of homosexuals but about showing the world—especially outside businesses—that "we've stopped arguing."[90] Walta's "Come Together Colorado" proposal attracted high-profile support. At a press conference introducing the compromise, Walta was joined by representatives from the Colorado Springs Chamber of Commerce, the local branch of the NAACP, and Colorado College, as well as by several religious leaders. But he had trouble getting support from activists on either side of the conflict. Many gay rights activists regarded Walta's compromise with skepticism, concerned by its inclusion of exemptions for small businesses and religious organizations. Christian right activists, for their part, never even considered signing on. CFV attacked "Come Together Colorado" as "worse than repeal."[91] Walta withdrew his proposal in March 1993. Lamenting its failure, he said that Colorado Springs needed to "chart a course between the two extremes" of the Christian right and the gay rights movement.[92] Though

Walta failed to find this elusive middle ground, other activists would have more success with this policy of self-conscious moderation.[93]

CFV used these efforts at repeal to legitimate the continuation of its activities after the election. Prior to the election, the organization's leaders pledged to dissolve CFV once the campaign was over. "This is a single issue as far as this amendment is concerned," said spokesperson Will Perkins.[94] But it soon became clear that their agenda went beyond one amendment. Over the next few years, CFV waged an ambitious campaign to protect "family values" in Colorado. Its leaders headed seminars in rural communities to teach locals about the dangers of gay rights; urged Colorado towns to adopt antigay "community standards resolutions"; and pushed for schools in Colorado Springs to implement a "sexual morality proposal" affirming heterosexual marriage.[95] In all its efforts, CFV eschewed the language of moderation for talk of battle, conflict, and conquest. "In opposing the homosexual agenda, there is no compromise," Kevin Tebedo told a crowd at one CFV seminar. "It will have to be defeated."[96]

CFV's staunchest opponent, the Citizens Project, rejected the language of warfare and instead emphasized the community's "significant basis of shared values." Its founders, married couple Amy Divine and Doug Triggs, styled themselves as "tired conservatives" rather than as liberals or progressives. Divine, Triggs, and other Citizens Project leaders also highlighted the diversity of their organization. In an editorial for the *Gazette Telegraph*, Citizens Project leader Richard Skorman wrote, "Diverse is a better adjective than divisive to describe Citizens Project. Some of us are deeply religious; others are not. Some of us are Republicans; others are Democrats or Independents."[97] The contrast with CFV—diverse rather than divisive—would have been obvious to readers. The signature initiative of the Citizens Project, the Dialogue Dinners, reflected the group's strategy of seeking consensus. These dinners brought together people from across the political spectrum to "explore our differences and our common ground." Organizing these dinners gave Citizens Project an opportunity to work with several of the city's evangelical churches and ministries, many of which wanted to put Amendment 2 behind them. Business organizations in the Springs, including Hewlett-Packard and the *Gazette Telegraph*, also lent their support to the Dialogue Dinners.[98]

As the Citizens Project was making allies in the business world, CFV was busy alienating that same community, undermining what could have been a powerful base of support. Business owners and leaders in the Springs may have been unhappy with the boycotts surrounding Amendment 2, but that does not mean they rejected the amendment itself. According to a poll taken by the Colorado Springs Chamber of Commerce in February 1993, almost 60 percent of its membership would vote for Amendment 2 if the election were held again.[99] But CFV fumbled away that support. At their Community Watch Seminars, CFV leaders suggested that activists consider picketing or boycotting "pro-homosexual" businesses.[100] Business leaders, already exhausted by talk of boycotts, exploded with anger at this apparent threat. The Economic Development Corporation, which had once courted evangelical groups, now held a press conference to denounce the "extreme" views on either side of the gay rights issue.[101]

Pressured by both liberal activists and the business community, CFV struggled to make headway in its campaign against gay rights. Its "community standards resolution" denouncing homosexuality and pornography received only a few thousand signatures, well short of the 25,000 it had aimed for.[102] School districts in Colorado Springs killed CFV's antigay "sexual morality proposal" by burying it in bureaucracy.[103] These setbacks were compounded by the mistakes of Kevin Tebedo, the organization's executive director. His aggressive Christianity—"I want to see the principles of God be imbedded in the lives of men," he told one interviewer—made it hard for CFV to shed its reputation for extremism.[104] Tebedo's ardent defense of Colin Cook, a therapist and "reformed homosexual" accused of engaging in phone sex with his clients, further embarrassed the organization. Tebedo resigned his position soon after the Cook fiasco, leaving CFV leaderless for almost two years.[105] CFV eventually selected Paul Jessen, pastor of the Colorado Springs Restoration Fellowship Foursquare Gospel Church, as its new executive director. Jessen's first press conference, held in December 1997, indicated that CFV had embraced its evangelicalism. Jessen declared that "we are guided by the words of our Lord who said we are to be the salt of the earth and the light of the world." When Tebedo made a similar statement during the Amendment 2 campaign, it was a serious gaffe. Now, these sentiments were the explicit policy of CFV.[106]

The 1999 campaign for mayor of Colorado Springs accelerated CFV's disintegration. After trying and failing to recruit a city council member to run for the position, CFV selected a candidate from its own ranks: Will Perkins, its longtime spokesperson. In some ways, Perkins made an ideal candidate.

He had lived in Colorado Springs since 1941 and had deep roots in the community. Decades of advertisements for his car dealership had made his name and face ubiquitous in the city. And his gentle, self-deprecating charm was recognized even by opponents.[107] But Perkins never escaped the shadow of Amendment 2—not that he tried very hard to do so. At one candidate forum, when an audience member asked a question about rights, Perkins quickly responded, "I'm opposed to government giving special rights to anyone based on how they have sex." This sparked a debate that continued until one audience member shouted, "We've had enough!"[108]

"We've had enough!" could have been the campaign slogan of Mary Lou Makepeace, the incumbent mayor. Makepeace had always been relatively friendly to gay rights; she had been the only city council member to support the 1991 antidiscrimination ordinance that covered sexual orientation.[109] One of her stated goals as mayor was to refurbish the city's reputation by putting the gay rights issue to rest. "I think we've come a long way in moving away from that [image]," Makepeace said of her efforts to help the Springs shed its conservative reputation.[110] Will Perkins was her ideal opponent: He symbolized everything she wanted the city to leave behind. On Election Day, April 6, 1999, voters affirmed Makepeace's vision. She defeated Perkins by about 10,000 votes, or by a margin of 44 percent to 31 percent, with 25 percent going to a third candidate. Makepeace explained these results as "a clear message to ourselves and the rest of the world that the Springs is not living up to its negative reputation."[111] Makepeace's victory was not necessarily an affirmation of gay rights. Rather, it suggested the desire of many in the Springs—on the left, in the center, and even some on the right—to move on from the issue, even if that meant leaving many important questions unresolved.

The election was a mortal blow to CFV. Paul Jessen resigned as executive director a few days after Perkins lost; no one ever replaced him.[112] The organization dissolved the following year. CFV existed for less than a decade, but in that short span it transformed Colorado politics, thrusting gay rights to the forefront of the state's agenda. It also left its mark on Colorado Springs, stamping that city with a reputation for ultraconservatism. But CFV's influence did not stop at the state border. The impact of Amendment 2 rippled across the United States, echoing and re-echoing in cities and states around the country.

The Colorado Model

Even as its support at home crumbled, CFV worked hard to sell its "Colorado Model" to antigay activists nationwide. *Gay Politics vs. Colorado*, written by CFV member Stephen Bransford, provided a book-length blueprint explaining this strategy. The book was blurbed by none other than Pat Buchanan, who had declared a "cultural war" at the 1992 Republican National Convention—a testament to CFV's national influence. *Gay Politics vs. Colorado* made an argument as straightforward as its title: Amendment 2 was a grassroots movement by ordinary Coloradans opposed to the "homosexual lobby." Bransford even dedicated his book to "the 53.6%," the percentage of the Colorado electorate who had approved the amendment. The book did, however, express regrets that the campaign had not focused more on Christian morality. "The Colorado approach," Bransford wrote, "recognized the fact that, like it or not, America has retreated from its Judeo-Christian roots."[113] This was the core of the Colorado Model: an effort to justify the antigay rights movement in secular terms without dampening the religious fervor of grassroots activists.

Gay Politics vs. Colorado was joined on the Amendment 2 bookshelf by *Refuge*, a "docu-novel" by CFV member Mark Olsen. A self-described "bohemian writer," Olsen believed the best way to get his message across was through a novel: "Jesus used stories to bring across the lessons that mattered the most," he explained.[114] *Refuge* centers on Vern Yates, a devout computer programmer living in Boulder; his wife, Gail; their nine-year-old son, John; and their four-year-old daughter, Heather. The novel is set in the near future, after Colorado passes a gay rights law that "made it a crime for someone who disapproves of homosexuality to exercise their freedom of association" and a hate crimes law that "made it illegal to speak negatively about homosexuality." Vern and John are forced to flee from their home after John inadvertently reveals to an undercover police officer that he is homeschooled. They escape to the Rocky Mountains, where fugitive Christians are rumored to operate. Their story is intercut with that of Gail and Heather, who, left behind, are trapped within the state's authoritarian human rights bureaucracy.[115] Another storyline follows Sonya, a "born-again pagan, butch dyke, and proud of it," who tracks Vern and John in hopes that, by capturing them, she can get a government job—and health insurance to pay for her AIDS medication.

Vern and John are eventually found by a former Boy Scout (the Scouts were disbanded for refusing to hire a member of NAMBLA, the North American Man-Boy Love Association) who guides them to "the refuge." The refuge's founder, a former Air Force officer, explains that he was inspired by the Underground Railroad to create an "Underground Bullet Train" to help fugitive Christians.[116] Vern hears the stories of Christian refugees: a minister who was jailed for refusing to attend sensitivity training; a woman whose husband killed himself after being bankrupted by a lawsuit from a gay ex-employee; a man whose fifteen-year-old son was inveigled into homosexuality by a gay high school counselor; and a man who walked in on a Scoutmaster performing oral sex on his five-year-old grandson. That last man, Frank, is one of the few figures in the book to explicitly call for violence. "Hidin' in the hills isn't gonna cut it," he tells Vern. "This is war, and we gotta fight it like a war."[117] Vern rejects this approach but accepts Frank's help in rescuing Gail and Heather. They succeed, though Frank dies in a shootout with the police. Sonya, badly injured when she attempts to stop Vern, reflects on the emptiness of her life and decides to return to Christ (and heterosexuality). The novel ends with Gail asserting that "the God I worship . . . is bigger than the government, bigger than the NEA, bigger than the police. He is capable, even, of healing this country I love, despite the incredible hatred and hypocrisy which has it in a stranglehold today."[118]

Olsen billed *Refuge* a "docu-novel," and the book's cover proclaimed that it was "fresh from today's headlines, packed with frightening facts." Each chapter began with a quote or news story demonstrating the supposed hidden agenda of the gay rights movement. Most of these quotes would have been familiar to regular readers of the *CFV Report*, which often highlighted inflammatory quotes from gay rights activists. Not only did Olsen borrow quotes from the CFV newsletter; he borrowed entire scenes. Vern's memory of a violent gay rights protest at his church, for instance, draws heavily upon a *CFV Report* article about a similar protest at a San Francisco church.[119]

This "docu-novel" style was meant to spur readers to action. Numerous characters in *Refuge* lament that they did not try to stop the gay rights movement when they had the chance. Vern reflects how he had dismissed Amendment 2 as the work of "paranoid fundamentalists."[120] Only after the Supreme Court strikes down Amendment 2 does Vern bother rereading the CFV literature kept in a box in his basement. "How had he missed all of it?" Vern thinks as he reads. "Here were direct quotes: homosexual manifestoes advocating the closing of churches, the silencing of political adversaries, the removal of children. Example after example."[121] Vern's belated revelation is echoed by many other characters. Vern's pastor laments his decision to avoid antigay rights activism. "I thought politics and the gospel had nothing to do with each other," he tells his congregation. "Now, seeing the way our church's ability to share the gospel has been hamstrung by these militant attacks, I realize I was wrong."[122] In case anyone failed to get the message, Olsen included an afterword urging readers to get involved: "Let's keep [this book] from becoming an awful prophecy of life to come in America."[123]

Gay Politics vs. Colorado and *Refuge* sought to broadcast the Colorado Model as widely as possible. CFV also targeted its message more strategically, aiming it at the national leadership of the Christian right. The Glen Eyrie conferences of 1993 and 1994 were CFV's most ambitious attempts to reach a national audience. The first conference, held at Glen Eyrie from April 30 to May 1, 1993, drew representatives from forty-five states. CFV spokesperson Will Perkins delivered the opening remarks, while CFV executive director Kevin Tebedo chaired the conference. Other lectures came from Douglas Kay, a political consultant who worked for Focus on the Family, and James Ryle, chaplain to the University of Colorado's football team.[124] This conference produced "The Colorado Model," a 200-page notebook containing lessons learned from the Amendment 2 campaign. The notebook gave readers an overview of the campaign, including a timeline and narrative history of the conflict. Also included was a "sample seminar workbook" with a sample speech, photocopies of useful articles, and even a list of "Things That Must Be Said in Interviews." An appendix included pro-Amendment 2 flyers and excerpts from antigay rights books like Enrique Rueda's *Homosexual Network*. A lengthy section on the "CFV Philosophical Model" explained that while most Americans found LGBTQ people "disgusting," they also felt that these people should not be discriminated against. "They are swing voters," the notebook asserted. "They want to vote for us, but they can't—they've been separated from their chests."[125] CFV borrowed this distinctive image from the Christian apologist C. S. Lewis, who used the phrase "men without chests" in his book *The Abolition of Man* to condemn modern educators who tried to disassociate the intellect from the emotions. As applied to the campaign against gay rights, "men without chests" meant it was not enough to arouse disgust about homosexuality. A successful campaign had to convince people that it was reasonable to vote on the basis of that disgust.

Building a bridge between voters' revulsion and their intellect meant framing antigay laws not as an attack on the rights of homosexuals but as a defense of the rights of others. "We're defending the fundamental freedoms of those who disapprove of homosexuality," as the notebook put it.[126] However, it also made clear that emphasizing fairness and rights would not preclude lurid discussions of homosexual behavior. "The Colorado Model" described gay sexuality in graphic terms (often prefaced with apologies to the reader) and linked homosexuality to criminality. It compared homosexuality to "arson, DWI, [and] rape" and LGBTQ people to Jeffrey Dahmer, Charles Manson, and the Boston Strangler.[127] Left unexplained was why, if homosexuality was so horrific, CFV was simply trying to prevent gays and lesbians from claiming "special rights" rather than trying to outlaw homosexuality entirely. Coherence, however, was not the goal. The goal was to give people as many ways as possible to rationalize their vote against gay rights.

"The Colorado Model" also demonstrated that CFV was only one part of a larger network of conservative Christian organizations. The notebook insisted that CFV was a grassroots movement, but it freely acknowledged the support CFV received from national organizations like Focus on the Family, the Eagle Forum, the Christian Coalition, the Traditional Values Coalition, and Concerned Women for America. The excerpts and book recommendations in the notebook drew from a vast antigay literature: books like Roger Magnuson's *Are Gay Rights Right?* and Lorraine Day's *AIDS: What the Government Isn't Telling You*. Also among the recommended books: David Noebel's *Understanding the Times*, a massive tome that explained modern history as an ongoing culture war between Christianity and secular humanism.

The next Glen Eyrie conference, held from May 16 to May 18, 1994, proved even more successful than the first. It drew forty organizations, including major ones like the Eagle Forum, the Christian Coalition, and the American Family Association, as well as lesser-known groups like Warriors Not Wimps for Jesus.[128] CFV tried to keep this meeting secret, but someone in the audience recorded several of the speeches and released the transcripts to two progressive newspapers in Colorado Springs. Everyone, not just attendees, could thus get a look at how the Colorado Model was supposed to work. The most noteworthy speech delivered at this conference came from John Eldredge, director of Focus on the Family's public policy division, who sketched the cultural environment that confronted Christian activists. According to Eldredge, American culture was defined by a celebration of individual autonomy, an emphasis on sexual gratification, and a belief that personal pain is the greatest evil imaginable. "What is left, then, for a majority of Americans, on a day-to-day basis, really are feelings," Eldredge told the audience. Advancing the Christian agenda in light of these realities required shrewdness and sensitivity. To demonstrate this point, Eldredge pointed to the example of Amendment 2. He contrasted CFV's approach with that of University of Colorado football coach Bill McCartney, who had condemned homosexuality as an abomination. "If Colorado for Family Values had made that the theme of their campaign," he said, "I doubt they would have succeeded as well as they did in the state of Colorado."[129] Strident denunciations of homosexuality might appeal to evangelicals, but activists needed to reach beyond that constituency to have any hope of victory.

The best way to do so, Eldredge said, was by using "what Americans consider to be the gospel truth . . . empirical science."[130] Eldredge's employer, Focus on the Family, was one of the nation's leading suppliers of antigay scientific knowledge.[131] Its only real rival was another attendee at the Glen Eyrie conferences: Paul Cameron, executive director of the Family Research Institute. Cameron, who held a PhD from the University of Colorado, churned out pamphlets with lurid covers and titles like *Child Molestation and Homosexuality* and *Murder, Violence, and Homosexuality*.[132] His extremism—he called for branding AIDS patients with indelible facial tattoos and flirted with the idea of "exterminating" all homosexuals—led even conservative surgeon general C. Everett Koop to denounce him as "one of the most dangerous men in America."[133] Focus on the Family, however, frequently used Cameron's research in its own publications.[134] And CFV welcomed him at its Glen Eyrie conference. Cameron, like Eldredge, emphasized the importance of using scientific facts rather than biblical quotations. But, speaking to a like-minded crowd, Cameron made clear that the struggle over gay rights was not about science but morality. "[What] we're looking at is a contest between good and evil, between the right way to do things and the wrong way to do things."[135] Scientific data mattered only for what it could contribute to this moral combat.

Paul Cameron, Focus on the Family, and CFV all hoped to make Colorado Springs the launching pad for a national movement that would, as John Eldredge put it, "roll back the militant gay agenda." Attendees at both conferences left Glen Eyrie confident that this goal was within their reach. The antigay rights movement seemed to be on the attack in the early 1990s, with the Springs leading the way. A *Washington Times* reporter who attended the second conference noted that "the anti-homosexual-rights movement finds itself in what has become the most active election year in its history," as conservative Christian activists across the country took up the Colorado Model.[136]

The first use of this model came in Cincinnati, where the conflict over gay rights played out almost exactly as it had in Colorado Springs. It began when the city council approved an ordinance expanding the city's antidiscrimination law to include sexual orientation.[137] Then came the backlash, which, though it was led by Protestant churches, organized under a secular name: Equal Rights, Not Special Rights (ERNSR). ERNSR gathered enough signatures to put an ordinance on the November 1993 ballot amending the city's charter to prohibit any law allowing people to make a "claim of minority or protected status, quota preference or other preferential treatment" on the basis of sexual orientation—an almost word-for-word copy of Amendment 2.[138] ERNSR also copied CFV's arguments, claiming that homosexuals did not deserve "protected status" because they were a privileged special interest group rather than a "true" minority.[139] To prove this point, the organization recruited an African American minister to serve as its spokesperson.[140] This strategy proved as effective in Cincinnati as it had in Colorado. On November 2, 1993, 62 percent of Cincinnati voters approved ERNSR's Issue 3, an even more resounding victory than that of Amendment 2.[141] One reason Issue 3 so closely resembled Amendment 2 was because CFV was intimately involved in the campaign. CFV trained several leaders of ERNSR, while Will Perkins made speeches in Cincinnati in support of Issue 3. CFV also provided 80 percent of the Cincinnati organization's campaign budget.[142] ERNSR's leader had good reason to say, "[CFV] has been an incredible help and resource."[143]

The battle over gay rights in Cincinnati was only the largest of several waged at the local level in 1993 and early 1994, almost all of which ended in victory for the "No Special Rights" movement. Gay rights activists recognized the urgency of this threat and scrambled to meet it. Surveys indicated that the Colorado Model had widespread appeal. A memo to the Human Rights Campaign Fund from a polling firm noted that, according to a national survey, "the most persuasive of their arguments is about special rights—that gay people have the same civil rights the rest of us have and this initiative just keeps them from getting additional special rights (56 percent convincing, 25 percent very convincing)."[144] The challenge was to neutralize the "No

Special Rights" slogan by making it clear that gays were still vulnerable to many forms of discrimination.

Local organizations mobilized to meet this challenge city by city and state by state. Like the Citizens Project in Colorado Springs, most of them did not explicitly identify themselves as progressive or liberal but rather chose generic names such as Basic Rights Oregon and Hands Off Washington.[145] National advocacy groups like People for the American Way, the American Civil Liberties Union, and the National Gay and Lesbian Task Force provided these local activists with information and resources.[146] The aim of these groups, both local and national, was to offer a vision of community more inclusive than that offered by the Christian right. As the pollster's memo to the Human Rights Campaign Fund noted, "Powerful values such as tolerance, community and unity compete with the radical right's dialogue on 'family values.' Making the case that gays and lesbians are part of our community 'just like everyone else' is convincing to our natural allies."[147] The Colorado Model emphasized division: "normal" people against gays. Its opponents responded by emphasizing community, inclusion, and unity.

Almost all the Amendment 2 clones failed, thanks in part to this counter-organizing but also because of the rules of politics. Of the dozen proposed statewide "No Special Rights" initiatives, only two ever came up for a vote. The rest either failed to gather enough signatures to make the ballot or were quashed by court ruling.[148] The only two states where Amendment 2 clones made the ballot in 1994 were Oregon and Idaho—states that, like Colorado, had easy ballot access laws and long traditions of direct democracy.[149] In those states, the counter-organizing paid off. Oregon voters had rejected the blatantly antigay Measure 9 in 1992; confronted with the toned-down Measure 13 in 1994, they rejected it as well. In Idaho, Proposition 1 was rejected by roughly 3,000 votes. It was a narrow margin, but this was a state that had not voted for a Democratic presidential candidate since Lyndon Johnson.[150]

The Colorado Model had come up short in electoral terms, but Amendment 2 still lived. Its fate would be determined not at the ballot box but in the courtroom. Progressive groups began preparing a legal challenge to Amendment 2 before it was even approved by voters. Only a week after the amendment passed, the Colorado Legal Initiatives Project and the Colorado branch of the ACLU announced their challenge at a press conference in Denver. The plaintiffs included the three cities whose gay rights ordinances would be overturned by the amendment: Aspen, Boulder, and Denver. The other plaintiffs were nine Colorado citizens, chosen to represent the human costs of the amendment.[151] One plaintiff, John Miller, taught Spanish language and culture at the University of Colorado at Colorado Springs. He had been active in the push for an antidiscrimination ordinance in Colorado Springs, a campaign that, ironically, led to the formation of CFV and the passage of Amendment 2.[152] The case—*Evans v. Romer*, named for plaintiff Richard Evans and for Colorado governor Roy Romer, who, despite his opposition to the amendment, was legally obligated to defend it—went before Judge Jeffrey Bayless of the Denver District Court in January 1993.

Bayless first had to make a speedy decision as to whether to grant an injunction against Amendment 2. Attorneys for the plaintiffs argued that the amendment would do irreparable harm to Colorado's gay and lesbian community if allowed to take effect. Bayless held several days of hearings on the question in January 1993, which gave both sides an opportunity to test their arguments.[153] The plaintiffs made a novel claim: Amendment 2 deprived gays and lesbians of the "right to equal political participation" by blocking the normal avenues for the passage of gay rights laws, which left the LGBTQ community vulnerable to harassment and violence. To dramatize this point, several plaintiffs took the stand to testify about their personal experiences with discrimination. Angela Romero, a Denver police officer, broke down in tears talking about the harassment she endured at work.[154] This argument convinced Bayless to place an injunction on the amendment until a full trial could be held later that year. When Colorado attorney general Gale Norton appealed the injunction to the Colorado Supreme Court, the court sided with Bayless.[155] These decisions suggested that the amendment faced an uphill struggle. In their rulings, both Bayless and the Colorado Supreme Court demanded proof that the amendment fulfilled a compelling state interest.

That question hung over the trial, which began in Bayless's courtroom in October 1993. Did Amendment 2 fulfill a compelling state interest, or was it simply bigotry? Answering this question meant delving into the motives of CFV leaders Will Perkins, Kevin Tebedo, and Tony Marco. In their depositions and testimony, all three insisted that they were motivated by secular reasons rather than some combination of bigotry and religion. "As far as this issue is concerned . . . it is not a religious issue," Perkins said in his deposition.[156] The plaintiffs' attorneys chipped away at these claims. This was easy to do in the case of Kevin Tebedo, who had been captured on tape asserting, "The authority of God says there's plenty wrong with homosexuality. Homosexuality is an abomination." Tebedo initially denied saying any such thing, only admitting to it after the examining attorney played the tape twice.[157]

However, the testimony presented in Bayless's courtroom went far beyond Amendment 2. The plaintiffs argued that LGBTQ people ought to be considered a "suspect class" akin to African Americans, which would entitle them to greater legal protection against discrimination. To make this case, their attorneys sought to prove, first, that homosexuality was immutable, and second, that LGBTQ people in the United States had endured centuries of discrimination.[158] One expert after another took the stand to provide evidence for these two claims. Richard Green and Judd Marmor, eminent psychiatrists, testified that sexual orientation was established early in life. George Chauncey, a historian of sexuality, described the history of persecution suffered by gays and lesbians: "Nausea, drugs, electroshock, and castration. Occasionally some lobotomies."[159] The defenders of Amendment 2 brought their own experts, befitting the Colorado Model's emphasis on science. But many of these experts were either disreputable or ill-prepared to discuss the intricacies of human sexuality. Attorney General Norton planned to call Paul Cameron as a witness and paid him $10,000 to prepare an affidavit. But Cameron's statistics were so questionable and his rejection by mainstream scientists so complete that the state decided against using his evidence.[160] Two political theorists, Harvey Mansfield of Harvard and Robert George of Princeton, spoke in generalities about the importance of traditional values, but they could not supply the kind of data provided by the scientists and historians on the other side of the case.[161]

Among the expert witnesses who testified in favor of Amendment 2 was James Davison Hunter, the sociologist who gave the culture war its name. As with the Alabama textbook case years earlier, Hunter did only cursory research on the subject: He read an issue of the *Denver Post*, examined several polls from the National Opinion Research Center, and asked a graduate student to search the LexisNexis legal database for litigation related to gay rights. He claimed, however, that in-depth preparation was unnecessary, given that what was happening in Colorado was just one more example of the process he had so thoroughly described in *Culture Wars*. On cross-examination, Hunter insisted he had "no opinion about Amendment 2" and that his only goal in testifying was to help produce a "serious and substantive debate in which people can be persuaded." His contribution to the defense of Amendment 2 was the claim that homosexuals, far from being powerless victims of oppression, were in fact a politically powerful interest group. Amendment 2 was not an exercise in bigotry but a reasonable attempt to restrain the power of the gay lobby.[162]

Bayless was not persuaded. He declared the amendment unconstitutional in December 1993, finding that it infringed upon the right to political participation.[163] The Colorado Supreme Court concurred with Bayless, concluding that the "promotion of public morality" did not constitute a "compelling governmental interest."[164] CFV, outraged, denounced the court for "outlawing the expression of 2,000 years of Judeo-Christian ethics regarding sexual behavior" and warned that the decision would normalize "not only homosexuality, but also adultery, fornication, polygamy, incest . . . sado-masochism, cross-dressing, pedophilia, bestiality, [and] necrophilia."[165] The plaintiffs celebrated their victory, but their euphoria gave way to anxiety when the United States Supreme Court decided to take the case. Less than a decade earlier, in *Bowers v. Hardwick* (1986), the high court had upheld a Georgia law criminalizing sodomy. The court had grown only more conservative since then. Amendment 2, gutted by the Colorado judiciary, was suddenly returned to life.

The significance of *Romer v. Evans*, as the Amendment 2 case was called when it reached the US Supreme Court in 1995, was evident from the volume of amicus briefs filed in the case. Numerous conservative organizations filed briefs defending Amendment 2, including Focus on the Family, the Oregon Citizens Alliance, and, of course, CFV.[166] Briefs against the amendment were filed by (among others) unions, gay rights organizations, and LGBTQ-friendly religious groups. One of these briefs, written by Harvard law professor Laurence Tribe and signed by several prominent legal scholars, dispensed with arguments about political participation and made a simpler claim: Amendment 2 was a "per se violation of the Equal Protection Clause" and thus was facially invalid.[167] This claim would prove very persuasive to the court.

Many of the justices seemed uncomfortable with Amendment 2's sweeping nature. Their questions at the oral argument set expertise aside in favor of commonsense reasoning. Many of the questions to Colorado solicitor general Timothy Tymkovich dealt with hypothetical situations involving gay rights. "Would a homosexual have a right to be served in a restaurant?" John Paul Stevens asked. The justices also seemed unsure of the amendment's purpose. "Well, what is the problem?" David Souter asked Tymkovich, trying to determine why the amendment was necessary. "What is the problem that you supposedly have been having?" The questions were not entirely one-sided. Antonin Scalia pressed Jean Dubofsky, the plaintiffs' attorney, on how to square her argument with the court's prior ruling in Bowers v. Hardwick. But the tenor of the questions was clear, giving hope to the amendment's foes.[168] On May 20, 1996, the court issued a 6–3 decision striking down Amendment 2 as a violation of the Equal Protection Clause. Anthony Kennedy's opinion held that the amendment's scope far outweighed its purported aim: "Its sheer breadth is so discontinuous with the reasons offered for it that the amendment seems inexplicable by anything but animus toward the class it affects." Laurence Tribe's amicus brief clearly influenced the justice's opinion. Like Tribe, Kennedy concluded that the amendment, far from being modest in its consequences, singled out homosexuals and made them "strangers to the law."[169]

Antonin Scalia's dissent breathed the language of culture war. Scalia opened by declaring, "The Court has mistaken a *Kulturkampf* [German for "culture war"] for a fit of spite." Amendment 2 was, he claimed, a reasonable attempt by Colorado voters to signal their disgust with homosexuality and their rejection of the elites who supported it. The amendment was simply their attempt to counter the "disproportionate political power of homosexuals." To prove this point, Scalia cited Hunter's affidavit. The dissent accepted the basic idea of the Colorado Model: Amendment 2 was a defensive measure, taken to keep liberal culture from imposing itself upon traditional values.[170] The culture war thesis had not carried the day, but the dissent demonstrated that it had found a receptive audience among at least a few members of the nation's highest court.

Romer v. Evans slammed the door on the national "No Special Rights" crusade and redirected these efforts to the campaign against same-sex marriage. Legal recognition of same-sex marriage, which even gay rights advocates had once seen as improbable, abruptly entered the realm of the possible when the Hawaii Supreme Court ruled in 1993 that the state's prohibition on same-sex marriage might violate the Hawaiian constitution. Conservatives responded by mobilizing against same-sex marriage at the state and national levels. They succeeded in passing the Defense of Marriage Act in 1996, which defined marriage as a union between a man and a woman.[171] Gary Bauer, director of the Focus on the Family–affiliated Family Research

Council, linked the act to *Romer*: "In *Romer vs. Evans*, the U.S. Supreme Court struck down Colorado's Amendment 2 and showed little regard for the right of people to govern themselves. . . . The Defense of Marriage Act sends a message to the Supreme Court and other courts that they cannot replace morality with immorality in the nation's laws."[172] Conservatives may, in fact, have given up on the Colorado Model too quickly. In 1998, the US Supreme Court upheld Issue 3, the Cincinnati initiative based on Amendment 2, by letting stand a lower court ruling that found that Issue 3 served "a litany of valid [state] interests."[173] The only difference between Amendment 2 and Issue 3 was that the former prohibited homosexuals from making any "claim of discrimination" while the latter did not. Given the weight that Kennedy's *Romer* opinion placed on "discrimination," Issue 3 may have been a path not taken for the campaign against gay rights.

By that point, however, many of those who had fought for the Colorado Model had lost their stomach for combat—at least in Colorado Springs, where, in the wake of the *Romer* decision, there was a concerted effort to smother the conflicts of the preceding years beneath the language of consensus. Several prominent religious leaders, including conservative figures like James Dobson, signed a message that appeared in the *Gazette Telegraph* only a few days after the *Romer* decision, calling upon everyone in the city to "work together to develop our area into a community of understanding and unity in the face of individuality and difference."[174] Even the *Gazette Telegraph* itself, which had supported Amendment 2, now implored readers to "come together as friends and as fellow citizens of the same community where Amendment 2 was born."[175] In Colorado Springs, the politics of consensus trumped those of culture war.

4

UPWARD, CHRISTIAN SOLDIERS

Reverend Warren Watties had a message for his congregation. He reminded them of their duty to evangelize, because "those not born again will burn in the fires of hell." It was a bracing message, but hardly an unusual one. Watties was, after all, a minister of the Foursquare Gospel Church, a Protestant denomination whose statement of faith declares that "soul winning is the one big business of the church on earth" and that the "unbelieving" shall be cast into "a lake that burns with fire and brimstone."[1] What *was* unusual was the venue. Watties was not preaching to congregants in a Foursquare Gospel Church but to Air Force Academy cadets during Basic Cadet Training (BCT), the brutal training regimen that all cadets had to endure the summer before their first year at the academy.

Ordinarily, his message would have gone unheard by anyone outside the Air Force Academy, located just north of Colorado Springs. But in the summer of 2004, when Watties delivered this sermon, students and faculty from Yale Divinity School were intermingled with the assembled cadets. The academy's leadership had asked Kristen Leslie, a professor of pastoral care at Yale, to visit BCT and evaluate the academy's response to the problem of sexual assault.[2] Leslie and a team of divinity school students found that BCT was suffused with evangelical Christianity. They reported that Protestant cadets were "encouraged to return to tents, proselytize fellow BCT members, and remind them of the consequences of apostasy." Leslie and MeLinda Morton, a Lutheran chaplain at the academy, wrote a memo to the academy's chief of chaplains warning of the "stridently Evangelical themes" and the "overwhelmingly Evangelical tone of general Protestant worship" at BCT.[3] Leslie and Morton did not intend to make their concerns public, but their memo was obtained and publicized by Mikey Weinstein, an attorney and academy graduate conducting his own investigation into the school's religious climate. Weinstein, frustrated by the academy's slowness in addressing the issue, took matters into his own hands by compiling a list of "evangelical incidents" at the academy and sending it to the Colorado Springs *Gazette*.[4] Weinstein's stratagem sparked a furious debate over the place of religion at the Air Force Academy. Four separate commissions eventually investigated the "religious atmosphere" at the school, while Congress held multiple hearings on the issue.

How did the academy become a bastion of evangelical Christianity? Given that the furor over evangelicalism coincided with the war on terror, some observers explained it as a consequence of the crusading spirit promoted by President George W. Bush, himself a devout evangelical. But the process began long before the Bush administration—indeed, its origins coincided with the origins of the academy itself. The academy was established during the religious revival of the 1950s and reflected that era's priorities. Its founders wanted the new institution to shape the souls of the cadets as well as their minds and bodies. Accordingly, they gave religion a central place at the academy, in a literal sense: The campus, after 1963, was dominated by the seventeen-spired Cadet Chapel. The chapel also dominated the religious lives of cadets, who were required to attend services there under penalty of expulsion. But the academy's control over religious life crumbled in the late 1960s and early 1970s under outside pressure. When a court struck down the mandatory chapel requirement as unconstitutional, its decision shattered the academy's religious establishment. Evangelical Christians moved fastest to pick up the pieces. Evangelical organizations like the Navigators, Campus Crusade for Christ, and the Officers' Christian Fellowship worked with allies among the faculty and staff to create a new, de facto religious establishment.

Evangelicalism thus kept alive the idea upon which the Air Force Academy was founded: that piety, patriotism, and power were inextricable from one another. Long after almost all ecumenical Protestants, and indeed many military leaders, had abandoned this idea, evangelical Christians continued to hold tightly to this Cold War inheritance. They believed that one way to make their faith winsome was to demonstrate its utility—in this case, its utility in preparing officers to fight on behalf of the United States. But this story involves change as well as continuity. Even as evangelicals at the Air Force Academy continued to insist that Christianity was essential to the making of good soldiers, they changed the language in which they expressed this idea, invoking the vocabulary of religious freedom. This language legitimated the influence of evangelicalism at the academy by effacing the role of authority. Talk of religious freedom obscured the power that faculty held over cadets and that cadets held over one another. This chapter thus contributes to a growing literature on religion and the US military by demonstrating the challenge of disestablishing religion within an authoritarian, hierarchical institution like the military.[5]

A Monument to the Faith of a Nation

The United States Air Force Academy was founded at the zenith of America's twentieth-century religious revival. The decade following World War II was (if statistics are to be believed) the most devout period in US history. Worship attendance soared, while religious denominations undertook massive construction programs that dotted the landscape with new churches, schools, and synagogues.[6] The federal government encouraged this revival: Congress voted to add "under God" to the Pledge of Allegiance; multiple senators and representatives introduced constitutional amendments declaring the United States a Christian nation; Dwight D. Eisenhower attended the first National Prayer Breakfast and gave his stamp of approval to religious projects like the "Declaration of Dependence on God."[7] Many political and military leaders believed that this revival ought to be cultivated in the armed forces; American soldiers, they thought, needed religious instruction to stiffen their resolve in the war against communism.[8]

The Air Force Academy reflected this assumption that religion was essential to military preparedness. Its stated aim was to shape souls as well as minds and bodies; the first volume of the academy's official history, written the year the institution opened, noted that the "high importance of religion in the life of the cadet and all Academy personnel was recognized very early" in the planning process.[9] The task of inculcating religion in the lives of cadets fell to the academy's chaplains. Gen. Hubert Harmon, the first superintendent, decided that these chaplains would be military officers rather than (as was the case at other service academies) civilian volunteers. Accordingly, the Air Force Academy chaplains did not hesitate to link military values with religious ones. Their sermons at the weekly chapel services—which cadets were required to attend for their first three years at the academy—conflated loyalty to the United States with obedience to God. Col. John S. Bennett, the academy's first Protestant chaplain, instructed cadets in a September 1955 sermon, "Those of us who have dedicated our lives to the military service belong to God, our Shepherd, and we belong to our country."[10] The chaplains' influence extended beyond their Sunday messages and into the everyday lives of cadets. If, for instance, a cadet sought to resign, the academy would not accept his resignation until he conferred with a chaplain.[11] The chaplains recognized the vast scope of their responsibilities. Col. Constantine Zielinski, the first Catholic chaplain, described his job as "doing everything within my power to further character guidance of the cadets in my Chapel Flight."[12] Chaplains were more than ministers; they were spiritual guardians.

Religious diversity posed a problem for the chaplains. Like the leaders of many American institutions in the 1940s and 1950s, the academy's leadership conceived of the United States as a tri-faith nation composed of Protestants, Catholics, and Jews.[13] They tailored the academy's religious policy to fit this idea. On arriving at the school, cadets filled out a card stating their religious preference, on the basis of which they were sorted into one of three "flights": Protestant, Catholic, or Jewish. The "Protestant" category proved troublesome. The first class at the academy included cadets from twenty-four Protestant denominations, including Methodists, Baptists, Episcopalians, Presbyterians, Lutherans, Congregationalists, Christian Scientists, and even one "agnostic." Compounding the problem was the divide between liturgical and nonliturgical Protestants; the latter made up about 85 percent of the Protestant cadets, but that still left a substantial number whose religious tradition required them to regularly receive Communion.[14] Moreover, the academy's leaders recognized that the challenge of accommodating diversity would grow as the number of cadets increased.[15] John Bennett, the academy's first Protestant chaplain, addressed the issue by creating his own order of worship, one that would (in theory) accommodate all Protestant denominations. That Bennett apparently saw no issues with crafting an entirely new form of worship testifies to the authority the chaplains held.

The Cadet Chapel embodied that religious authority. The contract for designing the academy went to Skidmore, Owings & Merrill, a firm whose size and prestige had earned it the nickname "The General Motors of Architecture."[16] Walter Netsch, an employee of the firm, designed the chapel, taking his inspiration from the Gothic cathedrals of France. He envisioned a building that would dominate the campus the way cathedrals once dominated medieval communities.[17] His original design, a modernist structure of glass and aluminum, received harsh criticism from the public—and, more ominously, from the congresspeople who controlled the academy's funds.

The ensuing conflict over the chapel's design reveals the political significance of religion in the Cold War–era United States. No matter which side people took in this debate, they all agreed on one thing: The chapel was not just a place of worship but a national symbol. Politicians, seeking a vision of the American soul, carefully scrutinized the chapel's design, and most of them did not like what they saw. When Skidmore, Owings & Merrill unveiled Netsch's initial plan in 1955, congressional critics responded with jeers. Senator A. Willis Robertson (D-VA) spoke for many when he denounced it as "an assembly of wigwams."[18] Such attacks led the architecture firm to withdraw Netsch's proposal in favor of a placeholder design featuring a steeple and stained-glass windows. However, John O. Merrill, who oversaw the academy project, insisted that the firm did not intend to re-create a New England chapel on the campus, saying, "The New England chapel was a small meeting house and its pattern could not be adopted to a building to accommodate 1,500 persons. It would be like a ten-foot-high dog."[19] It turned out that many congresspeople wanted a ten-foot-high dog. When Netsch's new design, revised but still very modern, was unveiled in 1957, his critics went on the attack once again, with Representative Errett Scrivner (R-KS) leading the charge. Netsch proposed a chapel with nineteen spires; Scrivner thought that was eighteen too many. "One spire is good," he said, "but why should there be a polished aluminum cathedral with 19 spires?" Scrivner's mention of "polished aluminum" pointed to the heart of the problem. For many congresspeople, the chapel's nineteen spires and aluminum exterior simply did not look like a church. Those who defended Netsch, meanwhile, believed aluminum was exactly the right material to express a fusion of religious faith and technological power. Rising to speak in the chapel's favor, Representative Alfred Sieminski (D-NJ) remarked, "[The] boys fight and die in aluminum planes.... They can worship in aluminum if they can die in it, can they not?" But Scrivner's claims momentarily carried the day. On August 6, 1957, the House voted 102–53 to adopt his amendment prohibiting the use of any appropriated funds to pay for the chapel's construction.

The next day, Scrivner pressed his case, urging colleagues to approve the amendment and defer construction on the chapel until the architects came up with a new design that was more "in keeping with the true solemnity of religion." Other representatives echoed his argument, suggesting Netsch's design violated their instinctive understanding of what a church should be. Representative Porter Hardy (D-VA) stated, "I certainly don't profess to be an authority on design, but I do know that this offends my concept of what a house of worship should look like." To counter this argument, a letter from Secretary of the Air Force James Douglas, read on the floor by Representative George Mahon (D-TX), sought to make Netsch's design legible as a church: "The exterior of the structure and the larger chapel are strongly reminiscent of the Gothic cathedrals that still contribute so much beauty to Western Europe and to so many American universities."[20] With Douglas's endorsement, the House reversed its vote from the previous day and approved funds for the chapel, despite continued grumbling from Scrivner and others.[21]

The Cadet Chapel's final design gave concrete form to Cold War religiosity. It embodied the "Protestant-Catholic-Jew" conception of American religion; though the architects originally considered building separate chapels for each faith, as was the case at the United States Military Academy, they ultimately decided to incorporate all three chapels into a single building—with, however, a Protestant chapel that was larger than the Catholic and Jewish chapels combined, a concession to the demographic realities of the United States.[22] Construction on the chapel proceeded slowly, much to the frustration of the chaplains. At one point, when it seemed as if funding for construction might be cut, Protestant chaplain John Bennett wrote an angry letter of protest invoking the taken-for-granted importance of religion: "When we provide an Officers Club ... and take the position that people can worship God any place ... we have minimized the value of religion in the lives of our cadets and we have substituted a matter of political expediency for principle, something we would deplore among the cadets themselves."[23] The chapel was finally completed in late 1963. Its dedication ceremony, held

The United States Air Force Academy Cadet Chapel, an icon of Cold War religiosity.
Courtesy of the Library of Congress, Prints and Photographs Division.

in September of that year, celebrated the fusion of Christianity and military power. Secretary of the Air Force Eugene Zuckert called the chapel "an unmistakable dynamic symbol to the world that the United States is a nation under God." The principal address, delivered by the Air Force chief of chaplains, hailed the chapel as a "monument to the faith of a nation and a symbol of the strength of a nation."[24] Long after those speakers were gone, their message remained, written into the Protestant chapel's interior. Its decor blended liturgical elements with the symbols of the aerospace age—the ends of pews, for instance, were modeled to look like airplane propellers, and the cross hanging in its transept resembled a sword. If cadets ever forgot that obedience to God was joined with obedience to the United States, they could always recall it to mind by reciting the "Cadet Prayer": "Make me an effective instrument of Thy peace in the defense of the skies that canopy free nations."[25]

Observers recognized the symbolic importance of the chapel even as they divided over its aesthetic quality. The architectural critic Allan Temko savaged the building, calling it a "social and spiritual fiasco" and "our first militant monument to Mass Cult."[26] Temko was so brutal because he believed the chapel's designers had failed to rise to the occasion: "As a national religious monument, crowning the largest assemblage of serious modern architecture yet commissioned by the federal government, and as a unique expression of the democratic ethos accommodating Protestant, Roman Catholic, and Jew within a single enclosure, the Air Academy Chapel was bound to be one of the most meaningful American buildings of its time." But instead, the architects had created something meaningless and banal.[27] The *Architectural Record* was far kinder in its assessment, but it concurred with Temko on the symbolic significance of the chapel: "By means of a different kind of architecture, and at a different time, this chapel appears likely to become a national shrine, as did the chapel at West Point."[28] Whether one loved or hated the chapel, one had to recognize that it mattered.

Prior to the chapel's completion, the academy had begun relaxing its control over the religious lives of cadets. This process unfolded slowly and unsteadily over the course of several years. In the first year of the academy's existence, with the chaplains struggling to meet the needs of Protestant cadets who belonged to liturgical denominations, the Episcopal bishop of Colorado asked Protestant chaplain John Bennett for permission to conduct services for Episcopalian cadets. Bennett refused, saying he did not want to establish a precedent by allowing civilian clergy to minister to cadets.[29] Hubert Harmon, the superintendent, endorsed Bennett's decision, informing the bishop that if they allowed him to conduct services they "would [then] have a moral obligation to follow this same policy with all religious groups."[30] The Episcopal Church was rebuffed again in 1957, when the rector of a Colorado Springs church asked the academy to set aside two acres of land for the construction of an Episcopal chapel. The superintendent rejected the request, reasoning that if the academy gave land to the Episcopalians, other Protestant denominations would demand the same treatment. Given that the academy anticipated "that there would be over 40 different Protestant sects represented in the Cadet Wing, an impossible situation would develop."[31] But though the academy would not permit outside religious groups on campus, it eventually allowed cadets to leave campus to attend services in Colorado Springs. Beginning in January 1959, first classmen (seniors) were permitted to attend Sunday services in the Springs rather than chaplain-led services on campus. Second classmen (juniors) were granted this privilege one Sunday each month.³² The academy relaxed its restrictions even further the following year, allowing all students except first-year cadets to attend services in the Springs.³³

With the Cadet Chapel completed, however, the academy tightened its control over the religious lives of cadets. The day after the chapel's completion, the academy's chief of staff wrote to the commandant of cadets, the officer in charge of cadet life, to explain that all students except first classmen were now required to attend chapel on campus. Cadets could still go to services in town, but only after attending services at the Cadet Chapel. The academy's official historian explained the new policy matter-of-factly: "Logically, with the completion of superior facilities for all cadet religious services, the Academy closely scrutinized chapel attendance practices."³⁴ The Cadet Chapel was a symbol of American's religious devotion, so it stood to reason that it was the best place for cadets to worship.

Even among the service academies, the Air Force Academy stood out for the strictness of its requirements. Not that either the Naval or Military Academy were particularly lenient: Both had traditions of mandatory chapel attendance stretching back to the first half of the nineteenth century. Furthermore, both institutions strongly reasserted this tradition in the early years of the Cold War. A statement from the Naval Academy, written in 1946, was typical: "In the molding of the character required of future leaders, it is considered that attendance at Divine Worship is essential."³⁵ In response to anyone who might criticize this policy as a form of coercion, the academies had a ready answer: Students were aware of the mandatory chapel requirement when they applied for admission and so forfeited their right to protest.³⁶ One's freedom to choose ended on entering the academy. However, by the late 1960s, even Annapolis and West Point were allowing students some leeway on chapel attendance. Rather than attend religious services, students could spend their Sunday mornings discussing morals and ethics in a small group setting arranged by the academies. The Air Force Academy offered no such alternative.³⁷

The Air Force Academy's new, even stricter attendance policy aroused a storm of protest, much to the surprise of academy leadership. The parents of several cadets complained to their congressional representatives, who in turn raised the issue with then-superintendent Lt. Gen. Robert H. Warren. Warren's only response was to reiterate the new policy. Other voices of protest came from the Colorado Springs religious community. In October 1963, seven Protestant pastors in the Springs wrote to the Air Force's Department of Chaplains and Personnel to express their concern about "the abridgement of the constitutional rights of USAF Academy Cadets to worship according to the dictates of their conscience." The pastors pointed out that the new policy might run afoul of the Supreme Court's recent *Engel v. Vitale* decision, which prohibited mandatory teacher-led prayer in public schools.[38] Their protest brought further attention to—and criticism of—the new policy. A *Washington Post* editorial supported the Colorado pastors and derided the academy's "homogenized non-denominational services."[39] Leaks from within the academy also expressed discontent with mandatory chapel. One Air Force cadet, in an anonymous letter to the *Denver Post*, complained that the chapel program was nothing but "a show for Academy visitors." "I find atheism more attractive than trying to put God in my life in such a vain, hollow way," the disgruntled cadet wrote.[40] The Air Force waved off these complaints, with the Air Force chief of chaplains remarking that the academy was "not a voluntary community."[41] At the academy, obedience to religious authority remained inseparable from obedience to military authority.

Disestablishment

Liberal Protestants played a key role in challenging mandatory chapel at the service academies. This included Protestant military chaplains—a population that, as Ronit Stahl's recent work on the chaplaincy has shown, were acutely aware of the problem of religious freedom in the armed forces.[42] The August 1964 edition of *The Chaplain*, published by and for Protestant chaplains, included an editorial denouncing "compulsory chapel attendance" at the service academies.[43] One Navy chaplain wrote to the secretary of the Navy protesting the requirement that naval enlistees attend worship services every week. Inverting the language of the Cold War, he condemned mandatory worship as akin to the coercion practiced "by our ideological enemies in the Cold War."[44] Liberal Protestant publications like the *Christian Century* also pressured the armed forces to give up the practice. The *Century* framed the issue as a clash of two cultures, military and religious, rejecting the Cold War–era assumption that the two forces necessarily complemented one another: "Academy officials, operating from a philosophy which exalts force, may be incapable of understanding the ineffectiveness of force in producing religious understanding."[45] This editorial earned the *Century* a congratulatory letter from an Air Force officer previously stationed at the Air Force Academy, who suggested that cadets there loathed mandatory chapel.[46]

Even as the academy's leadership dismissed these complaints in public, in private they were searching for a secular justification for mandatory chapel. They were well aware that judges had begun striking down other forms of state-sponsored religion established in the early Cold War, as happened in the *Engel* case. Robert Warren's successor as superintendent, Lt. Gen. Thomas S. Moorman, asked the academy chaplains to develop a defense of the chapel policy that did not rely on religious claims. Col. Harold D. Shoemaker, a Protestant chaplain, obliged the superintendent by providing him with an argument that reframed chapel attendance as a "cultural"—and thus secular—act rather than a religious one. Cadets, the chaplain wrote, needed to learn how to make "value judgments" that transcended "the immediate decisions of strategy and attacks." Learning those values required "the fullest exposure to the cults, creeds, and codes of western Judaeo-Christian civilization." Invoking "civilization" transformed a sectarian act into a universal one.[47] Moreover, Shoemaker argued, though cadets were required to attend chapel, they were not required to "perform an internal act of worship" while attending. Religion was something that happened inside oneself. If a practice was purely external, it was secular.[48] Moorman clearly approved of this argument, because he repeated much of it verbatim in correspondence defending the chapel policy.[49]

This defense could not stave off the inevitable legal challenge. The American Civil Liberties Union led the effort to pry apart religious and military obedience at the service academies. The ACLU first challenged mandatory chapel at the Air Force Academy in 1959, when its executive director wrote a letter to the secretary of the Air Force objecting to the policy as a violation of the First Amendment's Establishment Clause. He received a brusque reply from the chief of Air Force chaplains, who dismissed the complaint by noting that mandatory chapel was necessary to help cadets develop the "proper moral stature." Besides, the chaplain wrote, chapel attendance was hardly mandatory, given that cadets volunteered to attend the academy.[50] Reluctant to press the matter during a nationwide religious revival, the ACLU did not pursue the issue. By the 1960s, however, the organization had become more willing to challenge government-mandated religious practice. Stymied for several years by its inability to find a plaintiff with standing to sue, in 1970 the organization finally convinced several students at the US Naval and Military

Academies to join a class action lawsuit challenging the chapel policies at the service academies. The Air Force Academy took this threat seriously. The superintendent, Lt. Gen. Albert P. Clark, sought to head off the challenge with a "New Look" policy that allowed cadets to attend services at religious institutions in Colorado Springs rather than at the Cadet Chapel. Because this policy still required cadets to attend some kind of service, whether on campus or in the Springs, it contained a subsection intended as an inoculation against charges of religious compulsion: "A cadet is not required to worship at the service he attends."[51] Once again, the academy distinguished between external, secular "attendance" and internal, religious "worship."

Ingenious as it was, this distinction eventually failed to convince the courts. But it briefly seemed as if the chapel policy might survive the ACLU's lawsuit. In July 1970, a judge of the District Court of the District of Columbia rejected the challenge to mandatory chapel. This court's ruling accepted the claim that "the primary effect of required attendance is secular in that it enables those who will one day hold command positions to gain an awareness and respect for the force religion has on the lives of men."[52] This was exactly the distinction the service academies sought to make: between mandatory attendance, which was permissible, and mandatory worship, which was not. Leaders at the academies scrambled to build on this favorable ruling. At a meeting held in March 1971, they discussed plans to find witnesses who could testify that mandatory chapel attendance was a secular practice. One representative from the Navy noted that his service was applying "high level pressure" to recruit "top commanders, chiefs of staff, service secretaries, and academy superintendents" to vouch for the "secular effect of chapel attendance."[53] Indeed, in making the case for mandatory chapel, government attorneys laid such emphasis on its secular nature that some chaplains grumbled about the "downgrading" of religion.[54] Even these strenuous efforts to secularize the chapel proved fruitless, however. The US Court of Appeals for the District of Columbia circuit reversed the judge's initial ruling by a 2–1 vote in June 1972. While granting that cadets needed some knowledge of religion, the majority opinion held that the service academies had failed to prove that mandatory chapel attendance was the best way to impart this knowledge.[55] The US Supreme Court declined to hear the case, allowing the lower court's decision to stand—and shattering the religious establishment that had dominated the Air Force Academy since its founding.

Chaplains and officers at the academy claimed the decision would have no effect on the institution's religious program, but the statistics suggested otherwise. The change was abrupt: In January 1973, cadets returned from their winter break to find that they no longer had to attend chapel each week. According to the academy chaplains, chapel attendance dropped by one-third the first Sunday after the Supreme Court declined to hear the case.[56] The chaplains insisted (at least in public) that the religious program was as strong as ever, possibly even stronger. "It seems we have lost in quantity but gained in quality," said one. "Those who are attending [chapel] voluntarily do so with a greater sense of commitment and devotion than before." Chaplains also claimed that, while attendance at chapel might have declined, more cadets than ever before were participating in religious activities like Bible study classes. An academy press release asserted that, contrary to predictions that the end of mandatory chapel would sound the "death knell of organized religious programs" at the school, "cadet religious programs are still going strong and most chaplains feel the situation is better than before."[57] By the end of the 1970s, however, it was clear that the court rulings had transformed religion at the academy. In a 1977 interview with the Colorado Springs *Gazette Telegraph*, the academy's senior chaplain admitted that attendance had been declining at chapel services since 1973, a trend he predicted would only accelerate. The chaplain also gloomily noted that growing numbers of cadets were indicating "No Preference" when asked their religious identity on entering the academy, a practice held over from the days of mandatory chapel.[58] Replacing the academy's religious establishment with a "religious free market" had done nothing to spur the growth of religion at the school, at least in raw numbers.[59]

Reestablishment

The end of mandatory chapel did promote one form of religion, however: It empowered evangelical parachurch ministries at the academy. These groups had been present at the academy since 1965, when the Fellowship of Christian Athletes established a chapter there. The Fellowship of Christian Athletes was soon attracting about 30 cadets to weekly Bible study groups and over 100 cadets to special events, like a speech by Minnesota Vikings quarterback Fran Tarkenton.[60] The organization was soon joined by other

Christian groups, many of them evangelical, including the "Baptist Student Union, Methodist Cadet Fellowship, Presbyterian Cadet Fellowship, and the Catholic Newman Club."[61] As of 1971, over 1,000 cadets were taking part in seventeen different ministries.[62] The Officers' Christian Fellowship, headquartered near Denver, and the Navigators, headquartered only a few miles away in Colorado Springs, had a particularly strong presence on campus.[63] These organizations were well positioned to take advantage of an academy policy instituted after the end of mandatory chapel. Starting in the mid-1970s, cadets were allowed to spend their Monday evenings attending religious instruction classes on campus. This program was dubbed SPIRE—Special Programs in Religious Education—early in the 1980s.[64] At first only chaplains could teach SPIRE classes, but the academy eventually extended that privilege to outside groups. Most of the organizations involved in SPIRE were evangelical, including the Navigators, Campus Crusade for Christ, Officers' Christian Fellowship, and Youth with a Mission. Several hundred cadets attended SPIRE programs each week as of the early 1990s.[65] The chaplains, who had once jealously guarded their access to the spiritual lives of cadets, now shared that access with Christian ministries.

Guest speakers also injected evangelical Christianity into the academy's religious life. Outside speakers had been part of the school's religious program since its founding, but from the 1980s onward these events took on an increasingly evangelical tone. Starting in 1984, for instance, the chaplains sponsored annual revivals that featured speakers from evangelical institutions like the Southern Baptist Theological Seminary. Hundreds of cadets attended these revivals.[66] Contributing to this trend was the growing cluster of evangelical ministries in Colorado Springs, many of which provided the academy with speakers for religious events. Jim Irwin, former astronaut and founder of the parachurch ministry High Flight, addressed the academy several times.[67] James Dobson of Focus on the Family served as guest speaker at the academy's Protestant baccalaureate service in 1993, only a few months after his ministry arrived in the Springs.[68] And in 2000, Jerry White, president of the Navigators, spoke at the academy's celebration of the National Prayer Breakfast.[69] The city's evangelical megachurches also took part in the academy's religious life. Gary Huckabay, pastor of Woodmen Valley Chapel, spoke often at retreats for Protestant cadets, while the New Life megachurch regularly ran shuttles that took academy cadets to its Friday night services.[70]

Though the chaplains increasingly yielded their authority to outside ministries and churches, there was one area where they retained exclusive access to cadets: Basic Cadet Training, often referred to as "Beast," the brutal training regimen required of all incoming cadets. Prospective students spent the summer prior to their first year at the academy being pushed to their physical and psychological limits under the supervision of fourth-year cadets. Chaplains had long recognized that BCT was an ideal place to minister to cadets. Starting in the 1960s, the chaplains held daily devotionals during BCT and mingled with the incoming cadets during their few moments of downtime. These efforts seemed to yield fruit. As of 1975, the chaplains could claim that "about 98 per cent" of basic cadets attended Protestant or Catholic services.[71] This ministry of presence, already strong, intensified in the 1990s. The chapel program instituted a new policy that assigned one chaplain to each squadron of cadets for the entirety of BCT; some of these chaplains even took part in the grueling physical challenges of basic training.[72] By 1998, the academy's commandant of cadets confidently declared that at BCT there "were more chaplains about than anywhere else on earth."[73] The BCT program had replaced the chapel services as the place where chaplains exerted the greatest influence on cadets. Years later, Kristen Leslie and her team would note the consequences of this shift.

The academy's leaders looked at these trends—the evangelicalism of SPIRE and the muscular religion of BCT—and saw a way to advance their new agenda: character development. "Character" was a key word at the academy in the 1990s, for two reasons. First, the academy sought to redefine its mission in a post–Cold War world by embracing a "back-to-basics" educational philosophy. The "basics" included the development of proper character.[74] Second, a sexual assault scandal rocked the academy in the early 1990s. Public awareness of the scandal began when several female cadets reported to the superintendent, Lt. Gen. Bradley Hosmer, that they had been sexually assaulted by classmates during their time at the academy. Hosmer, who believed the problem was caused by a lack of "mature judgment" among cadets, responded by establishing the Center for Character Development at the academy in July 1993.[75] Hosmer hoped to find a place for religion in the academy's new character-building program. He had been part of the academy's first graduating class and had experienced mandatory chapel attendance firsthand. With this in mind, he floated the possibility of restoring mandatory chapel "under the rubric of training." Hosmer asked the academy's legal department and chaplaincy for their thoughts on the matter. The legal department, while granting the importance of "religious training" to "well rounded officers," pointed out that any attempt to reinstitute mandatory chapel would be fruitless unless the courts reconsidered the 1972 ruling that had struck down the policy.[76]

The response from senior chaplain James E. Price was more hopeful—and more revealing. Price suggested that the best way to promote religion among the cadets was not mandatory chapel but "mandatory OPPORTUNITY to experience religious activities." This meant giving the cadets more free time, which would make it easier for them to attend religious events like Bible study sessions. To prove his point that more free time yielded more religious practice, Price's memo included a chart showing that attendance at chapel services during BCT exercises, when chaplains were readily available and chapel services were held every morning, regularly exceeded 1,000 people each day.[77] Price's perception of BCT as the ideal religious environment was telling. Students may have flocked to chapel during BCT, but this was at least partly because chapel services offered one of the few respites from the physical and psychological pressure of training. That Price saw this high-pressure atmosphere as a time of maximum religious freedom suggests that the academy's leadership, including its chaplains, overlooked the role of coercion in the school's religious life.

As the academy placed greater emphasis on character development, chaplains took up the language of "character" to keep their program relevant. Changes in the chaplaincy's mission statement revealed the program's changing priorities. The mission statement for the 1990–91 academic year committed the chaplaincy to providing a "comprehensive religious program at the Air Force Academy."[78] The academy established the Center for Character Development in 1993; by the following year, the chaplaincy had changed its mission to "provide for and support spiritual and character development through the free exercise of religion and pastoral care."[79] But the chaplains also took care to demonstrate that their program would contribute to, rather than simply duplicate, the work of the Center for Character Development. The language of "spirituality" provided that necessary distinction. The official history of the chaplaincy explained that, while the Center for Character Development provided a "cognitive" approach to character, the chaplaincy engaged the "affective, emotional, and spiritual aspects" of the cadet to ensure that character was truly "internalized."[80] Some chaplains even suggested that spirituality could serve as a sort of back door for religion to return to the academy. A "Chaplain Service Supplemental Plan to the Strategic Plan for Character Development at the Air Force Academy," prepared in January 1997, argued that, while not every cadet had a "religion," they all had "spirituality," which encompassed "all those factors, values, and relationships that underlie each individual human personality."[81] Treating spirituality as a universal attribute, one that chaplains could nurture in cadets, would restore the chaplaincy to the position of influence it held prior to the end of the mandatory chapel policy.

Meanwhile, evangelical Christians at the academy were growing more assertive, blurring the line between parachurch ministries and the academy's staff and faculty. Starting in 1991, a division of Campus Crusade for Christ called Christian Leadership Ministries took out an ad in the academy's newspaper every December. The ad declared, "We believe that Jesus is the only real hope for the world. If you would like to discuss Jesus, feel free to contact one of us."[82] Dozens of faculty and staff put their names to this message. Among them was Fisher DeBerry, coach of the academy's football team. DeBerry's on-field success won him national attention, but he insisted that his greatest concern was not wins and losses but helping his players become "better people."[83] He believed the best way to do so was through a healthy infusion of religion, a belief he attributed to his Christian upbringing in South Carolina. DeBerry regularly prayed with his team and held "weekly spiritual gatherings on Friday nights during the season." "One of the pillars of the academy is spirituality," he explained, and so while a player did not need to be a Christian, he did need "some kind of character-led force in his life."[84] As so often happened at the academy, terms like "spirituality" and "character" generally translated to "Christianity." For despite his protestations to the contrary, DeBerry left a distinctly sectarian stamp on his program. Every game at Falcon Stadium began with a prayer delivered by a chaplain over the PA system; a chaplain accompanied the team to all the Falcons' away games; and, most notoriously, DeBerry hung a banner in the locker room declaring, "I am a member of Team Jesus Christ."[85] He borrowed the phrase "I am a member of Team Jesus Christ," also known as the "Competitor's Creed," from the Fellowship of Christian Athletes, one of the first evangelical organizations to have a presence at the academy. DeBerry belonged to the Fellowship, as did almost every member of his team. It was an indication of how evangelical organizations re-created a de facto religious establishment at the academy after the de jure establishment crumbled.

Few at the academy objected to these trends, and those who did were mostly ignored. Martin Cook, a professor in the philosophy department, raised concerns about the "fundamentalist" influence on campus in a letter written to the secretary of the Air Force in October 1997. Cook warned that the power of conservative Christians at the academy imposed a de facto religious test on the faculty. His letter reached the chief of the Air Force chaplains, who contacted the academy's senior staff chaplain seeking information "to assist him in formulating a response to Dr. Cook's allegation." The senior chaplain replied with a document, prepared for the Center for Character Development by another academy chaplain, that distinguished between parochial "religion" and universal "spirituality." This document suggested that only spirituality, defined as a "metaphysical consideration of that which leads us to a desire for meaning," could provide the proper foundation for character development. Ultimately, no action was taken in response to Cook's warning.[86] The slipperiness of the term "spirituality" allowed it to cover what might otherwise have been considered a violation of the Establishment Clause.

Even at this point, evangelical Christians did not constitute a majority of either cadets or staff at the academy. As of the 2001–2 academic year, the number of cadets participating in explicitly evangelical SPIRE programs stood somewhere between 200 and 300. Though not insignificant, that number was still less than 10 percent of the student body.[87] Evangelicals wielded influence not through numbers but through superior organization; there were no countervailing forces to the parachurch ministries present on campus. Yet even that was not enough on its own. The academy's hierarchical nature meant that the power of evangelical Christians ultimately depended on their relationship with the institution's leadership. As Hosmer's inquiry about restoring mandatory chapel suggests, many of these leaders would have happily accepted an expanded role for religion at the academy, provided it meshed with their agenda. The sexual assault scandal of 2002–4 was the moment evangelicals at the academy had been waiting for: the moment when the school's leaders, desperate to restore discipline, gave their imprimatur to evangelicalism.

The academy's leadership had known since at least the early 1990s that male cadets were harassing and sexually assaulting their female classmates.[88] But leaders took few concrete steps to respond, and so the problem festered until 2002, when the family of a thirteen-year-old girl who had been sexually assaulted by a cadet brought the case to the attention of the academy's board of trustees.[89] What followed was, according to the academy's official history, "what might well be the most serious crisis since [the academy's] establishment."[90] This scandal empowered evangelical Christians in two ways. First, it led to a near total change in the academy's leadership. The new commandant of cadets, Gen. Johnny Weida, was a devout evangelical who used his position to promote evangelical Christianity. One of his first acts as commandant was to send a school-wide email alerting cadets to the upcoming National Day of Prayer.[91] Soon afterward, he sent a "commander's guidance" informing cadets that they were "accountable first to your god." And at a Protestant chapel service during BCT exercises, Weida taught the cadets a new chant: He would say "Airpower!" to which evangelical cadets would respond "Rock, sir!" Weida told the assembled cadets that, when their classmates asked about the meaning of this unusual chant, they could use it as an opportunity to evangelize.[92]

The second factor that empowered evangelicals was the emphasis placed on "culture" as both the cause of and solution to the sexual assault crisis. The panel convened by the Department of Defense to investigate the crisis concluded that a "breakdown in values" had caused the assaults. Solving the crisis would mean re-inculcating "core values" in students.[93] For many evangelical Christians at the academy, this sounded like an invitation to improve the character of cadets through evangelization. A later report noted that "senior leaders" at the academy viewed the sexual assault scandal as a consequence of "moral deficiencies that could be corrected only with religious (primarily Evangelical Christian) moral values."[94] If evangelical Christianity improved the moral fiber of cadets, then it ought to be welcomed, even encouraged.

This was the atmosphere Kristen Leslie and her students stepped into in the summer of 2004. And this was the atmosphere that Mikey Weinstein relentlessly publicized. Revelations about the power of evangelical Christianity at the Air Force Academy led to multiple investigations into the academy's religious climate, all of which reached different conclusions. First to examine the issue was a delegation led by Shirley Martinez, the Air Force's deputy assistant secretary for equal opportunity. Martinez and her delegation visited the academy for three days in December 2004 and published their report the following March, concluding, "We did not find overt indications of a crisis in regards to religious insensitivity/intolerance nor did we note any consistent signs of rampant discrimination on the basis of religion." But their report nonetheless noted that some cadets felt "bombarded" with religious invitations and that, even during their relatively brief visit, they saw evidence of religious insensitivity and intolerance among both cadets and faculty. They diagnosed the academy as suffering not from discrimination but from a lack of understanding, a problem that could be solved by giving cadets sensitivity training.[95] Like the investigation into the sexual assault scandal, the Martinez report suggested that both the cause of and solution to the academy's religious problems lay in the realm of "values."

The watchdog organization Americans United for Separation of Church and State reached the opposite conclusion. This group's report declared that "religious practices" at the academy constituted "egregious, systemic, and legally actionable" violations of the Establishment Clause. Its report emphasized that religious discrimination at the academy involved not only chaplains but also faculty, staff, and cadets. Its allegations included intense proselytizing by evangelicals, sectarian prayers held at mandatory academy events, and denial of requests to attend religious events off-campus on Saturdays rather than Sundays. And it noted that proselytizing, rather than the work of a "few rogue individuals," was promoted by authority figures like commandant of cadets Johnny Weida and football coach Fisher DeBerry.[96] Where the Martinez report found a culture of misunderstanding, Americans United found a culture of evangelization—a culture, moreover, that came straight from the top.

The third report came from the National Conference on Ministry to the Armed Forces (NCMAF), a nonprofit that recruited and endorsed clergy to serve as military chaplains. The five-person NCMAF delegation visited the academy for several days in June 2005, interviewing almost 200 personnel and cadets. The delegation members agreed with Americans United that Weida and DeBerry had overstepped their boundaries. Their report also noted that representatives from evangelical organizations like Campus Crusade were present on campus throughout the week, rather than only during scheduled SPIRE classes. Despite these observations, the NCMAF delegation reached the same conclusion as Martinez's delegation: Religious sensitivity training would solve the problem.[97]

The highest-profile investigation was the *Report of the Headquarters Review Group concerning the Religious Climate at the U.S. Air Force Academy*, usually referred to as the "Brady Report" after its leader, Lt. Gen. Roger A. Brady. Brady led a sixteen-member task force (whose membership was not made public) that visited the academy in May 2005. Brady's team interviewed faculty, cadets, and staff and also met with twenty-five different focus groups, including several groups of cadets organized by religious affiliation. The Brady Report, issued June 22, 2005, concluded that there was no "overt religious discrimination" at the academy. Yet many of the details in the report seemed at odds with this conclusion. The focus groups revealed that cadets of different religious identities had vastly different experiences. Jewish cadets expressed discomfort with the school's religious climate. One remarked, "Freedom of religion does not exist if you are not a Christian." Some cadets in the Protestant focus groups, by contrast, complained that the academy had become too "politically correct" and that they were the ones being discriminated against. A similar divide emerged in the one-on-one interviews. One cadet said that "evangelical Christians are under constant attack and scrutiny solely on account of their beliefs." On the other hand, a faculty member claimed that "religion permeated this place like nothing I had ever seen before in the Air Force." Equally revealing was the report's discussion of the academy's annual Cadet Social Climate Surveys. Between 1995 and 2000, religion consistently ranked among the most positively rated areas in the survey. But these results concealed a significant amount of unease. A survey taken in the fall of 2004 found that "30% of non-Christian cadets responding believed that Christian cadets are given preferential treatment" and that "over 50% of all cadets responding agree that religious slurs/comments/jokes are used." The Brady Report nonetheless concluded that these were problems of perception rather than of discrimination.[98] Religious minorities may have felt discriminated against, but their feeling was simply that, a feeling rather than reality.

Given the academy's national prominence and its role in the ongoing war on terror, the religious issue soon spilled over into partisan politics. This was, after all, the era of what historian Steven Miller calls the "second evangelical scare"—a backlash against the conservative religiosity of George W. Bush and his evangelical allies.[99] No number of investigations, task forces, and reports could keep the debate over religion at the academy sealed off from this broader conflict. Inevitably, Congress waded into the matter. In June 2005, the same month that Brady's task force issued its report, Representative David Obey (D-WI) proposed an amendment to the 2006 Department of Defense Appropriations Act that asked the Air Force's leadership to address "inappropriate proselytizing" at the academy.[100] Republicans quickly rose to attack Obey's amendment as a threat to religious freedom. Representative Todd Tiahrt (R-KS), a staunch Christian conservative, asserted that the "men and women of our military have the right to freely practice their religion, and Congress has a solemn duty to protect their rights." But opponents of the amendment did not have a monopoly on claims of religious freedom. Many Democrats invoked the ongoing war in Iraq as a reason to defend the religious freedom of cadets. Americans were fighting and dying to protect this freedom abroad, so it was incumbent on Congress to protect it at home.[101] The debate over Obey's amendment turned on the question: Whose religious freedom was under threat? The Air Force cadets who were evangelizing, or the cadets who might be subject to that evangelization? The Republican-controlled House opted for the former, rejecting the amendment that would have limited proselytizing at the academy.[102]

This was not Congress's last word on the subject. On June 28, 2005, little over a week after the House rejected Obey's amendment, a subcommittee of the House Committee on Armed Services convened a hearing on the religious climate at the Air Force Academy. Roger Brady and Kristen Leslie both testified, as did Jack D. Williamson, the chaplain who had led the NCMAF investigation. Written testimony came from MeLinda Morton and Johnny Weida. Congressional debate over Obey's amendment had focused on the meaning of religious freedom. Testimony before the subcommittee dealt with a related question: At what points does religious insensitivity shade into something more insidious? Brady, echoing his report, argued that the "lack of awareness" displayed by some evangelical faculty, staff, and cadets did not amount to anything malicious. Indeed, the offenders were usually motivated by "the best of intentions." Williamson concurred with Brady, saying that the NCMAF team saw more insensitivity than intolerance. Leslie dissented. Evangelical Christianity, she suggested, was woven in the culture of the academy. The problem was not that some cadets evangelized aggressively; it was that the academy's leadership tacitly endorsed this practice. However, most of the questions from the congresspeople avoided issues of power and authority and returned to the matter of religious freedom. Representative John Hostetler (R-IN), who had angrily denounced Obey's amendment, now attacked the proceedings as a threat to the religious freedom of evangelical cadets. Representative Walter Jones (R-NC) was more temperate in his criticism but no less firm: "I strongly believe in religious freedom, and I hope you understand my grave concerns about the forces that would try to limit it."[103] The subcommittee mostly served to demonstrate how thoroughly the issue of religion at the academy had become entangled with the partisan politics of the era.

For all the passions aroused by this issue, the matter was never really concluded, let alone solved. It simply faded from public attention. Mikey Weinstein broadened his focus from the academy to the armed forces in general, founding the Military Religious Freedom Foundation to continue his fight against proselytizing in the military. MeLinda Morton was abruptly transferred from Colorado Springs to Okinawa; she responded by resigning from the Air Force and later joined Weinstein's foundation. Johnny Weida was rotated to a new position rather than disciplined, though he was denied a promotion to major general.[104] As for the Air Force Academy itself, it appeared that the mix of public scrutiny and sensitivity training tamped down the most aggressive forms of evangelizing. It was hard to draw firm conclusions beyond that. Diana Schemo, a journalist who spent a year following cadets at the academy, noted that evangelical organizations like the Navigators and Campus Crusade still had a strong presence on campus.[105] A delegation of Air Force officials visited the academy in 2011 to see what progress had been made on the religious climate. They found that religious minorities, among both the cadets and faculty, felt "far freer than even five years ago to be open about their beliefs." On the other hand, some "religiously-devout cadets" now complained that the "climate is too secular and is overly restrictive of their free expression." If anything united the cadets, it was the feeling that the academy was unfairly being "put under a microscope."[106] Yet this problem was likely insoluble. The academy had been under a microscope since its founding. Like Colorado Springs itself, the Air Force Academy was a symbol to which evangelicals—and many others—turned their eyes.

5
THE INVISIBLE WAR

"I believe God has chosen Colorado Springs." So said the Reverend Ted Haggard in August 1998 at the grand opening of the World Prayer Center. The prayer center was a triumph of both Christianity and technology. Its underground "nerve center" was packed with phones, computers, and fax machines that could receive requests for prayers from around the globe. These requests would be sorted and delivered to intercessors: people who would spend up to eight hours a day praying in special rooms at the prayer center. The World Prayer Center was only one facet of the evangelical empire Ted Haggard was building in Colorado Springs. He was also pastor of New Life Church, which in 1998 claimed over 6,000 congregants; within ten years it would expand to over 14,000. Haggard's influence grew with his church. In 2003, he was elected president of the National Association of Evangelicals. And in 2005, *Time* magazine named him one of America's most influential evangelicals.[1]

Haggard used his position to preach the gospel of spiritual warfare. Christianity has always encompassed a variety of ideas about evil spirits. In the latter half of the twentieth century, a network of Protestant ministers and writers crystallized some of these ideas into a discipline they called "spiritual warfare," which entailed using intense and often public prayer to combat demonic forces. Haggard and many other evangelicals in Colorado Springs presented their city as a laboratory where spiritual warriors could develop new techniques for use in their ongoing war against evil. Their ranks swelled during the 1990s, as the Springs attracted numerous ministries that specialized in spiritual warfare.

The arrival of C. Peter Wagner, professor at Fuller Theological Seminary and the nation's leading advocate of spiritual warfare, cemented the city's reputation as the center of this religious movement. Colorado Springs was now home to two of the movement's most important figures. Wagner was the theorist and publicist, the man who spread the gospel of spiritual warfare in countless books and seminars.[2] Haggard was the pastor, the man who founded his church upon its principles. Both men rose to the top of the evangelical world by virtue of their intelligence, charisma, and hard work (and, they insisted, their use of spiritual warfare). Wagner taught at Fuller Theological Seminary for decades, while Haggard served as president of the National Association of Evangelicals. They achieved the goals to which the first generation of evangelicals had aspired: media attention, political influence, and intellectual respectability.

Colorado Springs thus makes an ideal place to consider spiritual warfare as both concept and practice. There, theories developed by people like Wagner were implemented by people like Haggard. Examining this history reveals the significance of Pentecostal and charismatic traditions within American evangelicalism, a fact that can be obscured by an overemphasis on Billy Graham and his milieu.[3] Conservative Protestants throughout the twentieth century, including many who proudly identified as evangelicals, were quite comfortable with the notion that demons were an active force in the world. The spiritual warriors of Colorado Springs were simply adding a popular gloss to ideas that were common in the evangelical world, rather than—as some of their critics alleged—creating something new. If there *was* something new in the activities of Wagner, Haggard, and their allies, it was the way they yoked these ideas to a political agenda that was colored by Cold War triumphalism and that celebrated the power of free market capitalism.

Wrestling with Dark Angels

Spiritual warfare grew out of the "charismatic renewal" within twentieth-century Christianity. Charismatic Christians believed in the power of the

Holy Spirit to work miracles in the modern world, contrary to those who argued that the era of miracles was over.[4] The charismatic renewal had deep roots in Anglo-American Protestantism. The Keswick Conferences held in Great Britain in the last decades of the nineteenth century served as a gathering point for Protestants who believed that God's power could still erupt into everyday life. Pentecostalism, distinguished by its enthusiastic embrace of the gift of tongues, emerged in the United States in the first decade of the twentieth century and spread rapidly around the globe.[5] These were among the precursors of the charismatic renewal, which began in earnest in the United States and United Kingdom late in the 1950s.[6] Charismatics believed that spirit-filled Christians could work miracles, including divine healing, prophesying—and casting out demons.

A preoccupation with demons ran through the history of the charismatic renewal like a black thread. Welsh evangelist Jessie Penn-Lewis, identified by one historian as the "most accomplished lady speaker associated with Keswick," spent the final decades of her career urging Christians to recognize and resist Satan's wiles. Her *War on the Saints*, written with fellow evangelist Evan Roberts, described the demonic world as a hierarchy of spirits under the lordship of Satan; these spirits could fool, entrap, and possess people, even devout Christians.[7] Donald Grey Barnhouse, pastor of Philadelphia's Tenth Presbyterian Church and a popular radio preacher, delivered a series of talks on demonic powers that were published after his death as *The Invisible War*. Barnhouse, like Penn-Lewis, emphasized both the ceaseless machinations of Satan and the hierarchical nature of his forces.[8] However, perhaps the most important contribution to the emerging discipline of spiritual warfare came from a man with no connection to the charismatic movement. C. S. Lewis, professor of English literature at Oxford, achieved unexpected success with *The Screwtape Letters*, a novel framed as a series of letters from a devil to his nephew, a "junior tempter," explaining how to lead humankind to perdition. Lewis's devils worked with a light touch, controlling humans through suggestion and manipulation rather than possession. Nonetheless, Lewis insisted on the reality of these evil spirits. Later advocates of spiritual warfare often quoted a passage from the novel's preface: "There are two equal and opposite errors into which our race can fall about devils," Lewis wrote. "One is to disbelieve in their existence. The other is to believe, and to feel an excessive and unhealthy interest in them."[9] Generations of spiritual warriors would repeat this quote to assure readers that they were guilty of neither error.

C. Peter Wagner played a key role in turning these general ideas about demonic power into a distinct discipline called "spiritual warfare." Born in New York City in 1930, Wagner received a master of divinity degree from Princeton Theological Seminary and a master of theology degree from Fuller Theological Seminary before spending a decade as a missionary in Bolivia.[10] On returning to the United States in 1971, Wagner joined Fuller's School of World Missions. There, he taught alongside Donald McGavran, whose efforts to apply social science to mission work pioneered what became known as the church growth movement. McGavran believed it was possible to identify groups of people who were particularly receptive to the gospel and who could be converted en masse.[11] Wagner carried on McGavran's message, eventually becoming the Donald A. McGavran Professor of Church Growth at Fuller. But his interests gradually expanded beyond church growth. Early in the 1980s, Wagner and a California pastor named John Wimber began teaching a class at Fuller titled "MC510: Signs & Wonders."[12] Wimber and Wagner did more than simply teach about miracles; they gave students an opportunity to work wonders in the classroom. MC510 became one of Fuller's most popular courses—and one of its most controversial. The seminary's leadership investigated the course and issued a lengthy report that, while granting the possibility of miracles in the present, declared that these wonders were "not appropriate to the Fuller academic setting."[13] Though the seminary discontinued MC510, Wagner continued to explore the world of wonders. He concluded that these "spiritual gifts" were the key to church growth, noting that "effective evangelism in today's world is accompanied by manifestations of supernatural power."[14] If Christians applied the lessons of spiritual warfare, he suggested, the 1990s would witness the "greatest harvest of souls since the death and resurrection of Jesus."[15] Wagner put himself forward as an expert who could help Christians realize the possibility of limitless growth.

Wagner's affiliation with Fuller Theological Seminary reveals an important truth: Spiritual warfare emerged from eminently respectable evangelical institutions.[16] The Lausanne Congress on World Evangelization, held in Manila in 1989, was one such institution.[17] Wagner proposed that "20–25 elite intercessors"—that is, people particularly skilled in spiritual warfare—meet during the Manila conference to pray around the clock for its success.[18] Ben Jennings, a high-ranking employee of Campus Crusade for Christ, put Wagner's idea into practice, organizing the "prayer warriors" who gathered in Manila.[19] Among those present at these intense prayer sessions was Bill

Bright himself, president of Campus Crusade, who healed one of the intercessors after she suffered a seemingly fatal asthma attack—at least as recalled by Wagner, who attributed the asthma attack to demonic interference. Wagner recalled Bright exclaiming, "We have a lot of power! We should use it more often!"[20] The apparent success at Manila led to the creation of the "Spiritual Warfare Network," whose subtitle gave a sense of its purpose: "A Post-Lausanne II in Manila Group Studying Strategic Level Spiritual Warfare." The Spiritual Warfare Network was organized by John Robb of World Vision, another key neo-evangelical institution. Its first meeting, held in Pasadena in 1990, brought together pastors, writers, and academics who would go on to become key figures in the spiritual warfare movement. They included Charles Kraft, a professor of anthropology at Fuller; Jack Hayford, pastor of the Pentecostal Church on the Way in Van Nuys, California; and Cindy Jacobs, president of the Generals of Intercession ministry (and future resident of Colorado Springs).[21]

Wagner gave spiritual warfare credibility among evangelical writers and thinkers; Frank Peretti popularized the concept for the masses, introducing it to millions of readers with his novels *This Present Darkness* and *Piercing the Darkness*.[22] Peretti grew up in the small community of Vashon, Washington. The son of an Assemblies of God minister, Peretti served briefly as a youth pastor in the 1970s. As of the early 1980s, however, he was working on a ski assembly line and living with his wife in a cramped trailer. He was also struggling to publish a novel. Fourteen publishers rejected Peretti's manuscript before Crossway Books, a Christian publishing ministry, picked it up.[23] *This Present Darkness* appeared in 1986 and sold slowly at first. But word of mouth boosted sales, as did enthusiastic endorsements by popular evangelical musicians Amy Grant and Michael W. Smith.[24] By 1988, *This Present Darkness* had reached the top of the Evangelical Christian Publishers Association's bestseller chart. It ultimately sold millions of copies, as did its 1989 sequel, *Piercing the Darkness*.

Peretti's books enfolded a Christian message within the trappings of a secular horror novel. *This Present Darkness* was set in the college town of Ashton, described as "typically American—small, innocent, and harmless, like the background for every Norman Rockwell painting." But a pair of newcomers to the town sense "the true substratum of Ashton . . . a very special kind of evil."[25] These visitors are not ordinary humans but angels, dispatched to Ashton to counter demonic activity there. Peretti's narrative shifts between the physical world and the spiritual realm overlaid upon it, with most human characters only dimly aware of the angels and demons swarming around them. The novel's spiritual protagonist, the golden-haired angel Tal, is opposed by Rafar, the demonic "Prince of Babylon." In the human realm, Hank Busche, youthful pastor of the Ashton Community Church, struggles to spread the gospel in the face of demonic resistance, while Marshall Hogan, editor of the local paper, delves into a conspiracy that spans the spiritual and worldly planes. Busche and Hogan's human nemeses include the local police chief; the pastor of the town's respectable Protestant church; and a psychology professor who teaches courses like "In the Beginning Was the Goddess." Hogan discovers that these villains are pawns of the globe-spanning Omnia Corporation, which seeks to buy Ashton College and make it into a hub for the "Universal Consciousness Society." The spiritual and material stories converge at a meeting of the college trustees, where Hogan reveals the diabolical machinations of the Omnia Corporation while Busche's congregation provides the necessary "prayer cover" for Tal and his angels to vanquish the demons.

Piercing the Darkness is essentially the same story, now set in Bacon's Corner, a town that, like Ashton, is notable only for its lack of notability: "[Just] one of those little farming towns far from the interstate, nothing more than a small hollow dot on the AAA road map."[26] Once again, the novel features two human heroes opposed by a conspiracy of worldly and otherworldly forces. The role previously played by Hank Busche is now filled by Tom Harris, a teacher at a Christian academy who faces legal trouble after he rebukes a demon-possessed student. The lawsuit against him is brought by the "American Citizens Freedom Association," a thinly disguised stand-in for the American Civil Liberties Union: "That infamous association—one could say conspiracy—of professional, idealistic legal technicians, whitewashed, virtuous, and all-for-freedom on the exterior, but viciously liberal and anti-Christian in its motives and agenda."[27] Meanwhile, Sally Beth Roe, a burned-out former New Ager, flees from assassins working for a satanic cult called "Broken Birch." Once again, both plots eventually converge, as the American Citizens Freedom Association and Broken Birch are revealed as tools of a conspiracy that seeks to replace Christianity with a "global consciousness." And, once again, the book ends with a clash on the physical and spiritual planes. Sally Beth Roe exposes the conspiracy, forcing the resignation of a Supreme Court justice affiliated with the American Citizens

Freedom Association, while Tal, again leading the angelic hosts, shatters the demonic control over Bacon's Corner.

Both novels epitomize the counter-subversive tradition in American culture—the notion that traditional American values are being undermined by a secretive cabal.[28] Any community, no matter how idyllic it seemed, sheltered dark forces working ceaselessly for its destruction. Anyone could be an agent of the enemy, even a member of one's own church. At one key point in *Piercing the Darkness*, the virtuous members of the Good Shepherd Church discover and expel a "demonized" congregant. Marshall Hogan warns the Christians of Bacon's Corner, "We have concrete evidence that there's some witchcraft or Satanism in the area, some organized heavier form of occultism like a coven, a secret society, whatever. And that means there are people—and I mean normal-looking people, everyday people you'd never suspect—that belong to this group."[29] Victory is won by rooting out these subversive forces. Once Ashton and Bacon's Corner are cleansed of their "spiritual filth," they return to their original, pristine moral state, a world of happy families living behind white picket fences. The link between this worldview and conservative politics was obvious to Peretti's publishers, who described *This Present Darkness* as "a book for the so-called moral majority."[30]

Peretti's concern with purifying communities reflected an important aspect of spiritual warfare: the idea that demons could possess specific areas. "The entire globe is organized under principalities, corresponding to earthly governments," Donald Grey Barnhouse wrote in *The Invisible War*. "If there is a Prince of Persia and a Prince of Greece, we may not be astonished if there is a Prince of Russia or a Prince of India, a Prince of Britain and a Prince of the United States."[31] Later authors argued that specific demons ruled over specific geographic units. John Dawson, an evangelical missionary and member of C. Peter Wagner's Spiritual Warfare Network, played a particularly important role in introducing a new generation to the concept of territoriality.[32] His *Taking Our Cities for God*, published in 1989, argued that cities were the new frontier of evangelization.[33] Dawson painted a grim picture of urban life: "My city, Los Angeles, is crowded, expensive, violent and polluted," he wrote. "I would rather raise my children in rural isolation or suburban convenience, but Jesus has called me here. Jesus has always been attracted to dark places."[34] Dispelling this darkness required not social but spiritual action. Only intense prayer could break the grip of the demons that controlled the city.

Demons could control not only cities but also regions, countries, even entire cultures. This belief imparted a strange mix of cosmopolitanism and xenophobia to the literature of spiritual warfare.[35] Wagner, like many advocates of spiritual warfare, believed that Christians in Africa, Asia, and Latin America understood the importance of the supernatural far better than their counterparts in the United States.[36] To break down American skepticism regarding supernatural forces, Wagner filled his books and articles with stories from abroad that demonstrated the reality of demons. Many stories came from Argentina, a country Wagner referred to as his "principal laboratory."[37] Wagner regaled readers with stories of Carlos Annacondia, the revivalist whose "premediated, high-energy approach to spiritual warfare" transformed the country's spiritual climate, and of Edgardo Silvoso, who battled demons in one Argentine city after another. Silvoso had been educated at Fuller Theological Seminary and Multnomah School of the Bible in Portland, Oregon—an indication that American ideas about spiritual warfare flowed to the Global South just as often as the reverse.

But if foreign countries could provide valuable lessons, they were just as likely to provide cautionary tales. Wagner was open to learning from foreign evangelists like Annacondia and Silvoso, but he made it clear that there were limits to his openness. He condemned many foreign cultures as "corrupted" and "demon possessed" and bragged about smashing Indigenous artifacts that he had brought back from South America.[38] Many spiritual warriors also gloated about the injury or death of their foes. Wagner gleefully described the death of the "high priestess of the cult of San La Muerte" in the city where he was evangelizing: "Two weeks before the massive evangelistic thrust began in October, her bed caught fire. For some reason, the flames seemed to be selective. They consumed only the mattress, the woman, and her statue of San La Muerte!"[39] Wagner possessed a global vision of Christianity, but it was not a vision of universal brotherhood. It was of universal war, with Christians making violently contested incursions into enemy territory.

Militaristic language was inescapable in this literature. Wagner used it incessantly: The church was a "barracks for warriors," while pastors were "spiritual Green Berets" who engaged in "smart-bomb praying."[40] Wagner claimed he would prefer to use the language of sports rather than of war, but "I am not free to do this. The Bible itself describes our fight against the devil as warfare. . . . We are in a life or death struggle."[41] To reinforce this point, Wagner spoke often of the dangers of spiritual warfare. It is "not fun and games," he wrote. "It is not some kids running around in devil costumes on Halloween or a spooky horror movie on television."[42] Wagner sounded like a pacifist compared to men like George Otis, founder of a spiritual warfare ministry called the Sentinel Group (and another future Colorado Springs resident). Otis promised to provide readers with the "spiritual equivalent of the military's night-vision goggles" that would help them see the world as it really was, that is, as dominated by spiritual forces.[43] In books like *The Last of the Giants* (1991) and *The Twilight Labyrinth* (1997), Otis presented himself as a spiritual commando, traveling around the world to confront evil wherever it appeared.

What did authors like Otis, Wagner, and Peretti entreat their readers to do? The answer: not much. Otis's *Last of the Giants* was representative in this regard. After 200 pages of apocalyptic thunder, Otis told his readers how to enlist in this cosmic war: "The Sentinel Group has launched what we call our 20–20 Program. We plan to recruit thousands of no-nonsense individuals over the next several years who will contribute to the softening of enemy defenses in these spiritually resistant bastions in two ways: 1) by praying at least twenty minutes a week . . . and 2) by giving at least twenty dollars a month to support outreach to these territories."[44] There was no need to change one's life; a few minutes of prayer each day and a few dollars each month would suffice. Recommendations to buy products from other spiritual warriors were also common. The world of spiritual warfare experts was a small one, and they frequently cited one another's work, blurbed one another's books, and recommended one another's seminars. In practice, "spiritual warfare" often meant consuming the right goods or donating to the right organizations.

Spiritual warfare also meant seeing the world in a new way. First, one had to learn to recognize the "spiritual oppression" that settled upon places where demons held sway. Sometimes those cues were sensory, like a smell or a sound, but more often it was about interpreting one's own sense of unease as the result of a spiritual miasma. Second, one had to learn to recognize the results of prayer. Many spiritual warriors were plagued by the fear that their prayers were not accomplishing anything. Dutch Sheets, a prayer warrior who pastored a Colorado Springs church in the 1990s, wrote of his intense desire to know whether his prayers made a difference: "I need to know if that cyst on my wife's ovary dissolved because I prayed. . . . I need to know if I was spared in the earthquake because someone prayed. . . . I need to know if my prayers can make a difference between heaven and hell for some."[45] Accordingly, theorists of spiritual warfare urged readers to interpret geopolitical events in light of their prayer requests. Peter Wagner was particularly bold on this point; he never hesitated to read any event, from the fall of the Berlin Wall to the ouster of Panamanian dictator Manuel Noriega, as evidence of prayer's efficacy. In short, spiritual warriors had to learn to see miracles wherever they looked. Their discipline was less about acting upon the world than about reinterpreting things that had already happened.

This process had a distinct therapeutic element. Being a good spiritual warrior meant being in touch with one's feelings. "Many Christians seem almost to scorn emotions," wrote Cindy Jacobs, "fearful perhaps that a lack of control follows closely on its heels. If we deny emotion in prayer, however, we lose some depth of intercession, for we cannot pray the heart of God without fully joining his expression."[46] Reading Jacobs's books, one is struck by how much her version of spiritual warfare resembles therapy. An individual would work with "prayer partners," who would call to check in if they believed that person was feeling anxious or depressed. Demonic attacks were indicated not by *Exorcist*-style manifestations but by things like "mental anguish" and "unexplainable negative attitudes."[47] Indeed, sensitivity toward one's emotions was often regarded as a desirable trait for a spiritual warrior. For all their violent talk, spiritual warriors also valued the ability to cry. Wagner recounted weeping while thinking about how demons held sway over Japan.[48] Dick Eastman, president of Every Home for Christ, boasted of having to carry a tin of eye salve because of his tendency to weep uncontrollably while praying.[49]

Weeping over the sins of the world was encouraged, but that was as far as many spiritual warriors went in terms of a social ethic. If only the spiritual world mattered, why bother doing anything about the material world? Occasional urgings toward social involvement were inevitably overshadowed by dramatic declarations about the need for warfare prayer. As usual, Peter Wagner outdid everyone on this point. "The crime, gangs, poverty, abortion, racism, greed, rape, drugs, divorce, social injustice, child abuse and other evils that characterize my city of Pasadena, California, reflect Satan's temporal victories," he wrote. "[Social] and evangelistic programs will never work as well as they could or should by themselves if Satan's strongholds are not torn down."[50] This attitude was not unique to Wagner. Cindy Jacobs recalled how a prayer rally was disrupted by a "wild eyed man" with "legalism [oozing] from his voice" who decried those who do not "feed the poor and the homeless nor see the hurting." For Jacobs, this person was a villain, disrupting the prayerful unity of evangelicals and Pentecostals with quibbling objections; she approvingly noted that the ushers hustled him away.[51] The lesson from this story: Nothing should disrupt unity. "Unity" was a key term in the spiritual warfare movement, because unity was a prerequisite to church growth—and growth was what mattered most.[52] Stories about spiritual warfare made sure to mention, often by citing precise statistics, how victory in the spiritual realm led to rapid church growth.[53] Though they never stated it so baldly, many of the movement's leaders assumed that bigger was always better.

These aspects of spiritual warfare—its preoccupation with growth, its weak social ethic, its militarism—unsettled many people, including some evangelicals. Critics of spiritual warfare pointed to its lack of biblical precedent, forcing advocates to search through the Old and New Testaments for passages that lent support to their cause. They often cited Ephesians 6:12 as their warrant. In the King James Version, this verse asserts, "For we wrestle not against flesh and blood, but against principalities, against powers, against the rulers of the darkness of this world, against spiritual wickedness in high places." However, this evidence did not convince some skeptics.[54] Even those who accepted the general concept warned against its more extravagant manifestations. Clinton Arnold, a professor of the New Testament at Biola University, cautioned that true spiritual warfare dealt with eradicating vices rather than exorcising demons.[55] Evangelical critics were particularly frustrated by Peretti's novels, which they saw as gross oversimplifications. "At times it seems that human responsibility disappears—all evil is caused by demons and all good by angels," wrote a reviewer for *Christianity Today*.[56] Reviews from non-evangelical critics were even harsher. One described Peretti's novels as having a "Star Wars/Jonathan Edwards/NRA theology," while another dismissed them as a mixture of "Cotton Mather and Stephen King." Historian Robert Orsi called the books "rotten" and "pathetic," expressive of a "Christian death wish."[57]

These critiques did nothing to stop the flourishing of the spiritual warfare industry. Pastors, missionaries, and freelance writers turned out a steady stream of books with titles like *The Edge of Evil* and *Battling the Prince of Darkness*. Typically, these books were how-to manuals that explained the basics of spiritual warfare, enlivening their step-by-step instructions with stories of the supernatural. Conferences and conventions knit these experts into a self-conscious movement. In December 1988, for instance, Fuller Theological Seminary hosted an Academic Symposium on Power Evangelicalism in Pasadena that brought together Pentecostals and more traditional evangelicals.[58] And in February 1994, the Melodyland Christian Center in Anaheim hosted a "National Conference on Prayer and Spiritual Warfare." Attendees could take part in workshops like "Your Church Can Be a Winner in the Invisible War" and listen to lectures such as "Navigating the Twilight Labyrinth."[59] That all these conferences took place in Southern California testified to Peter Wagner's influence. His presence at Fuller made Pasadena the capital city of spiritual warfare.

But its position was not unchallenged, as Wagner himself recognized. In the May/June 1993 issue of *Ministries Today*, a magazine for charismatic Christian pastors, Wagner used his column to inform readers, "God has brought Colorado Springs into a remarkable season for his glory." God, Wagner wrote, "[has] installed a divine magnet to build a concentration of ministries that will serve His kingdom on the spiritual front lines as we move into a new millennium."[60] By the time Wagner's column appeared, he had already made several trips to the Springs. He addressed forty local pastors in September 1992 as part of a retreat sponsored by the Colorado Springs Association of Evangelicals. In January 1993, he appeared at the North American Conference on Strategic-Level Prayer held in the city.[61] That conference was hosted by New Life, the church Wagner credited with making the city a "spiritual magnet." Its pastor, Ted Haggard, was (Wagner wrote) the "de facto leader" of a network of pastors "equipped with a higher-than-average understanding of strategic-level spiritual warfare." These pastors, with Haggard in the lead, had broken Satan's power and opened their city for revival.[62]

The Gospel of Ted Haggard

Ted Haggard no doubt appreciated this praise. After all, he had founded his church to be a bastion for spiritual warriors. Haggard, an Indiana native, underwent a conversion experience in high school after hearing a speech by Campus Crusade founder Bill Bright. He attended Oral Roberts University, where he embraced charismatic Christianity and the gifts of the Holy Spirit. He was also deeply influenced by a college course on "Evangelicals and Communist Society," which impressed upon him the importance of missions.[63] On graduating, Haggard and his wife, Gayle, began working for World Missions for Jesus, a Christian ministry in West Germany that smuggled religious literature into communist countries. Next, they moved to Louisiana, where Haggard served as a youth pastor at Bethany Baptist Church.[64] Gayle Haggard's father pastored a church in Colorado Springs, and so the Haggards occasionally visited the city; during one visit in 1984, Haggard spent several days praying and fasting in a pup tent on Pikes Peak. This, he would later say, was the moment when he heard God's call to plant a church in the Springs. Haggard moved his family to Colorado that same year and, with help from his father-in-law's church, founded New Life. The new church held its first meeting (in the Haggards' basement) in January 1985.[65]

New Life grew rapidly, thanks to its appealing blend of exuberance and respectability. It embraced the informal style of worship common among charismatic churches: The music was simple and catchy, the dress was casual, and the sermons focused on practical matters. Befitting a charismatic church, worshippers sometimes danced in the aisles or spoke in tongues during services.[66] Still, New Life provided enough boundaries to win acceptance from middle- and upper-class audiences who might have spurned a more traditional Pentecostal church. Haggard took care to note, "We have a great number of business people and highly educated people that love the Lord and are responding. It is remarkable the type of solid people in this community that love the Lord." These "solid people" came to New Life in ever-growing numbers. At its founding, the church had 30 members; only two years later, in 1986, it boasted "700 adults and 300 children, with a budget of almost $500,000."[67] By 1992, New Life claimed 3,000 members. The church outgrew property after property as its congregation expanded. New Life first met in the Haggards' basement; then at a local Holiday Inn; then at various rented locations; and then, finally, at a property the church owned, a 75,000-square-foot building that could accommodate thousands.[68] By this point Haggard was marketing himself as a church growth expert. His first book, *Primary Purpose: Making It Hard for People to Go to Hell from Your City*, promised pastors that they too could make their city "a little slice of heaven on earth," just as he had done in Colorado.[69] A follow-up, *Dog Training, Fly Fishing, and Sharing Christ in the 21st Century*, offered pastors the key to unlocking "incredible potential in your community."[70] To Haggard, his church's rapid growth was due neither to chance nor to his own charisma but to techniques that other religious leaders could learn and apply.

Ted Haggard leads New Life congregants in prayer. Courtesy of the Denver Public Library, Western History Collection, RMN-027-8088.

"Warfare prayer" was the most important technique. Haggard declared, "Prayer consists of two primary functions: intimate communion with God, which includes praise; and effective confrontation with the devil, which is war."[71] There was no shortage of the latter in Colorado Springs. Haggard narrated his arrival in the Springs as a thrust into enemy territory. He told of threatening phone calls and of a demon-possessed woman who attacked him with a steak knife.[72] These stories resembled the tribulations undergone by righteous Christians in the novels of Frank Peretti. Haggard himself compared the experience to a "Frank Peretti book come to life."[73] Haggard also echoed Peretti when he said that Colorado Springs was a "pastor's graveyard" before his arrival. In Peretti's novels, virtuous pastors are run out of town and congregations collapse without explanation. The heroes of *This Present Darkness* and *Piercing the Darkness* reverse these trends through vigorous prayer; Haggard claimed to have done the same thing in Colorado. New Life conducted a campaign of "prayer walking" in which congregants walked through the city, praying for each neighborhood block by block and street by street.[74] Haggard also led marathon prayer sessions to combat the evil spirit he felt hovering over the city, finally breaking its power in one particularly intense session. Accounts of this sort were a staple of spiritual warfare literature.[75] So too were claims that warfare prayer could solve social ills. Haggard did not hesitate to make such claims about his own church. In his telling, New Life's warfare prayer had attracted Christian ministries to the city; spurred the growth of the city's churches; and even driven down rates of crime, divorce, and home foreclosure. The best available statistics did not bear out these claims, but Haggard was not making a sociological claim. He was telling a story of seizing territory from the devil.

Haggard did not attribute New Life's success *entirely* to warfare prayer. He also credited the church's organizational structure for its rapid growth. New Life encouraged its members to take part in small "cells" that met throughout the week. Haggard borrowed the cell concept from South Korean pastor David Yonggi Cho, whose Yoido Full Gospel Church in Seoul claimed hundreds of thousands of members.[76] Cho's church comprised thousands of cells, which were led by lay volunteers (usually women) and met regularly in the homes of congregants.[77] Haggard enthusiastically applied this system in the Springs. When individuals joined New Life, they were assigned to a "Discovery" cell. After spending several months in this cell, they could choose their own small group, picking from hundreds of options. Cells at New Life were organized by theme; many dealt with spiritual warfare. "Spiritual Warfare for Everyone" offered to teach attendees about "ground level warfare," "protective covering," and "protective warfare." Another group marketed itself to "strong prayer warriors for FRONT LINE SPIRITUAL WARFARE." No matter the topic, all these groups had one requirement: They had to grow. As the introduction to New Life's small group directory put it, "Growth is the sign of a truly healthy group."[78]

Haggard saw growth as a moral good. He suggested that small groups, and the growth they enabled, embodied the free-market principles that had won the Cold War. And he further suggested that a similar conflict was now taking place within Christianity, pitting the "top-down, rigid, chain-of-command styles that are characteristic of the old mainline and/or liberal denominations" against "independent networks that are more fluid and can freely strategize together and incorporate the best new ideas."[79] Haggard thus redrew the lines of the Cold War for a post–Cold War era. Conflating evangelicalism, democracy, and capitalism, he believed that New Life's growth betokened the triumph of these forces at home and abroad.

Haggard, like Peter Wagner, thought in global terms. He had always been interested in missions; before coming to Colorado, he and his wife had considered serving as missionaries in Calcutta or Mexico City.[80] The end of the Cold War led Haggard—along with many other evangelicals—to believe that the 1990s might usher in the evangelization of the whole world. But this sense of hope was intermingled with fears that the end of communism would empower a new enemy: Islam. American evangelicals had a long, complex, and often contentious relationship with the Islamic world.[81] Many evangelicals in the 1980s and 1990s, motivated by the Iranian Revolution and growing Muslim populations in Europe, began warning about the dangers of militant Islam. Among the loudest voices was George Otis, whose book *The Last of the Giants* denounced Islam as a form of paganism and spoke darkly about the growth of Muslim communities in the former Soviet Union.[82] Otis was an associate of Haggard's, and Haggard clearly shared his opinions on Islam.[83] In a 1993 interview, Haggard claimed that "I don't know any Islamic cultures that embrace civil rights the way we understand them."[84] The terrorist attacks of 9/11 only deepened his hostility toward Islam; he now associated the religion with "inciting hate, killing your enemy and using the poor."[85] But Haggard expressed confidence that Islam, or at least "fundamentalist Islam," could be defeated by the same forces that defeated communism: evangelicalism, capitalism, and American power.[86]

Achieving his expansive ambitions at home and abroad required Haggard to cultivate like-minded pastors. As he put it: "We recognize that one megachurch cannot change a city. . . . But when hundreds of churches working together embrace a common purpose, we see societal change."[87] He sought to instill this sense of common purpose through The Net, a coalition of evangelical churches. Member churches signed a "Declaration of Interdependence," which asserted, "There is only one church in Colorado Springs, and it meets in many locations." The Net organized prayer rallies, sponsored revivals, and oversaw an ambitious effort to distribute religious literature to every household in the Springs.[88] But Haggard aspired to be more than a leader of evangelicals. He wanted to be a leader within the city's broader religious community. With his charisma, charm, and instinct for finding consensus, he was well-equipped to do so. Only a few weeks after the 1992 Los Angeles riots, Haggard convinced several dozen Colorado Springs pastors to read his "Prayer for All Races" at their Sunday services, which asked congregants to confess, "I repent of any feelings or resentment, hatred, inferiority or supremacy that I may be harboring because of racial differences."[89] He sought to play a similar role in the wake of Amendment 2, bringing together church and parachurch leaders to sign a "Covenant of Mutual Respect" that appeared in the *Gazette Telegraph*. James Dobson of Focus on the Family, progressive minister James W. White, and Catholic bishop Richard Hanifen were among those who signed this commitment to "listen and learn from each other."[90]

Haggard's tireless promotion of his methods, his church, and himself paid dividends, elevating him first to local and then to national prominence. He became president of the Colorado Springs Association of Evangelicals less than a decade after arriving in the city.[91] By the mid-1990s, *Christianity Today* was celebrating him as one of "Fifty Evangelical Leaders 40 and Under."[92] His winsome personality and gift for the pithy quote made him a favorite of journalists; one New Life publication boasted that "Pastor Ted's influence ... has been noted by Bill Moyers, *U.S. News & World Report*, in the *Los Angeles Times, New York Times, Chicago Tribune, Washington Post, Denver Post, Charisma Magazine*, on ABC and NBC National News and by the BBC and International News Network."[93] Due in no small part to this media savvy, the National Association of Evangelicals selected Haggard as its president in 2002, giving him a national platform to preach his vision of an inclusive evangelicalism. "Evangelical does not mean any particular political ideology," Haggard declared, in hopes of reclaiming the term from its association with the Christian right.

This, ironically, was an association Haggard himself had promoted. Haggard generally took a cautious approach to political involvement. When the *Gazette Telegraph* ran an article suggesting he had endorsed Amendment 2, he quickly wrote an open letter to the paper protesting that he had done no such thing.[94] Still, his conservatism was evident to anyone paying attention. Though he did not endorse Amendment 2, he publicly criticized the idea of gay rights.[95] When a furor arose over the National Endowment for the Arts funding art that offended some Christians, Haggard suggested abolishing the agency and letting the free market take care of the arts.[96] He even allowed the radical anti-abortion organization Operation Rescue to host a workshop at New Life.[97] Haggard was, in short, a conservative Republican. Unsurprisingly, he welcomed the election of George W. Bush, a conservative Republican with close ties to the Christian right.[98] Haggard praised Bush in books and interviews, declaring in 2002 that Bush had "moved American power, influence, and prestige to a level it hasn't enjoyed any time prior to this."[99] He did more than simply boost Bush, however; he belonged to a group of prominent evangelicals whom the president consulted on political matters.[100] Less pugnacious than James Dobson, whose Focus on the Family headquarters was only a ten-minute drive from New Life, Haggard was no less conservative.

All of these concerns—spiritual warfare, evangelical unity, conservative politics—came together in Haggard's most ambitious project, the World Prayer Center. The idea for a "prayer center" came to him while fasting in a tent on Pikes Peak. There, on the mountainside, "God revealed to me a globe with a person in the center praying for all nations."[101] New Life's growth through the 1980s and 1990s enabled Haggard to realize this vision. In May 1992, he filed incorporation papers with the Colorado secretary of state for the "World Prayer Center, Inc.," described in the application as a "place to encourage prayer for the nations."[102] Work on the prayer center began in the fall of 1995. Haggard spoke of the project in expansive terms: "This will make Colorado Springs the center of the global prayer movement." It was indeed a huge undertaking; the prayer center complex, located on New Life's campus, ultimately cost over $5 million to build. Despite its size, the concept behind the World Prayer Center was simple, analogous to the "prayer chains" organized in many Christian churches. Frank Peretti explained the function of these chains in *Piercing the Darkness*: "Every participant had a list of all the other participants and their phone numbers. When you needed prayers for something, you called the next person on the list after yourself, who then called the next person on the list, who then called the next person, and so on. The whole church could be praying for a request in just a matter of hours any day of the week."[103]

The World Prayer Center amplified this technique a thousandfold with modern technology. Requests for prayer from around the world would arrive in the "nerve center" in the basement. Then, as one journalist described it, each request would be "evaluated, rated for urgency and then assigned to churches, ministries, and individuals via fax, e-mail or phone."[104] More people praying for a request would give it more efficacy. Bigger was better, though Haggard rarely stated the point so bluntly. Publicity for the center spoke in terms of huge numbers. One brochure proudly pointed to the "six miles of wiring and conduits" beneath the center, the "500-seat-auditorium," even the "2000 pound globe" hanging in the auditorium.[105] The World

Prayer Center's opening in September 1998 was suitably grand. It attracted not only religious leaders but also local politicians, including Mary Lou Makepeace, mayor of Colorado Springs, and Joel Hefley, the local congressman. "I believe that prayer truly has power," Hefley said in his speech. "I believe it has the power to change nations around the world."[106] This secular validation of evangelical ideas was everything Ted Haggard could have hoped for.

A Spiritual NORAD

It was everything Peter Wagner hoped for, too. He had spent years promoting projects that sought to harness the power of mass prayer, such as the AD2000 Movement. Led by Argentine pastor Luis Bush, AD2000 sought to unite Christians in prayer for the "10/40 window," a term Bush coined to refer to the region between the tenth and fortieth parallels north of the equator that was supposedly home to most of the world's "unreached peoples."[107] Wagner served as director of the "United Prayer Track" of the AD2000 Movement, coordinating efforts among hundreds of churches to direct their prayers at the 10/40 window.[108] The World Prayer Center gave concrete form to Wagner's vision of prayer as global warfare. When the center officially opened in September 1998, Wagner was on hand to declare, "God has called us to do air war in the invisible world." He likened this "air war" to the activities of the Air Force Academy and the North American Aerospace Defense Command (NORAD), both located only a few miles from the prayer center.[109] Proving his dedication to the ongoing "air war," Wagner moved the two organizations he led, Global Harvest Ministries and the Wagner Leadership Institute, into the World Prayer Center.[110] The world's leading advocate of spiritual warfare had set up his headquarters in Colorado Springs.

Wagner was also drawn to the Springs by his work with Fuller Theological Seminary. Fuller had maintained a presence in the city since the late 1970s, when it opened an "Institute of Youth Ministries" to help train staffers at Young Life.[111] The seminary began to expand its operations in the city in the 1990s. It dispatched Edgar Elliston, an associate dean, to the Springs in August 1994 to meet with representatives from local ministries and churches. New Life was particularly helpful, offering Fuller the use of classroom and office space in the church. Elliston recommended that the seminary take advantage of this enthusiasm by forming a local advisory board that would include representatives from "local churches, denominations, and missions or church agencies."[112] The task of carrying out Elliston's recommendation fell to Wagner, who was appointed dean of the Colorado Springs campus in the mid-1990s.[113]

Wagner made a "market survey" of Colorado Springs in 1996 to get a sense of his new home. He conducted it with his typical energy, meeting with dozens of ministry leaders and pastors. The results surprised him: There was, he discovered "not as much functional unity in the Colorado Springs evangelical community as might be supposed." Conversations with local evangelical leaders revealed deep divides within this community. Pastors were "indifferent," sometimes even "hostile" to the city's Christian ministries, seeing them as "a bit parasitic." Smaller evangelical churches viewed megachurches like New Life with a similar degree of suspicion. Wagner also noted a lack of leadership in the community. When he asked several of the city's evangelicals to name "the five most influential spiritual leaders in Colorado Springs," he found the results disheartening. People consistently identified Ted Haggard; Jim Tomberlin, pastor of Woodmen Valley Chapel, another nondenominational megachurch; John Stevens, pastor of First Presbyterian Church; and, to a lesser extent, Bernie Kuiper, the stern, Dutch-born pastor of Village Seven Presbyterian. "There was no fifth," Wagner glumly noted. No one mentioned any ministry leaders, not even James Dobson. And while organizations like the Colorado Springs Association of Evangelicals were working to unite the city's evangelical community, thus far they had enjoyed limited success.[114]

Yet within this general disunity, ministries dedicated to spiritual warfare formed a tightly knit subcommunity. Haggard and New Life drew many of these ministries to Colorado Springs in the 1980s and 1990s. The largest was Every Home for Christ, a ministry dedicated to warfare prayer and to the distribution of religious literature. Dick Eastman, its president, embraced a distinctly macho form of Christianity. As a youth pastor in California in the 1960s, when teenagers balked at the grueling prayer regimen he demanded, he responded with remarks like, "Don't tell me we have another prayer pansy in the group!"[115] Eastman carried this energy into his next project, Prayer Corps, modeled on the Peace Corps, which established "prayer centers" where young people could spend a year in intense prayer.[116] Eastman became president of Every Home for Christ in 1988; soon thereafter, he led its relocation from Los Angeles to Colorado Springs after a Focus on the Family employee alerted him to the Springs' advantages.[117] Like many ministry executives, Eastman simultaneously recognized the practical advantages of relocation and cast the move in providential terms. "God is up to something in the Springs, and that is very obvious to me when ministries began to be drawn to a place like this," he told an audience of Christian nonprofit executives in 1993.[118]

Like Wagner and Haggard, Eastman believed God had chosen Colorado Springs to play a key role in the global war against Satan. From his ministry's new home in the Springs, he enthusiastically endorsed efforts to direct prayer at the "10/40 window," a region he called "a spiritual prison." His book *The Jericho Hour* encouraged Christians to take part in the "air war" against the strongholds of darkness.[119] Every Home for Christ affirmed its commitment to Colorado Springs by investing $7.5 million in a new headquarters called the Jericho Center for Global Evangelism, which boasted two indoor chapels and a scale replica of Jerusalem's Western Wall.[120] Like the World Prayer Center, the Jericho Center testified to the city's importance in the geography of spiritual warfare.

Every Home for Christ was followed to the Springs by the Generals of Intercession, a ministry founded and led by Cindy Jacobs. Like many of the movement's leaders, Jacobs prayed with an intensity that sometimes disturbed even fellow evangelicals. She recounted that, while in college, some classmates had accused her of being possessed and subjected her to an hours-long attempt at an exorcism.[121] She and her husband founded the Generals of Intercession in Texas early in the 1980s. In 1993, the ministry relocated to Colorado Springs to join the city's growing community of spiritual warriors. Jacobs echoed Eastman in explaining the move: "Colorado Springs," she said, "has been chosen by God for a special purpose."[122] Yet she also believed that, while the Springs might be ordained by God, it was nonetheless vulnerable to the forces of evil. In a book coauthored with her pastor, Dutch Sheets, Jacobs wrote of visiting a bookstore in the Springs and finding its "New Age" section packed with occult books and paraphernalia. "My head swam at the thought of so much occult material in my nice, Christian-influenced city," she wrote. "I live in Colorado Springs, Colorado, where there are at least 135 ministries and several megachurches. Some people call it 'Wheaton West,' after the long-time center of the evangelical world, Wheaton, Illinois."[123] Colorado Springs, which often served spiritual warriors as a positive reference point, could also serve as a negative one, providing a lesson in how danger could lurk even in Christian communities.

The arrival of figures like Wagner, Eastman, and Jacobs in Colorado Springs raised Ted Haggard's profile still further. He had transformed his city into the capital of the spiritual warfare movement; he was pastor of one of the nation's largest churches; he was president of the National Association of Evangelicals; he was on friendly terms with the president of the United States. Introducing George W. Bush at a National Association of Evangelicals conference in Colorado Springs, Haggard joked about how much he and Bush had in common: "The only thing I have a grief with about our wonderful president is that he drives a Ford."[124] The 2004 elections seemed to confirm Haggard's influence. He declared that evangelicals were "going to determine the election," and the Bush campaign apparently agreed.[125] Pressured by evangelical leaders and by his advisers, Bush tried to win social conservatives' votes by calling for an amendment that would define marriage as the union of a man and a woman.[126] The strategy seemed to work; many analysts attributed Bush's narrow victory over John Kerry to massive evangelical turnout.[127] Haggard basked in the attention that followed Bush's victory. A lengthy profile in *Harper's* magazine, written by the journalist Jeff Sharlet, claimed, "No pastor in America holds more sway over the political direction of evangelicalism than does Pastor Ted, and no church more than New Life."[128]

As Haggard's political clout grew, so did his church. Construction of a mammoth "worship center" on New Life's campus began in 2004. The new building boasted an auditorium that stretched the length of a football field and a cupola that rose over 100 feet.[129] All that space proved necessary when New Life dedicated the worship center in January 2005. Over 7,000 people crowded into the center for the two-and-half-hour ceremony, which included videotaped tributes to Haggard from politicians, ministry leaders, and megachurch pastors.[130] That the inauguration of Haggard's new worship center coincided with the inauguration of George W. Bush, the president Haggard had helped reelect, seemed fitting. Through his charisma, his energy, and his vision, Haggard had made his church—and himself—a symbol of evangelical Christianity's political power. Evangelicals had long hoped to gain power by being winsome. Haggard, the most winsome of them all, seemed to have fulfilled that dream.

It turned out that Haggard had built his empire upon sand. The politics of gay rights that boosted Haggard in the 2004 elections ultimately destroyed him. Though never as zealous in his opposition to gay rights as

New Life Church moved from building to building to accommodate its growing congregation; the enormous church shown here opened in 2005. Courtesy of the Denver Public Library, Western History Collection, RMN-033-3982.

James Dobson, Haggard left no doubt as to where he stood on the issue: "God created sexuality to be part of mankind, but if we abuse it, we have to be willing to face the consequences."[131] When the issue returned to the forefront of Colorado politics in 2006, his stance was predictable. That year, proponents and opponents of gay rights placed clashing initiatives on the Colorado ballot. Initiative 43 would define marriage as being between a man and a woman, while Referendum I would establish same-sex domestic partnerships in Colorado. Like most of the state's evangelicals, Haggard strongly supported Initiative 43.[132] Yet even as Haggard campaigned against same-sex relationships, he was engaging in one of his own with Mike Jones, a gay male escort who lived in Denver. Haggard had been paying Jones for sex for three years; he also asked Jones to help him acquire crystal meth, which Haggard used in Jones's presence. Only in 2006 did Jones realize that the client who called himself "Art from Kansas City" was actually a prominent foe of gay rights. Jones took his story to the local NBC affiliate and to an alternative weekly newspaper; when they hesitated to publish his claims, he appeared on a Denver radio show and publicly accused Haggard. Jones was up-front about his motives: "I am doing this to expose the hypocrisy of Ted Haggard," he

The Invisible War

told producers at the television station. "I want to do this before the election, so, yes, I am doing this for political reasons."[133]

Many of Haggard's allies initially dismissed the accusation as a political stunt. James Dobson proclaimed that "it appears someone is trying to damage [Haggard's] reputation as a way of influencing the outcome of Tuesday's election." But the truth quickly came out. Only a few days after Jones went public, Haggard published a letter, read at New Life services on Sunday, November 5, telling his congregants, "I am a deceiver and a liar." He announced he would resign his position at New Life and submit to the oversight of several religious leaders, including Dobson, who would "guide me through a program with the goal of healing and restoration for my life, my marriage, and my family."[134] Haggard's life took a winding course after this ignominious exit. Essentially exiled from Colorado Springs, he and his family moved to Arizona, where for a time he sold insurance. Meanwhile, more stories of his sexual impropriety trickled out. Eventually Haggard returned to the Springs to found a new church, St. James, to "help others struggling through their seasons of crisis."[135]

New Life moved on as quickly as possible, hiring Brady Boyd, an associate pastor at a Dallas megachurch, to replace Haggard. Boyd said he would not seek the "limelight" as pastor, implicitly rejecting the way Haggard had operated.[136] While New Life remained by far the largest church in Colorado Springs, it never again had the public influence it did during Haggard's time as pastor. By this point the spiritual warfare movement itself was crumbling, at least in Colorado Springs. Peter Wagner, always in search of the next new thing, had moved on to promoting the "New Apostolic Reformation," a coalition of conservative churches.[137] Cindy Jacobs, George Otis, and Dutch Sheets all moved out of Colorado Springs. Haggard and Wagner's dream of making the city a "Spiritual NORAD" proved hollow. Spiritual warfare was too flimsy a foundation upon which to build an empire.

Conclusion
THE SANCTUARY

"Man, as many people as we have in this school here, we ought to take over Woodland Park," Andrew Wommack told a crowd gathered at Charis Bible College in May 2021.¹ He was not exaggerating. His ministry, which included both Charis and Andrew Wommack Ministries, was one of the largest employers in Woodland Park, a small community twenty miles northwest of Colorado Springs. Wommack had moved his ministry from Colorado Springs to Woodland Park for the same reason he had once moved from Texas to Colorado Springs: He needed space. His ministry purchased hundreds of acres in Woodland Park to make room for its enormous new campus and headquarters. Just as boosters once welcomed Christian ministries to Colorado Springs, a new generation of boosters welcomed Wommack and his hundreds of employees and students to Woodland Park. Both the town's mayor and the president of its chamber of commerce attended a ceremony to celebrate the construction of a new lecture hall; the president of the chamber exulted, "I've never had an opportunity to experience and be part of something that is going to have such a positive impact on our community."² But, as happened in Colorado Springs, the arrival of this ministry did more than just grow the economy. It had far-reaching implications for local and state politics. Wommack's speech about taking over Woodland Park was the culmination of a long-running conflict between his ministry and state officials over COVID-related restrictions on worship.³ Particularly galling to Wommack was the fact that the governor who imposed those restrictions, Jared Polis, was a gay man—indeed, the first openly gay man elected governor of a US state.⁴

Wommack's clash with Polis seemed to pit Colorado's past against its future. Reliably Republican throughout the 1990s and the most part of the next two decades, by 2021 the state had a Democratic governor, two Democratic senators, and a Democratic legislature. This shift leftward was visible even in Colorado Springs. George W. Bush won El Paso County by a margin of over 30 percent in 2004; in 2024, Donald Trump won the county by less than 10 percent. The city's religious community had changed as well. The institutions that gave the city its reputation as an "Evangelical Vatican" had folded, moved away, or radically changed. Focus on the Family not-so-gently ousted James Dobson after he made one too many forays into partisan politics. His replacement, Jim Daly, took a more conciliatory approach to cultural issues.⁵ Ted Haggard was long gone from New Life Church. Colorado for Family Values, creator of Amendment 2, was long gone as well, while the progressive Citizens Project, formed to oppose CFV, remained active in local politics.

What looked like the past, however, might actually be the wave of the future—if not in Colorado, then in the United States at large. Wommack is only one of many "spiritual warriors" who have enthusiastically thrown their support behind Donald Trump. The New Apostolic Reformation, a loosely aligned group of evangelical leaders who preach a conservative, patriarchal, and authoritarian form of Protestant Christianity, is a particularly important part of the Trump coalition.⁶ Wommack is a major player in this milieu. Born in Texas in 1949, he founded Andrew Wommack Ministries in Lamar, Texas, in 1978. The ministry's chief product was Wommack himself. Each month the organization mailed out tens of thousands of cassette tapes with recordings of his sermons. Wommack moved his ministry to Manitou Springs in 1980 and to Colorado Springs in 1993. As of 1996, it employed thirty people in the Springs and had an annual budget of $2.3 million—respectable, but far smaller than organizations like Focus on the Family.⁷ But the ministry underwent a startling growth spurt in the new millennium. Wommack branched out from cassettes and began a television program, *Gospel Truth*, which by 2021 was carried on dozens of television stations. The ministry shipped not only tapes but also CDs, DVDs, and books, sending out thousands of packages every day. A phone ministry with over 100 employees—many of them recent graduates of Charis Bible College—handled requests for prayer around the clock.[8]

The growth of Wommack's ministry coincided with his move into explicit political advocacy. Outraged by the Supreme Court's legalization of gay marriage in *Obergefell v. Hodges* (2015), Wommack wrote a "Declaration of Dependence upon God and His Holy Bible" denouncing "same-sex marriage, polygamy, bestiality, and all other forms of sexual perversion." His declaration appeared in hundreds of newspapers. In the wake of the 2020 election, Wommack lamented that "over 72 million people in the United States [voted] completely anti-Bible" and urged Christians to get involved in politics to stave off the "spirit of anti-Christ that is attacking all over the world."[9] The new campus in Woodland Park was meant to train Christians for this battle against the anti-Christ. Wommack gave it a telling name: the Sanctuary.

Is Andrew Wommack an evangelical? He is not a product of the neo-evangelical milieu; he has no connection to Youth for Christ, Wheaton College, or Billy Graham. Indeed, he did not attend college or seminary at all. What theological training he had came from Kenneth Copeland, one of the founders of the "prosperity gospel" movement.[10] Wommack and the movement he represents seem to mark a rupture in the history of American Protestantism, with post–World War II evangelicalism giving way to something new: more violent, more authoritarian, more open toward the supernatural.

Yet there are clear continuities between Wommack and the evangelicals who came before him. The historian Larry Eskridge has noted that scholars place too much emphasis on the "Moody-Wheaton-NAE-Graham-Fuller" nexus when defining evangelicalism, leading them to neglect the "Baptist-Pentecostal-Holiness-Church of Christ" influence on the evangelical tradition.[11] Andrew Wommack was a product of this world. So, too, were many of the people who transformed Colorado Springs into "Jesus Springs." Dawson Trotman of the Navigators may have been close with Billy Graham, but he was also influenced by the Pentecostal preacher Aimee Semple McPherson. Jim Rayburn of Young Life was educated at Dallas Theological Seminary, not Wheaton. James Dobson of Focus on the Family was raised in the American South and Southwest and was shaped by his upbringing in the Church of the Nazarene.[12] Ted Haggard went to Oral Roberts University, not Wheaton, and began his ministerial career at a Pentecostal church in Louisiana. In the "Evangelical Vatican," Holiness, Baptist, and Pentecostal traditions intermingled with neo-evangelicalism.

Wommack, then, is not a new kind of evangelical but an old evangelical in a new context. Like Dawson Trotman, Jim Rayburn, Billy Graham, and so many other evangelical leaders, Wommack seeks the Christianization of the United States. But Graham, Rayburn, and Trotman worked in an era when they could feel, with some justification, that they were speaking to a Christian population who simply needed to be recalled to their evangelical heritage.[13] Confident they could achieve this goal through persuasion rather than force, they operated through parachurch ministries that used modern advertising techniques to target distinct segments of the public. Colorado Springs became the "Evangelical Vatican" because its political economy was uniquely well suited to this approach.

Things had changed by the turn of the twenty-first century. Evangelicals had not abandoned their desire to Christianize the United States, but they now lived in an era of religious decline rather than religious dominance.[14] Though the United States remains more religious than other industrialized nations, religious attendance, participation, and belief are all decreasing.[15] Many (though not all) American evangelicals have responded by shifting from cultural persuasion to political power as their preferred means of Christianizing America. Consequently, they have bound their fate to that of the Republican Party.[16] Evangelical institutions promote Republican politicians, and the Republican Party advances the political agenda of evangelical Protestantism. This alliance was confirmed by overwhelming evangelical support for Mitt Romney in 2012 and for Donald Trump in 2016, 2020, and 2024. Evangelicals' willingness to vote in overwhelming numbers for a man who belongs to a religious tradition that many of them consider a cult, and then for a man who boasts of committing sexual assault and whose grasp of Christianity appears tenuous at best, demonstrates a widespread belief among evangelicals that politics is the best way to restore Christianity to its former position of power in the United States.

A new strategy requires new institutions and calls forth new leaders. The parachurch ministries that made Colorado Springs into "Jesus Springs" are certainly not irrelevant to American evangelicalism. Focus on the Family, Compassion International, the Navigators, and other such organizations retain the loyalty of many Christians. But they belong to another era, an era of uncontested American power, cultural conservatism, and religious dominance. That age is over, and so too is that stage in the history of evangelicalism. We now live in an era of democratic backsliding, cultural progressivism, and widespread secularization. This era will produce its own version of evangelical Christianity. What that will look like remains to be seen.

Notes

Abbreviations

ARCHIVAL COLLECTIONS

- ACLU American Civil Liberties Union Records, Seeley G. Mudd Manuscript Library, Princeton University, Princeton, NJ
- CP Citizens Project Papers, Pikes Peak Library District Special Collections, Colorado Springs, CO
- E v. R *Evans v. Romer* Collection, Western History Collection, Denver Public Library, Denver, CO
- GEPM Glen Eyrie Purchase Materials, Navigators Archives, Colorado Springs, CO
- GRI Group Research Inc. Records, Rare Book and Manuscript Library, Columbia University, New York, NY
- HJT Herbert J. Taylor Papers, Evangelism and Missions Archive, Wheaton College, Wheaton, IL
- IFAS Institute for First Amendment Studies Records, Special Collections, Tufts University, Medford, MA
- PW C. Peter Wagner Collection, Special Collections, Fuller Theological Seminary, Pasadena, CA
- RHC Regional History Collection, Pikes Peak Library District Special Collections, Colorado Springs, CO
- YLSB Young Life staff bulletins, Young Life Archives, Colorado Springs, CO

NEWSPAPERS AND PERIODICALS

CSBJ	Colorado Springs Business Journal
CT	Christianity Today
DP	Denver Post
FP	Free Press (Colorado Springs)
GT	Gazette Telegraph (Colorado Springs)
NYT	New York Times
RMN	Rocky Mountain News (Denver)

Introduction

1. "Birth of the Easter Sunrise Services," *GT*, April 7, 1944. The quote is from the King James Bible.

2. Ralph C. Taylor, "Colorful Colorado," *GT*, Garden of the Gods Sunrise Service Collection, Pikes Peak Library District Special Collections, Colorado Springs.

3. Atkins, "'Business Sense If Not Souls.'"

4. "Army to Join in Worship on Easter," *GT*, April 4, 1943, box 3, Scrapbook VII, El Paso County Newspaper Clippings in Scrapbooks—World War II, Special Collections and Archives, Colorado College, Colorado Springs.

5. "Record Crowd Visits Garden," *GT*, Garden of the Gods Sunrise Service Collection.

6. Eastman, *Jericho Hour*, 52.

7. D'Arcy Fallon, "Garden of the Gods Easter Celebration Filled with Sunshine," *GT*, April 1, 1991.

8. "Evangelicals to Plan Easter Rites at Memorial Park," *GT*, March 7, 1964.

9. Helen McMillan, "Worshipping on Long-Hallowed Ground," *Chamber Magazine*, March 1986, 8–11.

10. Jeff Sharlet, "Inside America's Most Powerful Megachurch," *Harper's*, May 2005, 41–54.

11. On the relationship between religion and foreign policy, see Ribuffo, "Religion in the History of U.S. Foreign Policy"; and Preston, *Sword of the Spirit*.

12. Handy, "Protestant Quest."

13. See, for instance, the discussions in Noll, Bebbington, and Marsden, *Evangelicals*.

14. Bebbington proposed this "quadrilateral" in *Evangelicalism in Modern Britain*. His definition has been adopted by the National Association of Evangelicals, which lists it on their website under "What Is an Evangelical?," accessed March 8, 2025, https://nae.org/what-is-an-evangelical.

15. Recent works in this vein include Butler, *White Evangelical Racism*; Curtis, *Myth of Colorblind Christians*; Vaca, *Evangelicals Incorporated*; Gloege, *Guaranteed Pure*; Du Mez, *Jesus and John Wayne*; Silliman, *Reading Evangelicals*; Dochuk, *Anointed with Oil*; and Hammond, *God's Businessmen*.

16. For a concise statement of this point, see R. Williams, "Review of *Divided by Faith*."

17. Hamilton, "Interdenominational Evangelicalism of D. L. Moody."

18. My definition is influenced by D. G. Hart's argument in *Deconstructing Evangelicalism*.

19. Sutton, "Redefining the History and Historiography on American Evangelicalism."

20. Scheitle, *Beyond the Congregation*; Wuthnow, *Restructuring of American Religion*, 100–131.

21. Markusen et al., *Rise of the Gunbelt*; Dias, "Great Cantonment."

22. McGirr, *Suburban Warriors*; Dochuk, *From Bible Belt to Sunbelt*; Lassiter, "Big Government and Family Values"; Dochuk, "'Heavenly Houston.'"

23. Schäfer, *Piety and Public Funding*, is an important examination of the political economy of American evangelicalism.

24. Herzog, *Spiritual-Industrial Complex*; Inboden, *Religion and American Foreign Policy*; Sutton, *American Apocalypse*.

25. Loveland, *American Evangelicals and the U.S. Military*.

26. Rogin, *Intellectuals and McCarthy*; Schrecker, *Many Are the Crimes*.

27. Whitehead and Perry, *Taking America Back for God*, 10.

28. The literature on Christian nationalism is substantial. For a review, see Gorski and Perry, *Flag and the Cross*.

29. Smith and Adler, "What Isn't Christian Nationalism?"; Sherkat, Lehman, and Julkif, "Mooring Christian Nationalism"; A. Lewis, "Christian Nationalism."

30. Herzog, *Spiritual-Industrial Complex*; Kruse, *One Nation under God*.

31. On the universality of Christian (or "Judeo-Christian") language in this era, see Wall, *Inventing the American Way*; K. Schultz, *Tri-Faith America*; and Gaston, *Imagining Judeo-Christian America*.

32. Hollinger, *Christianity's American Fate*; Zubovich, *Before the Religious Right*; Jones, *End of White Christian America*.

33. Sprague, *Newport in the Rockies*, 1–16. This book, though entertaining, should not be taken as the last word on the city's history.

34. "Founder Envisioned Colorado Springs," *FP*, June 11, 1967, from "Colorado Springs Politics and Government," Clipping Folders, Pikes Peak Library District Special Collections, Colorado Springs.

35. Abbott, Leonard, and Noel, *Colorado*, 82.

36. *Colorado Springs Weekly Gazette*, January 18, 1873.

37. Loevy, *Colorado College*, 11–27.

38. Atkins, "'Business Sense If Not Souls.'"

39. Noel and Norman, *Pikes Peak Partnership*, 93–122.

40. As an example: Penrose sent a congratulatory telegram to Governor William Spry of Utah when Spry refused to commute the death sentence of labor organizer Joe Hill. Noel and Norman, *Pikes Peak Partnership*, 46. Thomas G. Andrews places the early history of Colorado Springs in the context of Colorado's "labor wars" in *Killing for Coal*.

41. Goldberg, *Hooded Empire*, esp. 58.

Chapter One: The Miracle Place

1. Kay McDonald to "Dear Wrangler Club Members," May 15, 1948, box 69, folder 32, HJT.

2. "The Story of the Fire on Cheyenne Mountain," January 17, 1950, box 69, folder 32, HJT.

3. "Story of the Fire."

4. Guss Hill to "Dear Friend of Young Life," February 15, 1950, box 69, folder 32, HJT.

5. Nash, *Federal Landscape*.

6. Shermer, *Sunbelt Capitalism*.

7. Hamilton, "Interdenominational Evangelicalism of D. L. Moody."

8. On this dynamic, see Carpenter, *Revive Us Again*.

9. I take my definition of "parachurch ministry" from Shelley, "Parachurch Groups (Voluntary Societies)," quoted in Willmer, *Prospering Parachurch*, 13. On the long history of the parachurch movement, see Scheitle, *Beyond the Congregation*, 26–29.

10. See Carpenter's introduction to *Youth for Christ Movement*.

11. Marsden, *Reforming Fundamentalism*; Grem, "Business of Conservative Evangelicalism."

12. Billy Graham, "America's Hope," from Carpenter, *Early Billy Graham*.

13. Wuthnow, *Restructuring of American Religion*, 35–53.

14. Herzog, *Spiritual-Industrial Complex*, 75–108; Kruse, *One Nation under God*, 67–94.

15. Herzog, *Spiritual-Industrial Complex*, 109–34; Gunn, *Spiritual Weapons*.

16. D. Williams, *God's Own Party*, 20.

17. Turner, *Bill Bright and Campus Crusade for Christ*, 52.

18. Clarence Jones, "Radio: The New Missionary," in Carpenter, *Missionary Innovation and Expansion*, 102–3.

19. L. Cohen, *Consumers' Republic*, 292–344.

20. Turner, *Bill Bright and Campus Crusade for Christ*, 22.

21. Turner, *Bill Bright and Campus Crusade for Christ*, 71.

22. Cailliet, *Young Life*, 8; Senter, "Mother of the Parachurch High School Movement"; Kit Sublett, "An Adventure in Excellence," unpublished manuscript, Young Life Archives, Colorado Springs.

23. Sutton, *Aimee Semple McPherson*.

24. Jim Rayburn to "Dear Friends," September 20, 1947, box 69, folder 32, HJT.

25. Jim Rayburn to "Dear Fellow Members," April 5, 1947, box 69, folder 31, HJT.

26. Wallace Chappell, "Report on the Study of the Young Life Campaign," box 69, folder 38, HJT.

27. Ted M. Benson, "A Reply to Wallace Chappell's 'Report on the Study of The Young Life Campaign,'" box 69, folder 38, HJT.

28. For one example, see Bederman, "'Women Have Had Charge of the Church Work Long Enough.'"

29. Skinner, *Daws*, 39, 40, 101, 170.

30. Skinner, *Daws*, 137.

31. Skinner, *Daws*, 189.

32. Sutton, *American Apocalypse*, 47–78.

33. Pierard, "*Pax Americana*"; Miller-Davenport, "'Their Blood Shall Not Be Shed in Vain.'"

34. Shelley, "Rise of Evangelical Youth Movements."

35. Dawson Trotman, "America's Responsibility in the New World," *King's Business*, October 1944, 344–45, cited in Skinner, *Daws*, 248.

36. "Young Life Mass Meetings," Billy Graham Archives Collection, Young Life Archives, Colorado Springs.

37. Robert Hall Glover, "What Is a Faith Mission?," *Missionary Review of the World*, September 1935, 409–11.

38. Wright, *Old Fashioned Revival Hour*, 104–5, 131, 174.

39. YLSB, January 3, 1951.

40. Board Minutes, October 11, 1952, Young Life Archives, Colorado Springs.

41. Hammond, *God's Businessmen*, 66–71.

42. "Young Life Work Centers in Pikes Peak Region," *GT*, May 21, 1950.

43. John E. Mitchell to H. J. Taylor, May 19, 1947, box 69, folder 31, HJT.

44. H. J. Taylor to Dick Langford, May 27, 1947, box 69, folder 31, HJT.

45. C. Davis Weyerhaeuser to H. J. Taylor, June 9, 1947, box 69, folder 31, HJT.

46. Skinner, *Daws*, 57, 174.

47. Skinner, *Daws*, 275.

48. Skinner, *Daws*, 191.

49. Rayburn, *Diaries of Jim Rayburn*, 135.

50. Rayburn III, *Dance, Children, Dance*, 74.

51. The literature on Graham is voluminous; for an excellent introduction, see Wacker, *America's Pastor*.

52. "Instructions for Counsellors," February 14, 1953, box 1, folder 37, Navigators Collection, Evangelism and Missions Archive, Wheaton College, Wheaton, IL.

53. Glen Eyrie Purchase and Endowment Fund, Bulletin #1, June 13, 1953, GEPM.

54. Dawson Trotman, July 20, 1953, "Dear Gang" Letters, Navigators Archives, Colorado Springs.

55. Dawson Trotman to Lee Sundstrom, August 22, 1953, GEPM.

56. Colorado Springs Chamber of Commerce Annual Report, 1941, box 5, folder 39, H. Chase Stone Papers, Pikes Peak Library District Special Collections, Colorado Springs.

57. *Fort Carson*, 9–10.

58. Leo Zuckerman, "Springs Proudly Says It Has Everything Air Force Needs," *RMN*, April 11, 1954.

59. "Springs Gets Academy," *GT*, June 24, 1954; "Thanks to Chamber," *GT*, June 24, 1954.

60. Crampon et al., *Economic Survey of the Pikes Peak Region*, p. IX-1.

61. Atkins, "America's Theopolis," 129–30.

62. YLSB, October 18, 1944.

63. Bulletin to the Board of Directors no. 39, July 11, 1945, Young Life Archives, Colorado Springs.

64. YLSB, January 15, 1947.

65. YLSB, February 19, 1946; YLSB, April 24, 1946.

66. "Glen Eyrie Is Purchased by George Strake," *GT*, September 23, 1938.

67. "Open Headquarters at Star Ranch," *FP*, December 15, 1947; telegram from H. J. Taylor to Jim Rayburn, April 23, 1946, box 69, folder 31, HJT.

68. "Evangelist Graham Envisions Glen Eyrie as Bible Center," *FP*, May 30, 1953.

69. Dawson Trotman to Lee Sundstrom, August 22, 1953, GEPM.

70. Dochuk, "'Heavenly Houston'"; Walsh, "Right-Wing Popular Front."

71. Carpenter, in the introduction to *Missionary Innovation and Expansion*.

72. Clarence Jones, "Radio: The New Missionary," in Carpenter, *Missionary Innovation and Expansion*, 57.

73. Wright, *Old Fashioned Revival Hour*, 97.

74. Torrey Johnson and Robert Cook, "Reaching Youth for Christ," in Carpenter, *Youth for Christ Movement*, 15.

75. Cailliet, *Young Life*, 25.

76. Sublett, "Adventure in Excellence," 180.

77. Trotman to Sundstrom, August 22, 1953, GEPM.

78. "Dear Overseas Nav Gang," September 16, 1953, GEPM.

79. Notes from August 29, 1953, meeting at 509 (place name), GEPM.

80. "Story stuff," GEPM.

81. Letter to "Dear Freddie," September 18, 1953, GEPM.

82. "Dear Overseas Nav Gang," September 16, 1953, GEPM.

83. Skinner, *Daws*, 353.

84. H. K. Ellingson, "Star Ranch Will Be Scene of Camps of Young Life Group," *GT*, March 2, 1947.

85. Jim Rayburn to "Dear Fellow Members," April 5, 1947, box 69, folder 31, HJT.

86. Sublett, "Adventure in Excellence," 132.

87. Script for Star Ranch Colored Slides, Adults, 1947, YLSB; H. J. Taylor to "Dear Al," November 18, 1947, box 69, folder 32, HJT.

88. YLSB, January 28, 1947.

89. "Navigators Will Dedicate Glen Eyrie Headquarters," *GT*, July 30, 1963.

90. YLSB, December 2, 1946.

91. Glen Eyrie payment requirements, August 26, 1955, GEPM.

92. Glen Eyrie dedication—summary of conclusions and discussion, GEPM; "Navigators Will Dedicate Glen Eyrie Headquarters."

93. Sublett, "Adventure in Excellence," 161.

94. Young Life Annual Report, 1954, Young Life Archives, Colorado Springs; Byron Akers, "Young Life Gives Award to FBI Chief," *GT*, February 16, 1964. On the relationship between American evangelicals and Hoover's FBI, see Martin, *Gospel of J. Edgar Hoover*.

95. Jenkins, *Mystics and Messiahs*.

96. Braden, *These Also Believe*, 257–307; Donald Janson, "Conservatives at Freedom School to Prepare a New Federal Constitution," *NYT*, June 13, 1965, 66.

97. Bryan, *Psychic Dictatorship in America*.

98. "Ballards and 22 Reindicted in I AM Cult Investigation," *Los Angeles Times*, August 29, 1940; Failinger, "*United States v. Ballard*."

99. "The Answer," The San Francisco Group, May 1949, box 13, folder 3, Robert LeFevre Papers, University of Oregon Special Collections, Eugene.

100. "War Veteran Runs in 14th District," *Los Angeles Times*, February 21, 1950.

101. Letter from Milton Ellerin, April 21, 1959, box 144, folder 3, GRI.

102. Lichtman, *White Protestant Nation*, 221–22.

103. "Girl Scout Handbook Changes 'Tea-China' to 'Tea-India,'" *Baltimore Sun*, December 29, 1954; "Criticism Brings Changes in Girl Scouts' Handbook," *Washington Post*, December 30, 1954.

104. "Newsweek Magazine Prints Article about R. C. Hoiles," *GT*, October 16, 1947; "Making Money by Making Enemies," *Time*, April 19, 1963.

105. On Pegler, see Witwer, "Westbrook Pegler."

106. "Notes on Exemption Application," May 16, 1963, box 144, folder 3, GRI.

107. Robert Donner, "'Reds' in Education, 1950–1953," box 49, Billy James Hargis Papers, University of Arkansas Special Collections, Fayetteville; memorandum, December 29, 1958, box 144, folder 3, GRI.

108. "Men, Women Work Together to Build Freedom School," *GT*, September 23, 1956; "Freedom School Names Six Discussion Leaders," *GT*, March 12, 1957.

109. Robert LeFevre, "Autarchy versus Anarchy," box 144, folder 3, GRI.

110. LeFevre, *Nature of Man and His Government*, ch. 4.

111. LeFevre, *Nature of Man and His Government*, ch. 6.

112. "Freedom School Names Six Discussion Leaders"; Phillips-Fein, *Invisible Hands*, 53–56, 76.

113. On the ideology of the John Birch Society, see Mulloy, *World of the John Birch Society*.

114. Mulloy, *World of the John Birch Society*, 104; Jane Mayer, *Dark Money*, 39–47; Freedom School Form 990A, Return of Organization Exempt from Income Tax—1964, box 144, GRI.

115. Freedom School Form 990A, 1964, box 144, folder 3, GRI.

116. Timothy Williams, "Roger Milliken, 95, Conservative Tycoon," *NYT*, January 1, 2011; Freedom School Information Sheet, box 144, folder 3, GRI.

117. "Gazette Editor to Conduct Program for 47 Executives," *GT*, March 22, 1963; Roger Milliken to Robert LeFevre, February 5, 1962, box 144, folder 3, GRI.

118. Grant Records, box 144, folder 3, GRI.

119. Freedom School Form 990A, 1964, box 144, folder 3, GRI.

120. "1968 Bulletin—Rampart College," LeFevre, Robert T., Ernie Lazar FOIA Collection, accessed May 11, 2021, https://archive.org/details/lazarfoia.

121. "1965 Bulletin—Freedom School," LeFevre, Robert T., Ernie Lazar FOIA Collection, accessed May 11, 2021, https://archive.org/details/lazarfoia.

122. "Freedom School Names Six Discussion Leaders"; Janson, "Conservatives at Freedom School to Prepare a New Federal Constitution," *NYT*.

123. "What They Said in '63," box 144, folder 3, GRI.

124. "Three of Five 'Freedom School' Scholarship Winners Connected with the U.S. Armed Services," *FP*, April 16, 1963.

125. Janson, "Conservatives at Freedom School to Prepare a New Federal Constitution."

126. "Making Money by Making Enemies," *Time*, April 19, 1963.

127. "Ex-Students Rap 'Freedom School,'" *Rockford Morning Star*, October 23, 1959, reprinted by *FP*, November 10, 1959.

128. "Businessmen Hear Freedom School Expansion Proposal," *GT*, February 20, 1963.

129. "Chamber Board Upholds Committee Action to Welcome Rampart College," *GT*, March 19, 1963.

130. "TIME Blasts Hoiles," *FP*, April 16, 1963.

131. "Rampart College Plan Attacked in Springs," *DP*, May 15, 1963.

132. Dick Woodbury, "Springs C of C Deaf to Attack on School," *DP*, March 19, 1963.

133. "Colorado Springs without Daily Paper," *Colorado Springs Independent*, January 30, 1947; "For 75 Years, GT Has Kept Pace with Region's Growth," *GT*, June 29, 1947; "Union Sells Newspaper," *NYT*, August 2, 1951.

134. "The Libertarian Viewpoint," *FP*, March 14, 1963.

135. *A Free Press Report on the Freedom Philosophy* (pamphlet), 1963, GRI.

136. Hixson, *Search for the American Right Wing*, 68–69.

137. "Tornados, Floods Continue to Plague Pikes Peak Region," *GT*, June 18, 1965; "Damage at Freedom School above $150,000," *GT*, June 19, 1965; "Freedom School in Larkspur Long Gone, but Area Still Makes a Good Day-Trip," *Gazette* (Colorado Springs), May 19, 2006.

138. "College Getting Out of Woods," *Pomona (CA) Progress Bulletin*, October 17, 1968.

Chapter Two: Making Jesus Springs

1. "A Day in the Life of Focus," *Focus on the Family with Dr. James C. Dobson*, November 1993, box 28, folder 21, CP; Steve Rabey, "Thousands Help Dedicate New Focus Headquarters," *GT*, September 26, 1993.

2. For example, Schemo, *Skies to Conquer*, 6.

3. On the business aspect of evangelical Christianity, see Grem, *Blessings of Business*.

4. Atkins, "'Business Sense If Not Souls.'"

5. Schwarz, "Limiting Religious Tax Exemptions."

6. Crockett, "Problem of Tax Exempt Property."

7. Kemp v. Pillar of Fire, 94 Colo. 41 (Colo. 1933).

8. McGlone v. First Baptist Church, 97 Colo. 427 (Colo. 1935).

9. First Congregational Church of Fort Collins v. Wright, 131 P.2d 419 (Colo. 1942).

10. Brief of plaintiff in error, District Court, Records of *Young Life v. Commissioners of Chaffee County*, Colorado State Archives, Denver.

11. Testimony of Jim Rayburn, District Court, Records of *Young Life v. Commissioners of Chaffee County*.

12. "Reply brief of the plaintiffs in error," Records of *Young Life v. Commissioners of Chaffee County*.

13. Young Life v. Chaffee County, 134 Colo. 15 (Colo. 1956).

14. C.R.S. 39-3-101(e)(I), *Colorado Revised Statutes*, 1973.

15. General Conference of the Church of God v. Carper, 557 P.2d 832 (Colo. 1976).

16. Opening brief of the petitioner in the Supreme Court of Colorado, Records of *West-Brandt Foundation, Inc. v. Carper*, Colorado State Archives, Denver.

17. "Colorado Court of Appeals, No. 78–683," Records of *West-Brandt Foundation, Inc. v. Carper*.

18. At that point Christian Camping International was headquartered in Wheaton, Illinois. It relocated to Colorado Springs in 1993.

19. Amicus curiae in the Supreme Court of the State of Colorado, no. 80 SC279, Records of *West-Brandt Foundation, Inc. v. Carper*.

20. Young Life Campaign v. Patino, 122 Cal. App. 3d 559 (Cal. Ct. App. 1981).

21. Young Life v. Division of Employment and Training, 650 P.2d 515 (1982).

22. Appellant's opening brief, Court of Appeals, Records of *Maurer v. Young Life*, Colorado State Archives, Denver.

23. Answer brief of Young Life, Court of Appeals, Records of *Maurer v. Young Life*.

24. Answer brief of Young Life, Court of Appeals, Records of *Maurer v. Young Life*.

25. Maurer v. Young Life, 779 P.2d 1317 (Colo. 1989).

26. Senate Finance Committee hearing on SB237, March 2, 1989, Legislative History of SB237, Colorado State Archives, Denver.

27. William Frey testimony, Senate Finance Committee hearing on SB237, March 2, 1989, Legislative History of SB237.

28. Memo from Mary Anne Maurer to members of the House Finance Committee, RE: SB237, April 20, 1989, Legislative History of SB237.

29. Brian Weber, "Despite No New Taxes, Taxpayers Will Pay More," *GT*, May 21, 1989.

30. Senate Finance Committee hearing on SB237, March 7, 1989, Legislative History of SB237.

31. Memo to Citizens Project from Jack Paterson and Tony Massaro, March 24, 1995, box 26, folder 15, CP.

32. Noel and Norman, *Pikes Peak Partnership*, 199.

33. "Forecast '86: Colorado Springs," published by Schuck/Grubb & Ellis, RHC; "Forecast '85," published by the Schuck Commercial Brokerage Company, RHC; Dave Bamberger, "Economy: Booming or Bottoming Out?," *Chamber Magazine*, February 1984.

34. "The EDC's Other Full-Time Job Is Here at Home," *Chamber Magazine*, May 1985.

35. Bill Tutt, "The Chamber Salutes Our Military Friends," *Chamber Magazine*, May 1982.

36. "Final Environmental Impact Statement: Consolidated Space Operations Center," January 1981, Consolidated Space Operations Center file, Information Files, Special Collections and Archives, Colorado College, Colorado Springs.

37. Kris Newcomer, "Pentagon Picks Springs for Star Wars Test Site," *RMN*, June 26, 1986.

38. Jeffrey Manberg, "Speculating on an Earthly Space Boom," *NYT*, box 73, folder 2, Marshall Sprague Papers, Pikes Peak Library District Special Collections, Colorado Springs; Ken Western, "CSOC Sending Land Values into Orbit," *Colorado Springs Sun*, December 9, 1984.

39. Stephen Bobbitt, "Springs Leaders Praise Star Wars Test Center," *RMN*, June 26, 1986, and pamphlet published by SLB Company, Inc., both from the Consolidated Space Operations Center file.

40. Western, "CSOC Sending Land Values into Orbit"; Ken Western, "Counting Down to CSOC: Prairie People Ready to Take Giant Leap into Space Age," *Colorado Springs Sun*, December 9, 1984.

41. Amanda Ritchie, "Aerospace Giants Already Here," *GT*, September 13, 1983.

42. Western, "CSOC Sending Land Values into Orbit"; Wayne Heilman, "Economic Impact of CSOC on Area Unclear," *GT*, February 24, 1985; "Cities in Colorado and Texas Compete for the Unofficial Title of Space City," *Wall Street Journal*, January 15, 1986.

43. Patrick Yack, "Pentagon's $70 Million White Elephant," *DP*, April 5, 1987.

44. Dinah Wisenberg, "Defense Budget Sent to Reagan," *GT*, July 15, 1988.

45. Gray and Markusen, "Colorado Springs," 321.

46. "Colorado Springs Economic Development Council Annual Report, 1985," RHC; "Business," *GT*, July 30, 1989.

47. "Colorado Springs Real Estate Forecast, 1987," published by Schuck/Grubb & Ellis, RHC.

48. From the *GT*: Russ Arensman, "Theme Park, Resort Plans Unveiled," June 28, 1989; Russ Arensman, "Isaac: Park Should Be Built—and Built Here," June 28, 1989; Russ Arensman, "Liberty Park Officials Plan Mascots, TV Shows," July 2, 1989; Joanna Schmidt, "Liberty Park Design Work Might Delay Construction," March 10, 1990; Jerry Mahoney, "So Long, Liberty Park—Write When You Find a Home," March 8, 1992.

49. Wayne Heilman, "Profile of a Gambler," *GT*, December 15, 1985; Wayne Heilman, "A Tale of Two Cities," *GT*, December 15, 1985; Wayne Heilman, "Tucson Developer Has Option to Buy 'Future of Springs,'" *GT*, October 4, 1985; Wayne Heilman, "S&L Trying to Reduce Aries Loan," *GT*, January 11, 1989; Wayne Heilman, "Lender to Aries Facing Loss," *GT*, February 25, 1989; Andy van de Voorde, "Greed Acres," *Westword* (Denver), December 13–19, 1989; proceedings and reports of the Colorado Springs City Council, June 28 and July 12, 1988, RHC.

50. *Assessment of the Role of Key Groups.*

51. *Assessment of the Role of Key Groups*, 8–18.

52. Wayne Heilman, "Economic Proposals Draw Mixed Reviews," *GT*, May 4, 1988; Wayne Heilman, "The Path Not Taken: Most Officials Oppose Separating Chamber and EDC," *GT*, May 22, 1988.

53. Wayne Heilman and Russ Arensman, "Business Group More Independent," *GT*, August 24, 1988; Rocky Scott, Economic Development Corporation business plan for 1990/1991, in the author's possession.

54. Noel and Norman, *Pikes Peak Partnership*, 216; Douglas Stewart, "El Pomar," *Bull Sheet*, March 15–February 15, 1988, El Pomar file, Information Files, Special Collections and Archives, Colorado College, Colorado Springs.

55. William B. Tutt, oral history interview, September 21, 1984, box 78, Marshall Sprague Papers; Frank Zang, "Perfect Partners," *The Olympian*, May 1993, Vertical File, United States Olympic Committee Archives, Colorado Springs; F. Don Miller, "The United States Olympic Complex," *Chamber Magazine*, July 1982.

56. "Foundation Picks Springs," *GT*, December 11, 1983; Colorado Springs Economic Development Council annual report, 1985, RHC.

57. "An Interview with William Hybl, CEO of El Pomar Foundation," *CSBJ*, April 15, 1990; "El Pomar Grant to Establish Nonprofit Center," *CSBJ*, March 15, 1991.

58. John Weiss, "Colorado Springs: America's New Nonprofit Center," *Nonprofit Times*, October 1994, box 42, folder 59, IFAS.

59. Scott, Economic Development Corporation business plan for 1990/1991.

60. Mead, *Handbook of Denominations in the United States*, 209.

61. "Neddo Joins EDD Staff," *Chamber Magazine*, January 1985; "A Candid Conversation with Alice Neddo," *CSBJ*, March 15, 1990; Bill McKenzie, "Measure 9 May Harm Economy—or May Not," *Oregonian* (Portland), September 30, 1992.

62. Among the books that explored this crisis were Ronsvalle and Ronsvalle, *Behind the Stained Glass Windows*; Wuthnow, *Crisis in the Churches*; and Willmer, *Prospering Parachurch*.

63. Kathleen McLain, "SIM Missionary Group Will Move to Charlotte," *Charlotte Observer*, October 7, 1986.

64. Debbi Sykes, "Christian Organizations Flocking to Evangelical Pastures of Cary," *News & Observer* (Raleigh, NC), February 18, 1991.

65. "Youth for Christ Moving to Denver," *Religious News Service*, June 2, 1990.

66. D. Henry, *A. B. Simpson and the Making of Modern Evangelicalism*.

67. Kathleen Bowling, "Ministries Look for the Promised Land," *CT*, November 25, 1991.

68. Glenda Wenger to David Rambo, November 17, 1987, series 2, book 3, Relocation, RG901, Christian and Missionary Alliance Archives, Colorado Springs; Lorne Sanny to David Rambo, November 19, 1987, series 2, book 3, Relocation, RG901. On the significance of Wheaton in the evangelical world, see Hamilton, "Fundamentalist Harvard."

69. Agenda, January 11, 1988, series 2, book 4, Relocation, RG901.

70. "Report of Relocation Committee to General Council 1989," series 2, book 4, Relocation, RG901.

71. Paul Yaggy and Don Wyckoff, "Report of a Feasibility Study," June 1, 1989, box 70, folder 6, OC International Collection, Evangelism and Missions Archives, Wheaton College, Wheaton, IL.

72. Paul Yaggy, "Project Blue—An Interim Status Report," CN222, box 70, folder 6, OC International Collection.

73. "Project Blue—Decision Matrix Rankings," box 70, folder 6, OC International Collection.

74. Steve Rabey, "Missionary Group to Buy Office Building in Springs," *GT*, August 24, 1991.

75. Turner, *Bill Bright and Campus Crusade for Christ*.

76. Tom Morton, "Campus Crusade Keeps Springs in Running," *GT*, August 12, 1989; "Affordable Colorado Springs," *GT*, August 12, 1989.

77. Wayne Heilman, "Tiffany Square Leaseholder Sues Owners," *GT*, August 18, 1989; Tom Morton, "Campus Crusade Lured to Orlando," *GT*, September 7, 1989; Adelle Banks, "Campus Crusade Base Moving to Orlando Area," *Orlando Sentinel*, September 6, 1989; Adelle Banks, "Donated Land May Be Ministries New Home," *Orlando Sentinel*, June 22, 1990; Charles B. Shelden, "Editorial," *CSBJ*, November 15, 1989.

78. For Dobson's biography, see Tim Stafford, "His Father's Son," *CT*, April 22, 1988; on Focus on the Family in general, see Gilgoff, *Jesus Machine*.

79. Laura Stepp, "The Empire Built on Family & Faith," *Washington Post*, August 8, 1990; Peter Steinfels, "No Church, No Ministry, No Pulpit, He Is Called Religious Right's Star," *NYT*, June 5, 1990.

80. H. Stephens, *Family Matters*.

81. Joanna Schmidt, "Focus on the Family Moving to Springs," *GT*, June 15, 1990; John Dart, "Dobson's Influence Based on Family Issues," *Los Angeles Times*, April 2, 1988; Joanna Schmidt, "Ministry Move Will Boost Demand for Area Housing," *GT*, June 17, 1990.

82. Weiss, "Colorado Springs: America's New Nonprofit Center."

83. Joanna Schmidt, "Many in Devoted Flock Relocating with Ministry," *GT*, June 30, 1991; "Focus on the Family Completes Lease Negotiations," *CSBJ*, August 1, 1991.

84. Oral history with William Hybl, conducted by Amy Ziegler, July 24, 2007, Colorado Springs History Project (Oral Histories), Pikes Peak Library District Special Collections, Colorado Springs.

85. "Focus on the Family Relocates to Colorado Springs," *CSBJ*, July 1, 1990.

86. Wayne Heilman, "Briargate to Sell Prime Acreage," *GT*, October 26, 1988; "Focus Signs Land Contract," *GT*, September 27, 1991; Steve Rabey, "Focus to Dedicate New Home," *GT*, September 25, 1993.

87. Nancy Novosad, "The Right's New Messiah," *The Progressive*, December 1996.

88. Letter from James Dobson, May 1991, box 42, folder 62, IFAS.

89. Jan Ellen Spiegel, "EDC Swamped by California Tidal Wave," *CSBJ*, July 15, 1992; Joanna Schmidt, "California Company Follows Well-Worn Path to Springs," *GT*, September 25, 1992; D'Arcy Fallon, "The Good Life Lures People to Colorado," *GT*, March 10, 1993.

90. Steve Rabey, "Evangelical Groups Reach Out to World from Springs Home," *GT*, November 24, 1991; Joanna Schmidt, "Californians Find Good Life in Springs," *GT*, September 12, 1992.

91. "Christian Ministry Announces Move to Springs," *CSBJ*, September 1, 1990.

92. "Christian School Organization Leaves from Calif. for Springs," *CSBJ*, March 1, 1992; "Religious Organization Announces Move to Springs," *CSBJ*, July 15, 1991; "Missionary Organization to Relocate Locally," *CSBJ*, June 1, 1991.

93. Weiss, "Colorado Springs: America's New Nonprofit Center."

94. Rabey, "Evangelical Groups Reach Out to World from Springs Home"; Steve Rabey, "Springs-Based Christian Groups Growing Presence, Survey Shows," *GT*, February 26, 1994.

95. Gray and Markusen, "Colorado Springs," 327–28; Weiss, "Colorado Springs: America's New Nonprofit Center."

96. Terry Taylor to Doug Burleigh, January 25, 1989, and Jerry White and Terry Taylor to Burleigh, July 9, 1990, both from Denny Rydberg Presidential Collection, Young Life Archives, Colorado Springs.

97. Tom Morton, "Local Publishing Firm Gains Faith and Foothold in Difficult Market," *GT*, May 9, 1989; Steve Rabey, "Ministries Flocking to Springs," *GT*, December 20, 1992; Patricia Merritt, "Ministry Helps Men Find God's Path for Them," *Gazette*, April 5, 1997.

98. Rabey, "Evangelical Groups Reach Out to World from Springs Home"; Rabey, "Ministries Flocking to Springs"; Steve Rabey, "Area Christian Groups Continue to Grow in Size, Number," *GT*, February 27, 1994.

99. Rabey, "Evangelical Groups Reach Out to World from Springs Home."

100. Rabey, "Ministries Flocking to Springs."

101. Steve Rabey, "Ministry to Move to Colorado Springs—Radio Group to Bring 50 Jobs," *GT*, October 9, 1991; Steve Rabey, "Christian School Group Follows Springs Move of Focus on the Family," *GT*, February 20, 1992.

102. These statistics are from the Digital Atlas of American Religion, hosted by the Virtual Center for Spatial Humanities at Indiana University–Indianapolis. They come from examining "Largest Denominational Family per County" for El Paso County in the years 1980, 1990, and 2000. Accessed July 1, 2015, http://religionatlas.org (site discontinued).

103. Rabey, "Ministries Flocking to Springs."

104. "A Candid Conversation with Alice Neddo," *CSBJ*, March 15, 1990.

105. "MCI to Establish Division Headquarters in Springs," *CSBJ*, April 1, 1991; Charles B. Shelden, "Apple, MCI Signal Resurgence," *CSBJ*, April 1, 1991.

106. Shelden, "Apple, MCI Signal Resurgence."

107. US Bureau of the Census, "County Business Patterns Datasets," 1993, accessed July 3, 2014, www.census.gov/programs-surveys/cbp/data/datasets.html. For comparison, the figure was 1 percent in the city and county of Denver, 1.2 percent in Jefferson County, and 1.6 percent in Arapahoe County, the three other largest Colorado counties.

108. "Largest Colorado Springs Area Private-Sector Employers," *CSBJ*, July 15, 1991.

109. "Largest Colorado Springs Area Public Employers," *CSBJ*, March 15, 1991.

110. Rabey, "Evangelical Groups Reach Out to World from Springs Home."

111. "Business Harassment," *Freedom Watch* 1, no. 2 (September 1992), box 47, folder 7, CP.

112. "Single Teachers," *Freedom Watch* 1, no. 2 (September 1992), box 47, folder 7, CP.

113. "Pressure on Our Schools," *Freedom Watch* 1, no. 1 (July 1992), and "School Censorship," *Freedom Watch* 1, no. 2 (September 1992), both from box 47, folder 7, CP.

114. Steve Rabey, "Ancient Myths under Attack," *GT*, February 1, 1991.

115. David Skipworth to *High Mountain Sun*, n.d., box 43, folder 3, CP.

116. "Plaintiff's Memorandum Brief in Support of Response to Defendant," District Court, County of Teller, Case No. 92, CV59, July 6, 1992, box 43, folder 3, CP.

117. Order, District Court, County of Teller, Colorado, Case No. 92, CV59, Division 8, October 14, 1992, box 43, folder 3, CP.

118. Rabey, "Ancient Myths under Attack."

119. Warren Epstein, "Group Formed to Counteract Religious Right's Political Activism," *GT*, July 4, 1992.

120. "School Case Update," *Freedom Watch* 1, no. 2 (September 1992), box 47, folder 7, CP.

121. "Elections," *Freedom Watch* 1, no. 1 (July 1992), and Barry Horstman, "Christian Activists Using 'Stealth' Tactics," *Los Angeles Times*, April 8, 1992, both from box 47, folder 7, CP.

122. Rabey, "Area Christian Groups Continue to Grow in Size, Number."

Chapter Three: A Civil War of Values

1. Colorado for Family Values transcript, May 19, 1994, box 65, folder 41, IFAS.
2. For important discussions of the interplay between liberalizing trends in American culture and the conservative backlash to those trends, see Self, *All in the Family*; Hartman, *War for the Soul of America*; Jones, *End of White Christian America*; and R. Griffith, *Moral Combat*.
3. D. Williams, *God's Own Party*, is the best history of the relationship between conservative Christians and the Republican Party; see esp. 133–86. See also the essays collected in Green et al., *Religion and the Culture Wars*.
4. Rick Perlstein, "Behind the Right's Phony War on the Nonexistent Religion of Secularism," *Rolling Stone* (blog), April 25, 2012, www.rollingstone.com/politics/politics-news/behind-the-rights-phony-war-on-the-nonexistent-religion-of-secularism-238757/.
5. W. Eskridge, *Dishonorable Passions*, 280.
6. Bennett, *Defending Faith*.
7. Penabaz, *Crusading Preacher*, 46–47.
8. "Fact-File: David A. Noebel," October 1970, box 3, folder 48, Billy James Hargis Papers, University of Arkansas Special Collections, Fayetteville.
9. Redekop, *American Far Right*. The list of speakers is from Penabaz, *Crusading Preacher*, 232.
10. D. Williams, *God's Own Party*, 58.
11. William R. Bechtel, "Kindschi, Noebel Fight to Face Kastenmeier," *Milwaukee Sentinel*, September 5, 1962.
12. "The Scandal of Bogus Degrees," *CT*, May 9, 1960.
13. Penabaz, *Crusading Preacher*, 60.
14. Redekop, *American Far Right*, 24–25.
15. "A Life-Changing Experience," *GT*, June 11, 1978.
16. Charles Secrest, "Counterpoint," *Christian Crusade Weekly*, January 25, 1970, box 721, folder 8, ACLU.
17. "World Parish," *Los Angeles Times*, November 3, 1974.
18. "The Sins of Billy James," *Time*, February 16, 1976; Wendell Rawls Jr., "Sex Scandal Rocks Hargis Followers," *Philadelphia Inquirer*, February 22, 1976; Steve Gunn, "The Resurrection of Billy James Hargis," *Atlanta Constitution*, January 11, 1981.
19. Noebel, *Understanding the Times*.
20. Noebel, *Communism, Hypnotism and the Beatles*, 15.
21. Noebel, *Slaughter of the Innocent*, 7.
22. Noebel, *Homosexual Revolution*, 88.
23. Herman, *Antigay Agenda*.
24. Rueda, *Homosexual Network*, 4, 11.
25. Noebel, Lutton, and Cameron, *AIDS*, 5.
26. Dobson and Bauer, *Children at Risk*, 19–20.
27. Dobson and Bauer, *Children at Risk*, 32.
28. John D. Woodbridge, "Culture War Casualties," *CT*, March 6, 1995, 20–26.
29. James Dobson, "Why I Use 'Fighting Words,'" *CT*, June 19, 1995, 27–30.

30. Joseph Berger, "Peter Berger, Theologian Who Fought 'God Is Dead' Movement, Dies at 88," *NYT*, June 29, 2017.

31. Dudley Clendinen, "'Humanist' Schoolbooks Go to Court in Alabama," *NYT*, October 6, 1986.

32. Testimony of James Davison Hunter, October 7, 1986, 207–413, box 1698, ACLU.

33. The ruling was later published as a book with an introduction by conservative intellectual Richard John Neuhaus, himself an important proponent of the "culture war" idea. Hand, *American Education on Trial*.

34. Hunter, *Culture Wars*, 51.

35. Hunter, *Culture Wars*, 156.

36. Hunter, *Culture Wars*, 311–12.

37. Brint, "What If They Gave a War . . . ?"; Gilbert, "Cultural Skirmishes."

38. Scott, "Remaking Urban in the American West," 168–70; Timothy Lee Lange, "The New Left Almost Blew It," *The Nation*, July 20, 1974; certificate of election returns, May 7, 1974, box 11, "Plaintiffs exhibit" folder, *E v. R*; Judith Cummings, "Homosexual-Rights Law Shows Progress in Some Cities, but Drive Arouses Considerable Opposition," *NYT*, May 13, 1974.

39. Bill Briggs, "Mayor Backs Rights Bill," *DP*, October 11, 1990; Bill Briggs, "Denver Approves Anti-Bias Ordinance," *DP*, October 16, 1990; Kevin Flynn, "Civil Rights Bill Heads for OK," *RMN*, October 16, 1990.

40. Patricia Calhoun, "Off Limits," *Westword*, May 22–28, 1991; Alan Gottlieb, "8 Vying for 2 At-Large Seats on City Council," *DP*, April 29, 1991; Richard Heckmann, letter to *Denver Post*, December 15, 1990; Bill Briggs, "Denver to Vote on Gay Rights Petition," *DP*, March 16, 1991; "Down to the Election Wire," *RMN*, May 19, 1991; J. R. Moehringer, "Gay-Rights Supporters Savor Win," *RMN*, May 22, 1991; EPOC newsletter, June 1991, box 7, folder 11, Equality Colorado Records, Western History Collection, Denver Public Library.

41. Noebel, Lutton, and Cameron, *AIDS*, 60.

42. Andrew H. Malcolm, "New Efforts Developing against the Hate Crime," *NYT*, May 12, 1989; Andrew Rosenthal, "President Signs a Law to Study Hate Crimes," *NYT*, April 24, 1990; letter from Susan E. Anderson, Gay and Lesbian Community Center of Colorado, February 5, 1991, HB1059 Legislative History, Colorado State Archives, Denver.

43. Bransford, *Gay Politics vs. Colorado*, 18.

44. Bransford, *Gay Politics vs. Colorado*, 26.

45. Colorado Springs City Council proceedings, April 23 and June 25, 1991, RHC; Rich Laden, "Council Axes Gay Rights Plan," *GT*, April 24, 1991; Rich Laden, "Council Kills Anti-Discrimination Measure," *GT*, June 26, 1991; Bransford, *Gay Politics vs. Colorado*, 25–27; David A. Noebel, "The City of Colorado Springs Anti-Bias Proposal Background Materials and Facts," box 11, folder 13, CP.

46. Linda Castrone, "Couple's Lives of Sin Led to Gay Crusade," *RMN*, February 7, 1993.

47. "Community Invitees to Burleigh and Loux Luncheon," February 7, 1989, Denny Rydberg Presidential Collection, Young Life Archives, Colorado Springs; "Further Details on Persons Invited to the Dedication," May 9, 1963, GEPM; "Meet the Leaders Who

Assist the Local Staff," February 6, 1959, "Young Life—1957" folder, Navigators Correspondence, Navigators Archive, Colorado Springs.

48. Steve Rabey, "Clergymen Differ over Role in Tackling Election Issues," *GT*, October 31, 1992.

49. Bransford, *Gay Politics vs. Colorado*, 36; *Colorado Springs City Directory*, 1990 and 1993 editions, RHC.

50. Cronin and Loevy, *Colorado Politics and Policy*, 103–4; Dennis Polhill, *Initiative and Referendum in Colorado*, report published by the Initiative and Referendum Institute, University of Southern California (December 2006), www.iandrinstitute.org/REPORT%202006-4%20Colorado.pdf.

51. "Colorado," Initiative and Referendum Institute, www.iandrinstitute.org/Colorado.htm; Brian Weber, "Official English Proposal Cruising to Easy Victory," *GT*, November 9, 1988; Cronin and Loevy, *Colorado Politics and Policy*, 148–49.

52. Bransford, *Gay Politics vs. Colorado*, 39; "Amendment 2, the Untold Story," *RMN*, February 7, 1993. On the Oregon initiative, see Schultz, "Rise and Fall of 'No Special Rights.'"

53. Brian McCormick to Tony Marco, "RE: Analysis of Language in Amendment Initiative," June 13, 1991, CP.

54. Diane Alters, "Armstrong Faith Reaffirmed While Serving on Capitol Hill," *GT*, January 20, 1991; "The Former Senator Showed That One Could Be Devoutly Religious, and Still Be Elected," *RMN*, February 10, 1991; letter from Bill Armstrong, August 27, 1991, box 9, folder 17, CP.

55. Louis Aguilar, "Coach's Anti-Gay Remarks Defended," *GT*, February 14, 1992; J. R. Moehringer, "Anti-Gays: Coach OK's Brochure," *RMN*, February 9, 1992; Michael Romano, "McCartney Receives Reprimand," *RMN*, February 12, 1992; Michael Romano, "Protesters Denounce McCartney," *RMN*, February 13, 1992; Cara DeGette, "Where There's a Will, There's a Gay," *Colorado Springs Independent*, July 20–27, 1994.

56. Bransford, *Gay Politics vs. Colorado*, 51–52.

57. Angela Dire, "Petition Drive Pulls Out Stops," *GT*, May 3, 1992; Anne Windishar, "Gay Rights Pit Pastor against Pastor," *GT*, June 22, 1992.

58. Bruce Mirkin, "Hell-Raiser," *Los Angeles Reader*, box 10, folder 20, Equality Colorado Records; Jeff Mapes, "Order Banning Bias against Homosexuals Readied," *Oregonian*, August 28, 1987; Lauren Cowan, "Vote for Measure 8 Shocks Opponents," *Oregonian*, November 10, 1988.

59. "Homosexuals Are a Rich Class Demanding Special Rights at the Expense of True Minorities," *Freedom Journal*, n.d., box 1, folder 26, Hate-Free Oregon Records, Oregon Historical Society, Portland; "What's Wrong with 'Gay Rights'? YOU Decide!," box 1, folder 10, Chares F. Hinkle Collection, Oregon Historical Society, Portland; "What's Wrong with Special 'Gay Rights'? YOU Be the Judge!," box 9, folder 19, CP; "Controversial Researcher Focus of Rights Debate," *DP*, September 27, 1992.

60. "CFV Transcript, 1994," box 65, folder 41, IFAS.

61. Tony Marco, "Special Gay Rights Legislation," 1991, box 9, folder 15, CP; Colorado for Family Values, "Vote 'Yes' on 2!," n.d., box 10, folder 17, CP; Colorado for Family Values, "Protecting True Minorities," n.d., box 9, folder 17, CP.

62. "The Colorado Model," box 65, folder 3, IFAS.

63. Family Research Institute, "Is God Right about SEX?," n.d., box 9, folder 17, CP; Family Research Institute, "Medical Consequences of What Homosexuals Do," n.d., box 9, folder 17, CP; "What's Wrong with Special 'Gay Rights'? YOU Be the Judge!," box 9, folder 19, CP.

64. Peter Goldman et al., *Quest for the Presidency 1992*, 402–4; Patrick Buchanan, "Culture War Speech: Address to the Republican National Convention," August 17, 1992, Voices of Democracy, https://voicesofdemocracy.umd.edu/buchanan-culture-war-speech-speech-text.

65. Jeff Mapes, "Gay Rights Move toward Center Stage in Presidential Campaign," *Oregonian*, August 3, 1992.

66. HoSang, *Racial Propositions*, 205; Robin Toner, "Eyes to the Left, Democrats Edge toward Center," *NYT*, March 25, 1990; Greenberg, "Reorientation of Liberalism."

67. "Hatred Is Not a Family Value—Hospitality Is," transcript of Kevin Tebedo address, box 9, folder 3, CP.

68. "Focus Group Regarding Gay Rights Amendment," box 8, folder 20, Equality Colorado Records.

69. Michael Booth, "Gay-Rights Amendment Fight Costly, Heated," *DP*, October 29, 1992; Angela Dire, "Trailing in Polls, Backers Plan Blitz for Amendment 2," *GT*, October 17, 1992; Thaddeus Herrick, "Campbell, Clinton Will Win State, Poll Indicates," *RMN*, October 28, 1992; Gary Massaro, "Polls Show Amendment 2 Going Down to Defeat," *RMN*, November 4, 1992.

70. Dirk Johnson, "Colorado Homosexuals Feel Betrayed," *NYT*, November 8, 1992.

71. "Colorado No Protected Status for Sexual Orientation Initiative 2," Ballotpedia, accessed March 10, 2025, https://ballotpedia.org/Colorado_Amendment_2,_No_Protected_Status_for_Sexual_Orientation_Initiative_(1992).

72. Meyer, "State of Colorado."

73. Tomas Romero, "An Ugly Victory That Will Not Stand," *DP*, November 11, 1992.

74. Ed Quillen, "Could We Secede from the Springs?," *DP*, November 17, 1992.

75. Michael Booth and Jeffrey A. Roberts, "Amendment 2: CON," *DP*, September 19, 1993; Tomas Romero, "Latinos Caught in Amendment 2 Crossfire," *DP*, January 12, 1993.

76. Stone, *Gay Rights at the Ballot Box*, 65–67.

77. "Boycott Hardens Battle Lines," *GT*, January 4, 1993; Fred Brown, "Voters Unchanged on Amendment 2," *DP*, February 23, 1993.

78. Alan Gottlieb and Virginia Culver, "Evangelical Influx Splits Colorado City," Religion News Service, November 20, 1992; Ned Zeman, Michael Meyer, and Sherry Keene-Osborne, "No 'Special Rights' for Gays," *Newsweek*, November 23, 1992; Sandra D. Atkinson, "Bashing Gays—and Business," *Businessweek*, December 7, 1992; "New Hub for Family Values Movement," *Los Angeles Times*, December 19, 1992; Matt Smith, "Colorado Town as Mecca of Religious Right," *National Catholic Reporter*, December 25, 1992; Steve Rabey, "Amendment 2 Sharpens Clash over 'Gay Rights,'" *CT*, January 11, 1993; Steve Rabey, "Focus under Fire," *CT*, March 8, 1993; Paula Poundstone, "He Didn't Even Like Girls," *Mother Jones*, May/June 1993; Donna Minkowitz, "Ground Zero: Fear and Renewal in Colorado Springs," *Village Voice*, January 19, 1993; Donna Stumbo, "The State of Hate," *Esquire*, September 1993; Michael Meyer and Kenneth

L. Woodward, "Onward Muscular Christians!," *Newsweek*, March 1, 1993; "Colorado Springs: The Conservative Source," *The Economist*, March 5, 1994; Thomas Heath, "In Colorado Springs, Religious Groups Have Right of Way," *Washington Post*, December 25, 1994; Marc Cooper, "God and Man in Colorado Springs," *The Nation*, January 2, 1995; Richard John Neuhaus, "America's Spiritual NORAD," *First Things*, April 1995, 62–63; Jim Ipoco, "Fatigue on the Right," *U.S. News & World Report*, October 23, 1995; Michael Lewis, "Crucifixation," *New Republic*, July 8, 1996, 20–24.

79. Fred Brown, "Hope Springs Eternal," *DP*, February 17, 1993.

80. Maureen Harrington, "Gay Writer Cancels Denver Appearance," *DP*, November 11, 1992.

81. Angela Dire, "Boycott Keeps State Guessing," *GT*, November 30, 1992.

82. "Hate Crimes Policy and Colorado Boycott," memo from Barry Steinhardt to Board, Affiliates, and National Staff, January 28, 1993, box 2109, "Hate crimes policy and Colorado boycott" folder, ACLU; "GLAAD/USA Endorses National Boycott of Colorado Protesting Anti-Gay Amendment," November 23, 1992, box 22, folder 26, GLAAD Records, Human Sexuality Collection, Cornell University, Ithaca, NY; "Statement from NGLTF on the Colorado Boycott," December 21, 1992, box 107, folder 57, National LGBTQ Task Force Records, Human Sexuality Collection, Cornell University; Louis Aguilar, "Gay Rights Group Wants Boycott to Target Springs," *GT*, December 11, 1992; Michael Specter, "Anger and Regret in Aspen as Boycott Grows," *NYT*, December 30, 1992.

83. "Mayor Edward G. Rendell—Boycott of Colorado Statement," n.d., box 107, folder 55, National LGBTQ Task Force Records.

84. "Chamber Marks Ballot," *RMN*, October 16, 1992; "A Message from Apple Computer," n.d., box 9, folder 21, CP.

85. Louis Aguilar, "Leaders Work to Head Off Boycott Spread," *GT*, November 24, 1992; Louis Aguilar, "Denver Tells World: Don't Blame Us," *GT*, December 4, 1992; Joanna Schmidt, "Corporate 'Culture' at Stake, Firms Say," *GT*, February 21, 1993.

86. Jack Forrest, "Area Must Plan for New, Diversified Economy," *GT*, June 9, 1992; Jennifer Okamoto, "Springs Posturing to Withstand Defense Cuts, *GT*, May 31, 1992.

87. From the *GT*: Anne Windishar, "Minorities in Springs Seek Economic Boycott," January 19, 1992; Anne Windishar, "Minorities Say City Unfair with Contracts," April 29, 1992; Anne Windishar, "Some Wary of City's Lack of Diversity," May 25, 1992; Lu Pollard, "Race Relations in Colorado Springs: Where Do We Stand?," July 15, 1992.

88. Jerry Mahoney, "Amendment 2 Won't Help the Economy," *GT*, January 10, 1993; Jane Grandolfo, "Businesses in Springs Fight Fallout," *GT*, February 14, 1993; "Springs Deeply Divided over Amendment 2," *RMN*, March 18, 1993.

89. Joanna Schmidt, "Chamber Slogan Promotes Diversity," *GT*, March 11, 1993.

90. Jeff Thomas, "Finding Middle Ground—Amendment 2 Compromise a Battle," *GT*, March 7, 1993; Rich Laden, "Local Backing Called Key to New Plan," *GT*, February 5, 1993; Jerry Mahoney, "Strait Joins the Fray, Hoping to Find Compromise," *GT*, February 21, 1993.

91. Harvey Martz, "Colorado Springs Seeks Middle Way," *DP*, February 20, 1993; Jeff Thomas, "Finding Middle Ground," *GT*, March 7, 1993; Will Perkins, "'Compromise': Special Rights with a Brand New Name," *CFV Report*, March 1993, box 49, folder 7, CP.

92. Greg Walta, "Stakes High in Reconciling Differences over Amendment 2," *GT*, March 30, 1993.

93. On the power of "moderation" as a political strategy, see C. Howard, *Closet and the Cul-de-Sac*, esp. 13–14.

94. "Amendment 2 Sponsor Uses Newsletter to Fight Proposed School Curriculum," *GT*, February 20, 1993.

95. Louis Aguilar, "Town Told Gays Pose Threat," *GT*, March 27, 1993; letter from Will Perkins, 1995, box 9, folder 18, CP; Dick Foster, "5-County Petition Drive Targets Homosexuality, Pornography, Violence," *RMN*, July 20, 1995; Wendy Y. Lawton, "D-11 Urged to Adopt Policy on Morality," *Gazette*, January 9, 1997; "Perkins' Sexual Conduct Policy Draft/Proposal," box 13, folder 14, CP; Colorado for Family Values press release, January 21, 1997, box 13, folder 14, CP.

96. "A Word from Executive Director Kevin Tebedo," *CFV Report*, March 1993, box 49, folder 7, CP; Aguilar, "Town Told Gays Pose Threat"; Steve Rabey, "Group Warns of 'Militant' Gay Agenda," *GT*, June 27, 1993.

97. Richard Skorman, "Citizens Project Defends Civil Rights While Celebrating Our Diversity," *GT*, June 21, 1995.

98. *Freedom Watch* 3, no. 1 (January/February 1994), box 47, folder 10, CP; Food for Thought newsletters, box 44, folder 10, CP; interview with Nori Rost, Colorado Springs, June 9, 2015; phone interview with Glenn Paauw, February 5, 2018.

99. Jane Grandolfo, "Poll Shows Support for Compromise," *GT*, February 17, 1993.

100. Documents from CFV Boulder meeting, box 9, folder 20, CP; Thaddeus Herrick, "Springs Group Proposes Boycott," *RMN*, April 1, 1993.

101. Phone interview with Robert "Rocky" Scott, September 12, 2019; Louis Aguilar, "Business Groups Fight Boycott," *GT*, April 6, 1993.

102. "'Community Standards' Drive Stalled," *GT*, October 21, 1995.

103. "Statement on Current Practices in School District 11 in Response to Colorado for Family Values Postcards," box 13, folder 14, CP; Wendy Y. Lawton, "D-11 Balks at Affirming Only 'Traditional' Marriages," *Gazette*, May 20, 1997.

104. Greg Worthen, "Kevin Tebedo Talks," *Springs Magazine*, October 1995, box 9, folder 20, CP.

105. Virginia Culver, "Sessions with Gays Criticized," *DP*, October 27, 1995; Michael Booth, "Counselor to Answer for Charges," *DP*, November 10, 1995; James B. Meadow, "Founder of Family Values Quits," *RMN*, November 7, 1995.

106. "For Immediate Release: Colorado for Family Values Appoints Dr. Paul Jessen Executive Director to Lead Upcoming Push," December 10, 1997, box 10, folder 3, CP; "Press Conference Presentation of Dr. Paul Jessen for 12/10/97," box 10, folder 3, CP.

107. Michael Booth, "The Man Who Sold Amendment 2," *DP*, March 21, 1993; Raquel Rutledge, "Mayoral Candidates Share Backgrounds," *Gazette*, April 4, 1999.

108. Raquel Rutledge, "Gay Rights Revisited at Forum," *Gazette*, March 12, 1999.

109. Colorado Springs City Council proceedings, April 23, 1991, RHC.

110. Pam Zubeck, "Mayor Image," *Gazette*, April 4, 1999.

111. Raquel Rutledge, "Makepeace Wins Again," *Gazette*, April 7, 1999; Pam Zubeck, "Mayor's Victory a 'Clear Message,'" *Gazette*, April 7, 1999; Pam Zubeck, "Eastburn,

Colt, Skorman Elected," *Gazette*, April 7, 1999; Eric Gorski and Raquel Rutledge, "Swaying the Political Tide," *Gazette*, April 11, 1999.

112. Eric Gorski, "Executive Director Quits Family Values," *Gazette*, April 16, 1999.

113. Bransford, *Gay Politics vs. Colorado*, 229.

114. Ward Harkavy, "Free Willy," *Westword*, October 2, 1997.

115. Olsen, *Refuge*, 19–20, 64–65.

116. Olsen, *Refuge*, 86.

117. Olsen, *Refuge*, 114.

118. Olsen, *Refuge*, 185.

119. Olsen, *Refuge*, 18–20; "Homosexual Mob Attacks San Francisco Churchgoers," *CFV Report*, November 1993, box 49, folder 7, CP.

120. Olsen, *Refuge*, 36–37.

121. Olsen, *Refuge*, 39.

122. Olsen, *Refuge*, 49.

123. Olsen, *Refuge*, 190.

124. DeGette, "Where There's a Will There's a Gay."

125. "CFV Model Handbook," section II-2, box 65, folder 43, IFAS.

126. "CFV Model Handbook," section II-8, box 65, folder 43, IFAS.

127. "CFV Model Handbook," section III, box 65, folder 43, IFAS.

128. Mike Shaver, "CFV behind Closed Doors," *Freedom Watch* 3, no. 4 (July/August 1994), box 47, folder 10, CP.

129. CFV Seminar Transcript—5/16/1994, "Common Ground and Strategies," box 9, folder 19, CP.

130. CFV Seminar Transcript—5/16/1994, "Common Ground and Strategies."

131. Robert Knight, "Sexual Disorientation: Faulty Research in the Homosexual Debate," box 44, folder 77, IFAS.

132. "Paul Cameron Vita," box 1, folder 10, Charles F. Hinkle Collection.

133. Koop, *Koop*, 291.

134. H. Stephens, *Family Matters*, 156–93.

135. CFV Seminar Transcript, Institute for First Amendment Studies, box 65, folder 41, IFAS.

136. Valerie Richardson, "Anti-Gay-Rights Leaders Talk of Repeating 1993 Success," *Washington Times*, May 19, 1994.

137. Sarah Sturmon, "Votes in Place for Gay Rights," *Cincinnati Post*, November 25, 1992.

138. Al Andry, "Emotions Run Hot over Issue 3," *Cincinnati Post*, October 28, 1993.

139. Mark McNeil, "Homosexual Rights Fail Constitutional—and Spiritual—Tests," *Cincinnati Post*, October 21, 1993.

140. Phil Burress, "Petition Drives: Pros and Cons," n.d., box 1, folder 1, Ann Burlein Papers, Kenneth Spencer Research Library, University of Kansas, Lawrence.

141. Angela Dire, "Amendment 2 Strategy Tilts Elections in Other States," *GT*, November 4, 1993.

142. "PAC It In—Inquiring Minds Want to Know: Who Gave $390,000 to Issue 3?," *Cincinnati Enquirer*, April 20, 1994, box 9, folder 19, CP; "Springs Group Gives Money to Ohio Effort," *GT*, October 31, 1993.

143. Burress, "Petition Drives: Pros and Cons."

144. National Survey on Gay Rights, memo from Mellman, Lazarus, Lake, Inc., to HRCF, March 3, 1994, box 2, folder 7, Gary Smith Collection, Oregon Historical Society, Portland.

145. Lunch, "Christian Right in the Northwest."

146. "A Briefing Book Prepared by the ACLU Lesbian and Gay Rights Project," August 1993, box 4569, ACLU.

147. "The Radical Right," memo from Mellman, Lazarus, Lake, Inc., to HRCF, May 20, 1994, Gary Smith Collection.

148. John Gallagher, "Split Decision," *The Advocate*, box 9, folder 19, CP; letter from David Caton, chairman, May 5, 1994, box 65, folder 45, ISAF.

149. "Anti-Gay Rights Measures on Ballots in Only 2 States," Associated Press, July 12, 1994.

150. Mark O'Keefe, "OCA Falls Short," *Oregonian*, November 9, 1994; Kevin Richert, "Anti-Gay Initiative Lost, but Backers Pleased with Election Day," *Idaho Falls Post Register*, November 13, 1994.

151. Angela Dire, "Suit Fights Gay Rights Law Ban," *GT*, November 13, 1992; Angela Dire, "Six Plaintiffs Staying with Case to the End," *GT*, October 1, 1995.

152. "A Conversation with Professor and Gay Activist John Miller," *UCCS News*, Spring 1993, box 1, folder 2, John Miller Collection, Stephen H. Hart Research Center, Denver; Raymond McCaffrey, "Professor Goes about Business of Fighting Bias," *GT*, December 15, 1993; Jeff Thomas, "Amendment 2 Foes Prepare for Hard Sell," *GT*, September 26, 1995.

153. Louis Aguilar, "Amendment 2 in Limbo until Court Challenge," *GT*, January 15, 1993.

154. Rick Hills to Bruce Nichols, box 8, "Rick Hills memos" folder, *E v. R*; Louis Aguilar, "Gays Warn of Perils If Amendment Stands," *GT*, January 13, 1993.

155. Evans v. Romer, 882 P.2d 1335 (Colo. 1994).

156. Deposition of Will Perkins, October 1, 1993, box 1, folder 1, *E v. R*; Angela Dire, "Amendment Authors State Their Case," *GT*, October 16, 1993.

157. Trial transcript, *Evans v. Romer*, vol. 16, October 16, 1993, box 1, "Romer v. Evans summaries, transcripts" folder, *E v. R*; Angela Dire, "Special Rights' Tactic Now Called Irrelevant," *GT*, October 19, 1993.

158. Angela Dire, "Experts, Plain Folk Ready to Do Battle," *GT*, October 10, 1993.

159. Trial transcript, *Evans v. Romer*, vol. 12, October 12, 1993, box 1, "Romer v. Evans summaries, transcripts" folder, *E v. R*; Angela Dire, "Courtroom Battle Kicks into Gear," *GT*, October 13, 1993; Angela Dire, "Amendment Called Health Threat," *GT*, October 14, 1993.

160. Angela Dire, "Controversial State Witness to Testify through Affidavit," *GT*, October 13, 1993; "Norton: State Paid for Controversial Psychologist's Testimony about Gays," *GT*, September 16, 1994.

161. Trial transcript, *Evans v. Romer*, vol. 16, October 16, 1993; Angela Dire, "State Attorneys Wrap Up Defense of Amendment 2," *GT*, October 21, 1993.

162. Deposition of James Davison Hunter, October 7, 1993, box 1, "Jean Dubofsky" folder, *E v. R*.

163. Angela Dire, "Amendment 2 Unconstitutional," *GT*, December 15, 1993; "Analyzing the Bayless Decision," *CFV Report*, February 1994, box 49, folder 7, CP.

164. Angela Dire, "Amendment 2 Is Heating Up," *GT*, October 1, 1995.

165. Press release, "CFV Responds to Colorado Supreme Court Ruling," October 11, 1994, box 10, folder 2, CP.

166. *Romer v. Evans*, Brief Amicus Curiae of Colorado for Family Values in Support of Petitioners, filed April 21, 1995.

167. *Romer v. Evans*, Brief Amicus Curiae of Laurence H. Tribe, John Hart Ely, Gerald Gunter, Philip B. Kurland, and Kathleen M. Sullivan in Support of Respondents, filed June 9, 1995; Jeffrey Toobin, "Supreme Sacrifice," *New Yorker*, June 30, 1996.

168. *Romer v. Evans* Oral Argument—October 10, 1995, Oyez, www.oyez.org/cases/1995/94-1039; Jeff Thomas, "The Final Round—High Court Appears to Be Uneasy with Amendment 2," *GT*, October 11, 1995.

169. Romer v. Evans, 517 US 620 (1996) at 620–36.

170. Romer v. Evans, 517 US 620 (1996) at 637–53; Linda Greenhouse, "Colorado Law Void," *NYT*, May 21, 1996; Angela Dire, "This Colorado Cannot Do," *GT*, May 21, 1996.

171. Klarman, *From the Closet to the Altar*, 48–74.

172. Gary Bauer, "The Dangers of Same-Sex Marriage," *St. Louis Post-Dispatch*, September 9, 1996.

173. Equality Foundation v. City of Cincinnati, 54 F.3d 261 (6th Cir. 1995).

174. "A Message to the People of Colorado Springs," *GT*, May 21, 1996.

175. "Amendment 2 Falls, Its Concerns Unresolved," *GT*, May 21, 1996.

Chapter Four: Upward, Christian Soldiers

1. Foursquare Gospel Church, "Declaration of Faith," Foursquare.org, accessed February 22, 2024, www.foursquare.org/about/beliefs/.

2. Eric Schmitt with Michael Moss, "Air Force Academy Investigated 54 Sexual Assaults in 10 Years," *NYT*, March 7, 2003.

3. Kristen J. Leslie and MeLinda Morton, memorandum for Michael Whittington, "Subject: After Action Report: BCT II Chaplain Practicum Training," July 30, 2004, included as an appendix to *Report of the Headquarters Review Group*.

4. Pam Zubeck, "Year-Old Report Warned of Evangelical Tone at AFA," *Gazette*, April 20, 2005; Weinstein and Seay, *With God on Our Side*, 84. The newspaper had dropped "Telegraph" from its name in 1997.

5. Loveland's *American Evangelicals and the U.S. Military* remains the most comprehensive work on the subject. For recent works in this field, see Stahl, *Enlisting Faith*; Sutton, *Double Crossed*; and Graziano, *Errand into the Wilderness of Mirrors*. My thinking on the problem of disestablishment is indebted to Sullivan, *Prison Religion*.

6. Wuthnow, *Restructuring of American Religion*, 35–35; Zeller, "American Postwar 'Big Religion.'"

7. Kruse, *One Nation under God*, 67–126.

8. Loveland, *American Evangelicals and the U.S. Military*, 56–59; Herzog, *Spiritual-Industrial Complex*, 109–34.

9. Holt, Cannon, and Allen, *History, 27 July 1954–12 June 1956*, vol. 2, 1063–64.
10. Holt, Cannon, and Allen, *History, 27 July 1954–12 June 1956*, vol. 2, 1082–85.
11. Holt, Cannon, and Allen, *History, 27 July 1954–12 June 1956*, vol. 2, 1071–72.
12. Holt, Cannon, Cohen, and Dixon, *History, 13 June 1956–9 July 1957*, vol. 1, 497.
13. Schultz, *Tri-Faith America*; Gaston, *Imagining Judeo-Christian America*.
14. Holt, Cannon, and Allen, *History, 27 July 1954–12 June 1956*, vol. 2, 1066–68.
15. Holt, Cannon, and Wiley, *History, 10 June 1957–11 June 1958*, vol. 2, 783–84.
16. "Louis Skidmore, Architect, Dies," *NYT*, September 29, 1962. On the significance of the Air Force Academy to the history of architecture, see Nauman, *On the Wings of Modernism*.
17. Oral history with Walter Netsch, in *United States Air Force Academy 1954–2004*; "Models for Air Force Academy Shown at Colorado Site," *NYT*, May 15, 1955.
18. "With Steeple," *Time*, July 18, 1955.
19. "Radical Design Dropped for Air Academy Chapel," *NYT*, July 4, 1955.
20. *Congressional Record* 103 (1957): 13769–70, 13789–90, 13926–28.
21. "Air Force Gothic," *Time*, August 19, 1957.
22. Holt, Cannon, and Allen, *History, 27 July 1954–12 June 1956*, vol. 2, 1076; Hutchison, *Religious Pluralism in America*, 209–13.
23. Holt, Cannon, and Allen, *History, 27 July 1954–12 June 1956*, vol. 2, 1077–78.
24. "Address by Eugene Zuckert"; "Address by Robert P. Taylor"; Bill Olcheski, "Chiefs See Cadet Chapel Dedication," *Air Force Times*, October 2, 1963.
25. E. Miller, *Wild Blue U.*, 104.
26. "Mass cult" referred to middlebrow, middle-class culture and was almost always used in a derogatory sense. See Macdonald, "Theory of Mass Culture."
27. Allan Temko, "The Air Academy Chapel—A Critical Appraisal," *Architectural Forum*, December 1962, 75–79.
28. "Air Force Academy Chapel," *Architectural Record*, December 1962, 86.
29. Holt, Cannon, and Allen, *History, 27 July 1954–12 June 1956*, vol. 2, 1068.
30. Holt, Cannon, and Allen, *History, 27 July 1954–12 June 1956*, vol. 2, 1069.
31. Holt, Cannon, and Wiley, *History, 10 June 1957–11 June 1958*, vol. 2, 783–84.
32. Holt, Cannon, and Wiley, *History, 12 June 1958–30 June 1959*, vol. 3, 756.
33. Holt, Cannon, and Wiley, *History, 1 July 1959–30 June 1960*, vol. 1, 648.
34. Cannon and Wiley, *History, 1 July 1963–30 June 1964*, vol. 3, 293.
35. Quoted in John Babigan, "Compulsory Chapel at West Point and Annapolis: A Report to the Fund for the Republic," June 9, 1958, box 802, folder 9, ACLU.
36. Everett Post to John Pemberton, September 16, 1963, box 808, folder 2, ACLU.
37. George Foster, "Chapel Case Cause for Concern," *Air Force Times*, December 6, 1972.
38. Cannon and Wiley, *History, 1 July 1963–30 June 1964*, vol. 3, 293–94.
39. "On Marching to Church," *Washington Post*, May 17, 1964.
40. Quoted in "On Marching to Church."
41. "Duty to Pray?," *Newsweek*, February 24, 1964.
42. Stahl, *Enlisting Faith*, esp. 1–14.
43. "Editorial: Compulsory Chapel Attendance," *The Chaplain*, August 1964, box 809, folder 20, ACLU.

44. Memo from Roland W. Faulk to Paul Nitze, n.d., box 815, folder 7, ACLU.

45. "Protest Mandatory Chapel," *Christian Century*, April 1, 1964, 421.

46. William Paterson, "On Compulsory Chapel," *Christian Century*, September 23, 1964.

47. Beaman, *Transition of Religion to Culture*.

48. Harold D. Shoemaker, memo to the superintendent, in Cannon and Fellerman, document CHAP 5, *History, 1 July 1966–30 June 1967*, vol. 7.

49. Thomas S. Moorman, letter to Mrs. Doyle C. Ruff, December 22, 1966, in Cannon and Fellerman, *History, 1 July 1966–30 June 1967*, vol. 7.

50. Patrick Murphy Malin to James H. Douglas, August 5, 1959, and Terence P. Finnegan to Malin, August 18, 1959, both in box 803, folder 12, ACLU.

51. Fellerman, *History, 1 July 1970–30 June 1971*, vol. 1, 228–29.

52. Fellerman, *History, 1 July 1970–30 June 1971*, vol. 1, 228.

53. "Chapel Attendance Case" memo, document HC-5, in Fellerman, *History, 1 July 1970–30 June 1971*, vol. 7.

54. John P. MacKenzie, "US Asks High Court to Uphold Mandatory Chapel at Academies," *Washington Post*, October 31, 1972.

55. Anderson v. Laird, 466 F.2d 283 (D.C. Cir., 1972).

56. Fellerman, *History, 1 July 1972–30 June 1973*, 228–29.

57. "Air Force Academy Chapel Program Doing Fine."

58. "Cadets Indicating 'No Preference' in Religion," *GT*, November 11, 1977.

59. The evidence that religious pluralism stimulates religious participation is mixed. See Chaves and Gorski, "Religious Pluralism and Religious Participation."

60. Summary of Cadet Chapel activities, in Cannon and Fellerman, *History, 1 July 1966–30 June 1967*, vol. 7.

61. Cannon and Fellerman, *History, 1 July 1967–30 June 1968*, vol. 1, 520.

62. Chace, "Protestant Cadet Chaplain Program Highlights 69–70."

63. Spoede, *More Than Conquerors*, 73, 125; Loveland, *American Evangelicals and the U.S. Military*, 204.

64. Hoyt S. Vandenberg, Air Force Cadet Regulation 265-1, May 20, 1975, in Fellerman, *History, 1 July 1975–30 June 1976*, vol. 4; "Cadet Chaplains Present SPIRE 1983."

65. "Academic Year Historical Report."

66. "Semi-Annual History Report of the Command Chaplain Function"; Hubbard, "Semiannual Chaplain Historical Report, 1 July 1991–31 December 1991."

67. Oliver, *To Touch the Face of God*, 106–7; T. Moore, "Semiannual Chaplain Historical Reports, 1 January–30 June 1990."

68. Muenger, *History, 1 July 1992–30 June 1993*, vol. 1, 216–19.

69. Muenger, *History, 1 July 1999–30 June 2000*, vol. 1, 133.

70. Merrell, "Semi-Annual History"; T. Moore, "Semiannual History for the Office of Cadet Chaplain Activities, 1 January–30 June 1989"; Schemo, *Skies to Conquer*, 162.

71. *Falcon News* article, document HC-10, n.d, in Fellerman, *History of the United States Air Force Academy, 1 July 1973–30 June 1974*, vol. 6.

72. Price, "Annual History for the Staff Chaplain's Office."

73. Muenger, *History, 1 June 1997–30 June 1998*, vol. 1, 149.

74. Muenger, *History, 1 July 1989–30 June 1990*, vol. 1, 2–5.

75. Muenger, *History, 1 July 1992–30 June 1993*, vol. 1, 8–9.

76. Bradley Hosmer, letter to Judge Advocate and Office of the Chaplain; Judge Advocate to Hosmer; and James E. Price, letter to Hosmer, all in Muenger, *History, 1 July 1993–30 June 1994*, vol. 8.

77. Hosmer, letter to Judge Advocate and Office of the Chaplain; Judge Advocate to Hosmer; Price, letter to Hosmer.

78. T. Moore, "Semiannual Chaplain Reports, 1 July–31 December 1990," 3.

79. Price, "Annual History for the Staff Chaplain's Office, 1 July 1993–30 June 1994."

80. Caley, "History of the Cadet Chaplain Activities," 8.

81. Cote, "Chaplain Service (HC) Supplemental Plan," 2.

82. "Wise Men Still Seek Him," *Falcon Flyer*, December 3, 1992.

83. Douglas S. Looney, "Sky Kings: Where Falcons Dare," *NYT*, November 18, 1995.

84. Meri-Jo Borzilleri, "Spirituality Part of AFA Life," *Gazette*, June 20, 2005; DeBerry and Schaller, *For God and Country*, 24.

85. Borzilleri, "Spirituality Part of AFA Life"; Todd Jacobson, "Falcons Voted on Controversial Sign," *Gazette*, November 21, 2004.

86. David Cote, letter to William J. Dendinger, October 20, 1997, in Muenger, *History, 1 July 1997–30 June 1998*, vol. 6.

87. SPIRE numbers from Cadet Chapel Historical Report (n.d.), in Muenger, *History, 1 July 2001–30 June 2002*, vol. 7. Numbers on the entire student body from "Class Histories," *United States Air Force Academy*, accessed May 5, 2021, www.usafa.org/Heritage/Class_History.

88. Eric Schmidt, "Air Force Academy Zooms In on Sex Cases," *NYT*, May 1, 1994.

89. Michael Janofsky, "Air Force Begins an Inquiry of Ex-Cadets' Rape Cases," *NYT*, February 20, 2003.

90. Muenger, *History, 1 July 2002–30 June 2003*, 6–7.

91. Americans United for Separation of Church and State, "Report."

92. Americans United for Separation of Church and State, "Report," 6.

93. *Report of the Panel to Review Sexual Misconduct Allegations*.

94. Williamson, "Assessment Report," 4.

95. Department of the Air Force, "Staff Assistance Visit," 3.

96. Americans United for Separation of Church and State, "Report," 1.

97. Williamson, "Assessment Report."

98. *Report of the Headquarters Review Group*, 25, 31, 24.

99. S. Miller, *Age of Evangelicalism*, 135–44. See also Ribuffo, "George W. Bush."

100. "House Tempers Erupt over Religion at Academy," *Gazette*, June 21, 2005.

101. *Congressional Record*, June 20, 2005, H4759–H4767.

102. "House Tempers Erupt over Religion at Academy."

103. "Religious Climate at the U.S. Air Force Academy," 5, 19.

104. "Cadet Leader for Air Force Is Denied Promotion," *NYT*, August 3, 2005.

105. Schemo, *Skies to Conquer*, 161–62.

106. Patrick K. Gamble, "Assessment of Religious Climate at USAFA: Senior Leader Walk Around of USAFA," April 15, 2011, box 41, folder 8, Vertical File, Clark Special Collections, United States Air Force Academy, Colorado Springs.

Chapter Five: The Invisible War

1. "Ted Haggard," *Time*, February 7, 2005, http://content.time.com/time/specials/packages/article/0,28804,1993235_1993243_1993280,00.html.

2. There is no scholarly biography of Wagner, but aspects of his work are discussed in Berry, *New Apostolic Reformation*; Weaver, *New Apostolic Reformation*; Curtis, *Myth of Colorblind Christians*; and Rachel Tabachnick, "The Christian Right, Reborn," *Political Research Associates*, March 22, 2013, https://politicalresearch.org/2013/03/22/spiritual-warriors-with-an-antigay-mission.

3. Dayton, "'Search for the Historical Evangelicalism.'"

4. For an example of a "cessationist" argument by a major Protestant theologian, see Warfield, *Counterfeit Miracles*.

5. Bebbington, *Evangelicalism in Modern Britain*, 151–80; Wacker, *Heaven Below*; R. Stephens, *Fire Spreads*.

6. Bebbington, *Evangelicalism in Modern Britain*, 229–48; Reynolds, "Robert Walker's *Christian Life* Magazine"; Frank Farrell, "Outburst of Tongues: The New Penetration," *CT*, September 13, 1963, 3–7.

7. Hayward, "Lewis, Jessie Elizabeth Penn-"; Penn-Lewis with Roberts, *War on the Saints*.

8. L. Eskridge, "Barnhouse, Donald Grey"; Russell, "Donald Grey Barnhouse"; Barnhouse, *Invisible War*.

9. C. Lewis, *Screwtape Letters*, ix.

10. Hedges, "Wagner, Charles Peter."

11. Marsden, *Reforming Fundamentalism*, 239–42.

12. Luhrmann, *When God Talks Back*, 29–34.

13. Marsden, *Reforming Fundamentalism*, 294; Wacker, "Wimber and Wonders."

14. C. Peter Wagner, "Where the Action Is—That's Where the Growth Is Too," *Ministries Today*, May/June 1987.

15. C. Peter Wagner, "Fighting Principalities and Powers," *Ministries Today*, July/August 1990.

16. Rene Holvast argues that spiritual warfare is an evangelical phenomenon, rather than a Pentecostal one, in *Spiritual Mapping*.

17. On Lausanne's significance, see McAlister, *Kingdom of God Has No Borders*, 85–102.

18. C. Peter Wagner to Glenn Sheppard and Vonette Bright, September 22, 1988, and Sheppard to Wagner, September 27, 1998, both in box 212, folder 7, Robert Birch Papers, Evangelism and Missions Archives, Wheaton College, Wheaton, IL.

19. C. Peter Wagner to Leighton Ford, October 12, 1988, box 212, folder 7, Robert Birch Papers.

20. Wagner, *Warfare Prayer*, 39–43. Bright had a complex relationship with Pentecostalism. He endorsed some gifts of the spirit in the 1950s and 1960s but then changed his opinion and forbade Campus Crusade personnel from speaking in tongues. In the 1980s he changed course again and permitted glossolalia. Turner, *Bill Brights and Campus Crusade for Christ*, 86–92, 185–87.

21. Wagner, *Warfare Prayer*, 45. On World Vision, see King, *God's Internationalists*.

22. Silliman, *Reading Evangelicals*, 79–104.

23. Dan O'Neil, "The Supernatural World of Frank Peretti," *Charisma and Christian Life*, May 1989, 48–52.

24. On Grant and Smith, see Howard and Streck, *Apostles of Rock*, 75–78, 104–5.

25. Peretti, *This Present Darkness*, 11.

26. Peretti, *Piercing the Darkness*, 9.

27. Peretti, *Piercing the Darkness*, 71.

28. Davis, "Some Themes of Counter-Subversion"; Rogin, *Ronald Reagan*.

29. Peretti, *Piercing the Darkness*, 303–4.

30. Silliman, *Reading Evangelicals*, 68.

31. Barnhouse, *Invisible War*, 132. The "Prince of Persia" is a reference to Daniel 10:13, a favorite verse of spiritual warriors, in which an angelic messenger reports being hindered by "the prince of the kingdom of Persia" (NKJV).

32. Hardy and Roberts, "Youth with a Mission."

33. "Re-Drawing the Religious Publishing Map," *Publishers Weekly*, August 10, 1992.

34. Dawson, *Taking Our Cities for God*, 34.

35. Spiritual warfare took a somewhat different form outside the United States. See, for instance, Adelakun, *Powerful Devices*.

36. Wagner, *Warfare Prayer*, 80. Melani McAlister calls this assumption "enchanted internationalism" in *Kingdom of God Has No Borders*, 9–10.

37. Wagner, *Warfare Prayer*, 16.

38. Wagner, *Breaking Strongholds*, 70, 62–64.

39. Wagner, *Warfare Prayer*, 33–34.

40. Wagner, *Warfare Prayer*, 58, 115.

41. Wagner, *Territorial Spirits*, 4.

42. Wagner, *Territorial Spirits*, 7.

43. George Otis, "Spiritual Mapping," in Haggard and Hayford, *Loving Your City*.

44. Otis, *Last of the Giants*, 249.

45. Sheets, *Intercessory Prayer*, 23. On Sheets, see Tim Dickinson, "Meet the Apostle of Right-Wing Christian Nationalism," *Rolling Stone* (blog), September 1, 2022, www.rollingstone.com/politics/politics-news/new-apostolic-reformation-mtg-mastriano-dutch-sheets-1234584952/.

46. Jacobs, *Possessing the Gates of the Enemy*, 112.

47. Jacobs, *Possessing the Gates of the Enemy*, 159, 166, 173.

48. Wagner, *Warfare Prayer*, 137.

49. Jacobs, *Possessing the Gates of the Enemy*, 119.

50. Wagner, *Warfare Prayer*, 65.

51. Jacobs, *Voice of God*, 141–43.

52. Curtis, *The Myth of Colorblind Christians*, 78–108.

53. Wagner, *Warfare Prayer*, 22.

54. See, for instance, Wacker, "Wimber and Wonders."

55. Clinton E. Arnold, "Giving the Devil His Due," *CT*, August 20, 1990, 16–19.

56. Michael G. Maudlin, "Holy Smoke! The Darkness Is Back," *CT*, December 1989, 58–59. See also Corwin, "This Present Nervousness."

57. Vince Passaro, "Dragon Fiction," *Harper's*, September 1996, 64–71; Alissa Rubin, "Power Angels," *New Republic*, November 20, 1995, 20–21; Robert Orsi, "Onward Christian Soldiers: Blood and Guts in Sunday School," *Village Voice Literary Supplement*, July–August 1990, 15–16.

58. Wagner, *Wrestling with Dark Angels*, 6.

59. "National Conference on Prayer & Spiritual Warfare," box 26, folder 2, PW.

60. C. Peter Wagner, "A City's Season," *Ministries Today*, May/June 1993.

61. Steve Rabey, "Churchmen Gather for Prayer, Fasting," *GT*, September 12, 1992; "North American Conferences on Strategic-Level Prayer," *GT*, January 16, 1993.

62. Wagner, "City's Season."

63. Eric Gorski, "Reality Stems from Pastor's Vision," *Gazette*, December 22, 2002; Tim Stafford, "Good Morning, Evangelicals!," *CT*, November 2005.

64. "Church Briefs," *GT*, February 3, 1979; John Fetler, "At 2 Years Old, New Life Church Is Growing and Giving," *GT*, December 6, 1986.

65. "Troy Alcorn," *Gazette*, April 8, 2018, https://obits.gazette.com/obituaries/gazette/obituary.aspx?n=troy-alcorn&pid=188683177; Gorski, "Reality Stems from Pastor's Vision."

66. "Praise and Worship," New Life folder, Hall-Hoag Collection of Dissenting and Extremist Printed Propaganda, Special Collections, Brown University, Providence, RI.

67. Fetler, "At 2 Years Old, New Life Church Is Growing and Giving."

68. Steve Rabey, "Get Down with Jesus," *GT*, January 4, 1992; Fetler, "At 2 Years Old, New Life Church Is Growing and Giving"; Steve Rabey, "Born-Again Buildings," *GT*, October 5, 1991.

69. Haggard, *Primary Purpose*, 172.

70. Haggard, *Dog Training*, viii.

71. "New Life at Praise Mountain: Liberation through Prayer and Fasting," *GT*, February 22, 1987.

72. J. Lee Grady, "Piercing the Darkness," *Charisma*, October 1993, 20–27.

73. Haggard, *Primary Purpose*, 32.

74. Grady, "Piercing the Darkness."

75. Bob Beckett, "Practical Efforts toward Community Deliverance," and Victor Lorenzo, "Evangelizing a City Committed to Darkness," both in Wagner, *Breaking Strongholds in Your City*.

76. Wilson, "Cho, David (Paul) Yonggi"; Cox, *Fire from Heaven*, 221–26.

77. Comiskey, "Rev. Cho's Cell Groups."

78. New Life Church and Small Group Directory, Spring 1999, New Life folder, Hall-Hoag Collection of Dissenting and Extremist Printed Propaganda.

79. Haggard, *Dog Training*, 106. Since at least the 1970s, evangelicals have pointed to statistics on church growth to demonstrate their superiority to liberal Protestant churches. See S. Miller, *Age of Evangelicalism*, 14–16.

80. Fetler, "At 2 Years Old, New Life Church Is Growing and Giving."

81. Heyrman, *American Apostles*.

82. Otis, *Last of the Giants*.

83. For instance, Otis attended a conference on spiritual warfare hosted by New Life. "North American Conference on Strategic-Level Prayer," *GT*, January 16, 1993.

84. "Religious Leaders Debate Role of Church in Politics," *GT*, June 27, 1993.

85. Gorski, "Reality Stems from Pastor's Vision."

86. Stafford, "Good Morning, Evangelicals!"

87. Grady, "Piercing the Darkness."

88. Jaan Heinmets, "The Net—Serving Together," in Haggard and Hayford, *Loving Your City into the Kingdom*; Gillian Gaynair, "Rally Organized to Show Community Has a Prayer," *GT*, March 9, 1996; Steve Rabey, "Ministry to Canvass Springs," *GT*, September 30, 1993.

89. Steve Rabey, "Amen to Equality," *GT*, June 6, 1992; Ted Haggard, "A Prayer for All Races," *GT*, June 6, 1992.

90. "A Covenant of Mutual Respect," *GT*, April 22, 1993.

91. Rabey, "Churchmen Gather for Prayer, Fasting."

92. "Up & Comers: Fifty Evangelical Leaders 40 and Under," *CT*, November 11, 1996.

93. "About Pastor Ted," New Life folder, Hall-Hoag Collection of Dissenting and Extremist Printed Propaganda.

94. Ted Haggard, "Pastor Didn't Preach Politics," *GT*, March 10, 1993.

95. Dave Curtin, "Homosexuals Seek Anti-Bias Ordinance," *GT*, January 28, 1991; Dave Curtin, "All-Out Battle Waged over Gay Rights," *GT*, February 17, 1991; Anne Windishar, "Gay Rights Pit Pastor against Pastor," *GT*, June 22, 1992.

96. Linda Terhune, "A Taxing Time for the Arts," *GT*, October 14, 1990. On the broader conflict over the National Endowment for the Arts, see Hartman, *War for the Soul of America*, 191–98.

97. Tom Morton, "Abortion Foes Taught Protest Tactics," *GT*, August 27, 1989.

98. Ribuffo, "George W. Bush."

99. Haggard, *Dog Training*, 73.

100. Stafford, "Good Morning, Evangelicals!"

101. World Prayer Center brochure, box 29, folder 5, PW.

102. "World Prayer Center, Inc.," Colorado Springs Secretary of State, May 18, 1992, www.sos.state.co.us/biz/ViewImage.do?fileId=19921050431&masterFileId=19871610546.

103. Peretti, *Piercing the Darkness*, 30.

104. Michele Ames, "Prayer Central," *GT*, May 17, 1998.

105. World Prayer Center brochure, 181, box 29, folder 5, PW.

106. Susan Warmbrunn, "Center Will Link World in Prayer," *Gazette*, September 20, 1998.

107. McAlister, *Kingdom of God Has No Borders*, 144–58.

108. C. Peter Wagner, "The Gateway Cities," *Ministries Today*, January/February 1995; C. Peter Wagner, "Praying through the Window," *Ministries Today*, July/August 1993.

109. Warmbrunn, "Center Will Link World in Prayer."

110. World Prayer Center brochure, box 29, folder 5, PW.

111. Fuller Theological Seminary brochure, box 8, folder 7, PW.

112. Memo from Edgar J. Elliston to SWM Extension Committee, August 24, 1994, box 8, folder 7, PW.

113. Memo from C. Peter Wagner to Dudley Woodberry, "Letter of Understanding for Colorado Springs Assignment," February 1, 1996, box 8, folder 7, PW.

114. C. Peter Wagner to Russ Spittler et al., "Subject: Market Survey in Colorado Springs," November 26, 1996, box 8, folder 7, PW.

115. Eastman, *Purple Pig*, 25–26.

116. "Eastman to Explain 'Prayer Corps,'" *Greeley (CO) Tribune*, January 3, 1975.

117. "Our History," Every Home for Christ, accessed March 11, 2025, https://everyhome.org/what-we-do/history/; Tom Morton, "Christian Group Picks City," *GT*, August 28, 1990.

118. Steve Rabey, "God Has Plans for Springs, Executive Says," *GT*, March 4, 1992.

119. Dick Eastman, "Praying through the 10/40 Window," *Charisma*, October 1993, 28–37; Eastman, *Jericho Hour*.

120. Kamon Simpson, "Ministry Finally Has New Home in Jericho," *Gazette*, July 26, 2003; Mark Barna, "Christian Group Building Replica of 'Wailing Wall,'" *Gazette*, September 23, 2008.

121. Jacobs, *Voice of God*, 37.

122. Steve Rabey, "Duking It Out with the Devil," *GT*, September 25, 1993.

123. Jacobs and Sheets, *Deliver Us from Evil*, 17–18.

124. "President Has Rosy Future as TV Pitchman," *Gazette*, March 20, 2004.

125. Paul Asay, "Pulpit Power," *Gazette*, August 29, 2004.

126. D. Williams, *God's Own Party*, 256–63.

127. Kruse, "Compassionate Conservatism." As Kruse notes, claims about the importance of "values voters" were overblown. This category was more an artifact of exit poll methodology than a reflection of political reality.

128. Jeff Sharlet, "Inside America's Most Powerful Megachurch," *Harper's*, May 2005.

129. Paul Asay, "The Big House," *Gazette*, February 21, 2004.

130. Sharlet, "Inside America's Most Powerful Megachurch"; Paul Asay, "Church Breathes New Life into Service," *Gazette*, January 3, 2005.

131. Curtin, "All-Out Battle Waged over Gay Rights."

132. "Gay-Marriage Ban Sought," *Gazette*, February 2, 2006.

133. Jones with Gallegos, *I Had to Say Something*, 181.

134. Letter from Ted Haggard, reprinted in the *Gazette*, November 6, 2006.

135. Sarah Pulliam, "Haggard Reprimanded," *CT*, November 2007; "Passages," *CT*, April 2008, 14; "Man Says He Saw Haggard Perform Sex Act," *Gazette*, January 28, 2009.

136. Carol McGraw, "Pastor Could Get a Chance to Heal New Life," *Gazette*, August 1, 2007; Carol McGraw, "Boyd Gets New Life Job with 95% of Vote," *Gazette*, August 28, 2007.

137. Rene Holvast, *Spiritual Mapping*, 158.

Conclusion: The Sanctuary

1. Steve Rabey, "Andrew Wommack Urges Christians to 'Take Over' Woodland Park, Teller County," *Gazette*, June 1, 2021.

2. Debbie Kelley, "Not All Happy with Charis Project," *Gazette*, July 10, 2015.

3. "Colorado AG Threatens to Stop Bible Conference," *Charisma News,* July 7, 2020, https://charismanews.com/news/us/colorado-ag-threatens-to-stop-bible-conference/; "Colorado Drops Suit against Andrew Wommack Ministries," *Charisma News,* December 21, 2020, https://charismanews.com/news/us/colorado-drops-suit-against-andrew-wommack-ministries/; "Colorado Governor Declares Churches Essential," *Charisma,* December 10, 2020, https://mycharisma.com/culture/politics/colorado-governor-declares-churches-essential/.

4. Polis got his start in politics by opposing Amendment 2. William Schultz, "How Colorado Did a 180 on Gay Rights," *Washington Post,* December 17, 2018, www.washingtonpost.com/outlook/2018/12/17/how-colorado-did-gay-rights/.

5. H. Stephens, *Family Matters,* 194–96; Sarah Pulliam Bailey, "Refocusing on the Family," *CT,* July 2011; Noel Black and Jake Brownell, "Wish We Were Here, Episode 10: After the Evangelical Vatican," Colorado Public Radio, December 4, 2015, www.cpr.org/podcast-episode/wish-we-were-here-episode-10-after-the-evangelical-vatica; Daly and Batura, *ReFocus.*

6. Stewart, *Power Worshipers*; Posner, *Unholy*; Weaver, *New Apostolic Reformation*; Berry, *New Apostolic Reformation*; Gagné, *American Evangelicals for Trump*; Rachel Tabachnick, "The Christian Right, Reborn," *Political Research Associates,* March 22, 2013, https://politicalresearch.org/2013/03/22/spiritual-warriors-with-an-antigay-mission; Kathryn Joyce, "How Christian Nationalism Drove the Insurrection: A Religious History of Jan. 6," *Salon,* January 6, 2022, www.salon.com/2022/01/06/how-christian-nationalism-drove-the-insurrection-a-religious-history-of-jan-6/.

7. "Religion Notes," *GT,* June 19, 1993; Dennis Huspeni, "Cassettes Carry Wommack Ministry's Message," *GT,* October 19, 1996.

8. "Broadcast Schedule," Andrew Wommack Ministries, accessed March 11, 2025, www.awmi.net/video/tv-broadcast-schedules/usa-tv/; "The Power of Partnership Never Fails," Andrew Wommack Ministries, May 12, 2021, www.awmi.net/video/featured/?episode=the-power-of-partnership-never-fails.

9. Andrew Wommack, "Declaration of Dependence upon God and His Holy Bible," accessed March 11, 2025, https://s3.amazonaws.com/truthandliberty/files/Declaration-of-Dependence-with-background.pdf; "Where Do We Go from Here? Lessons from the 2020 Elections—Episode I," Andrew Wommack Ministries, November 13, 2020, www.awmi.net/video/featured/?episode=where-do-we-go-from-here-lessons-from-the-2020-elections-episode-1.

10. Steve Rabey, "Truth & Liberty Coalition Expands Culture War to 30 Colorado School Boards," *Ministry Watch,* November 6, 2023, https://ministrywatch.com/truth-liberty-coalition-expands-culture-war-to-30-colorado-school-boards/. On Copeland's broader significance, see Bowler, *Blessed,* 78–82.

11. L. Eskridge, *"Money Matters."*

12. Dowland, *Family Values,* 87–88.

13. Grant Wacker, in his biography of Billy Graham, astutely notes that Graham wanted both to win arguments *and* to avoid confrontation. Wacker, *America's Pastor,* 216. Graham could pursue these seemingly contradictory goals because he assumed American culture was essentially Christian and thus believed that his audience simply needed to be called back to a faith that they already held.

14. Kasselstrand, Zuckerman, and Cragun, *Beyond Doubt*; Bruce, *Secularization*.

15. Hollinger, "Religious Tide's Withdrawing Roar"; Voas and Chaves, "Is the United States a Counterexample to the Secularization Thesis?"

16. D. Williams, *God's Own Party*; Young, *We Gather Together*; Du Mez, *Jesus and John Wayne*; Dochuk, *From Bible Belt to Sunbelt*.

Bibliography

Primary Sources

ARCHIVES AND MANUSCRIPT COLLECTIONS

ARKANSAS
   Fayetteville
      University of Arkansas Special Collections
         Billy James Hargis Papers, MC1412
CALIFORNIA
   Pasadena
      Special Collections, Fuller Theological Seminary
         C. Peter Wagner Collection, Collection 181
COLORADO
   Colorado Springs
      Christian and Missionary Alliance Archives
         Relocation, RG901
      Clark Special Collections, United States Air Force Academy
         Command Histories
         Vertical File
      Navigators Archives
         "Dear Gang" Letters
         Glen Eyrie Purchase Materials, MS005
         Navigators Correspondence, MS007

Pikes Peak Library District Special Collections
    Banning-Lewis Ranch Records, MSS0098
    Citizens Project Papers, MSS0307
    Clipping Folders
    Colorado Springs History Project (Oral Histories)
    Garden of the Gods Sunrise Service Collection, MSS0060
    H. Chase Stone Papers, MSS0051
    Marshall Sprague Papers, MSS0050
    Regional History Collection
Special Collections and Archives, Colorado College
    El Paso County Newspaper Clippings in Scrapbooks—World War II
    Information Files
Starsmore Center for Local History, Colorado Springs Pioneer Museum
    Pikes Peak Justice and Peace Commission Records
United States Olympic Committee Archives
    Vertical File
Young Life Archives
    Billy Graham Archives Collection, MS2018-27
    Board Minutes 1950–1955
    Bulletins to the Board of Directors
    Denny Rydberg Presidential Collection, RG205
    Young Life Annual Reports
    Young Life staff bulletins

Denver

Colorado State Archives
    HB1059 Legislative History
    Records of *General Conference of the Church of God—7th Day v. Carper*
    Records of *Maurer v. Young Life*
    Records of *West-Brandt Foundation, Inc. v. Carper*
    Records of *Young Life v. Commissioners of Chaffee County*
    SB237 Legislative History
Denver Public Library, Western History Collection
    Equality Colorado Records, WH1787
    Evans v. Romer Collection, WH2102
Stephen H. Hart Research Center
    John Miller Collection, MSS01693
    Michael Booth Collection, MSS01691

ILLINOIS

Wheaton

Evangelism and Missions Archives, Wheaton College
    Herbert J. Taylor Papers, CN020
    National Association of Evangelicals Records, SC113
    Navigators Collection, CN007
    OC International Collection, CN222
    Robert Birch Papers, CN046

KANSAS
- Lawrence
  - Kenneth Spencer Research Library, University of Kansas
    - Ann Burlein Papers, MS43

MASSACHUSETTS
- Medford
  - Special Collections, Tufts University
    - Institute for First Amendment Studies Records, MS074

NEW JERSEY
- Princeton
  - Seeley G. Mudd Manuscript Library, Princeton University
    - American Civil Liberties Union Records

NEW YORK
- Ithaca
  - Human Sexuality Collection, Cornell University
    - GLAAD Records, MSS7679
    - National LGBTQ Task Force Records, MSS7301
- New York
  - Rare Book and Manuscript Library, Columbia University
    - Group Research Inc. Records

OREGON
- Eugene
  - University of Oregon Special Collections
    - Robert LeFevre Papers, Collection 202
- Portland
  - Oregon Historical Society
    - Charles F. Hinkle Collection, MSS2988-18
    - Gary Smith Collection, MSS2988-24
    - Hate-Free Oregon Records MSS2988-3

RHODE ISLAND
- Providence
  - Special Collections, Brown University
    - Hall-Hoag Collection of Dissenting and Extremist Printed Propaganda

PERIODICALS

The Advocate
Air Force Times
Architectural Forum
Architectural Record
Atlanta Constitution
Baltimore Sun
Businessweek
Chamber Magazine (Colorado Springs)
Charisma and Christian Life / Charisma
Charlotte Observer
Christian Century
Christianity Today
Cincinnati Enquirer
Cincinnati Post
Colorado Christian News
Colorado Springs Business Journal

Colorado Springs Independent
Colorado Springs Sun
Colorado Springs Weekly Gazette
Congressional Record
Denver Post
The Economist
Esquire
Falcon Flyer
First Things
Free Press (Colorado Springs)
Gazette Telegraph/Gazette
  (Colorado Springs)
Greeley (CO) Tribune
Harper's
Idaho Falls Post Register
King's Business
Los Angeles Times
Milwaukee Sentinel
Ministries Today
Missionary Review of the World
Mother Jones
The Nation
National Catholic Reporter
New Republic
News & Observer (Raleigh, NC)
Newsweek
New Yorker
New York Times
Oregonian (Portland)
Orlando Sentinel
Philadelphia Inquirer
Pomona (CA) Progress Bulletin
The Progressive
Publishers Weekly
Rocky Mountain News (Denver)
Springs Magazine
St. Louis Post-Dispatch
Time
U.S. News & World Report
Village Voice
Village Voice Literary Supplement
Wall Street Journal
Washington Post
Westword (Denver)

BOOKS AND OTHER PUBLISHED MATERIAL

"Academic Year Historical Report for the United States Air Force Academy Cadet/ Chaplains' Office." In *History of the United States Air Force Academy, 1 July 1996–30 June 1997*, vol. 7, edited by Elizabeth Muenger. Historical Division, 1998.

"Address by Eugene Zuckert." In *History of the United States Air Force Academy, 1 July 1963–30 June 1964*, vol. 3, edited by M. Hamlin Cannon and Elizabeth A. Wiley. Historical Division, 1965.

"Address by Robert P. Taylor." In *History of the United States Air Force Academy, 1 July 1963–30 June 1964*, vol. 3, edited by M. Hamlin Cannon and Elizabeth A. Wiley. Historical Division, 1965.

"Air Force Academy Chapel Program Doing Fine without Mandatory Attendance Program," August 21, 1974. In *History of the United States Air Force Academy, 1 July 1974–30 June 1975*, vol. 1, edited by Henry S. Fellerman. Historical Division, 1976.

Americans United for Separation of Church and State. *Report of Americans United for Separation of Church and State on Religious Coercion and Endorsement of Religion at the United States Air Force Academy*. Accessed April 5, 2018. www.christianfighterpilot .com/articles/files/aucomp.pdf.

Assessment of the Role of Key Groups in the Colorado Springs Economic Development Process. Fantus Company, 1988.

Barnhouse, Donald Grey. *The Invisible War*. Zondervan, 1965.

Bransford, Stephen. *Gay Politics vs. Colorado and America: The Inside Story of Amendment 2.* Sardis Press, 1994.

Bryan, Gerald B. *Psychic Dictatorship in America.* Truth Research Publications, 1940.

"The Cadet Chaplains Present SPIRE 1983." In *History of the United States Air Force Academy, 1 January 1983–31 December 1984*, edited by Elizabeth A. Muenger. Historical Division, 1985.

Cailliet, Emile. *Young Life.* Harper and Row, 1963.

Caley, Charles W., Jr. "History of the Cadet Chaplain Activities, 1 July 1995–30 June 1996." In *History of the United States Air Force Academy, 1 July 1995–30 June 1996*, vol. 6, edited by Elizabeth A. Muenger. Historical Division, 1997.

Cannon, M. Hamlin, and Henry S. Fellerman, eds. *History of the United States Air Force Academy, 1 July 1966–30 June 1967.* Historical Division, 1968.

Cannon, M. Hamlin, and Henry S. Fellerman, eds. *History of the United States Air Force Academy, 1 July 1967–30 June 1968.* Historical Division, 1968.

Cannon, M. Hamlin, and Elizabeth A. Wiley, eds. *History of the United States Air Force Academy, 1 July 1963–30 June 1964.* Historical Division, 1965.

Carpenter, Joel A., ed. *The Early Billy Graham: Sermon and Revival Accounts.* Garland, 1988.

Carpenter, Joel A., ed. *Missionary Innovation and Expansion.* Garland, 1988.

Carpenter, Joel A., ed. *The Youth for Christ Movement and Its Pioneers.* Garland, 1988.

Chace, Alston R. "Protestant Cadet Chaplain Program Highlights 69–70," May 22, 1970. In *History of the United States Air Force Academy, 1 July 1970–30 June 1971*, vol. 7, edited by Henry S. Fellerman. Historical Division, 1971.

Cote, David. "Chaplain Service (HC) Supplemental Plan to the Strategic Plan for Character Development at the Air Force Academy," January 21, 1997 (revised March 5, 1997). In *History of the United States Air Force Academy, 1 July 1998–30 June 1999*, vol. 7, edited by Elizabeth A. Muenger. Historical Division, 2000.

Crampon, L. J., Fred W. Ellinghaus, Donald F. Lawson, Ronald D. Lemon, and M. D. Miller. *An Economic Survey of the Pikes Peak Region.* The Bureau of Business Research, School of Business, University of Colorado Boulder, 1954.

Daly, Jim, and Paul Batura. *ReFocus: Living a Life That Reflects God's Heart.* Zondervan, 2012.

Dawson, John. *Taking Our Cities for God.* Creation House, 1989.

DeBerry, Fisher, and Bob Schaller. *For God and Country.* Cross Training, 2000.

Department of the Air Force. "Staff Assistance Visit to USAFA, 13–15 December 2004," March 25, 2005. Included as an appendix to the *Report of the Headquarters Review Group Concerning the Religious Climate at the U.S. Air Force Academy.* United States Air Force, 2005.

Dobson, James. *Dare to Discipline.* Tyndal House, 1970.

Dobson, James A., and Gary Bauer. *Children at Risk: Winning the Battle for the Hearts and Minds of Your Children.* Word Publishing, 1990.

Eastman, Dick. *The Jericho Hour.* Creation House, 1994.

Eastman, Dick. *The Purple Pig and Other Miracles: How Radical Young Intercessors Tapped into the Supernatural, Shook the World, and Inspired Today's Global Prayer Movements.* Charisma, 2011.

Fellerman, Henry S., ed. *History of the United States Air Force Academy, 1 July 1970–30 June 1971.* Historical Division, 1971.

Fellerman, Henry S., ed. *History of the United States Air Force Academy, 1 July 1972–30 June 1973.* Historical Division, 1974.

Fellerman, Henry S., ed. *History of the United States Air Force Academy, 1 July 1973–30 June 1974.* Historical Division, 1975.

Fellerman, Henry S., ed. *History of the United States Air Force Academy, 1 July 1975–30 June 1976.* Historical Division, 1976.

Fort Carson: A Tradition of Victory. Fort Carson Public Affairs and Information Office, 1972.

Haggard, Ted. *Dog Training, Fly Fishing, and Sharing Christ in the 21st Century: Empowering Church to Build Community through Shared Interests.* Thomas Nelson, 2002.

Haggard, Ted. *Primary Purpose: Making It Hard for People to Go to Hell from Your City.* Creation House, 1995.

Haggard, Ted, and Jack Hayford, eds. *Loving Your City into the Kingdom: City-Reaching Strategies for a 21st-Century Revival.* Regal Books, 1997.

Hand, W. Brevard. *American Education on Trial: Is Secular Humanism a Religion?* Center for Judicial Studies, 1987.

Henry, Carl F. H. *The Uneasy Conscience of Modern Fundamentalism.* William B. Eerdmans, 1947.

Holt, Edgar A., M. Hamlin Cannon, and Carlos R. Allen Jr., eds. *History of the United States Air Force Academy, 27 July 1954–12 June 1956.* Historical Division, 1957.

Holt, Edgar A., M. Hamlin Cannon, Victor H. Cohen, and Emory H. Dixon, eds. *History of the United States Air Force Academy, 13 June 1956–9 July 1957.* Historical Division, 1958.

Holt, Edgar A., M. Hamlin Cannon, and Elizabeth A. Wiley, eds. *History of the United States Air Force Academy, 10 June 1957–11 June 1958.* Historical Division, 1960.

Holt, Edgar A., M. Hamlin Cannon, and Elizabeth A. Wiley, eds. *History of the United States Air Force Academy, 12 June 1958–30 June 1959.* Historical Division, 1961.

Holt, Edgar A., M. Hamlin Cannon, and Elizabeth A. Wiley, eds. *History of the United States Air Force Academy, 1 July 1959–30 June 1960.* Historical Division, 1961.

Hubbard, Beryl T. "Semiannual Chaplain Historical Report, 1 July 1991—31 December 1991," June 8, 1992. In *History of the United States Air Force Academy, 1 July 1991–30 June 1992,* vol. 9, edited by Elizabeth A. Muenger. Historical Division, 1993.

Jacobs, Cindy. *Possessing the Gates of the Enemy: A Training Manual for Militant Intercession.* Chosen Books, 1991.

Jacobs, Cindy. *The Voice of God: How God Speaks Personally and Corporately to His Children Today.* Regal Books, 1995.

Jacobs, Cindy, and Dutch Sheets. *Deliver Us from Evil: Putting a Stop to the Occultic Forces Invading Your Home and Community.* Regal Books, 2001.

Jones, Mike, with Sam Gallegos. *I Had to Say Something: The Art of Ted Haggard's Fall.* Seven Stories Press, 2007.

Koop, C. Everett. *Koop: The Memoirs of America's Family Doctor.* Random House, 1991.

LeFevre, Robert. *The Nature of Man and His Government.* Laissez Faire Books, 2012. Google Books. Originally published in 1959.

Lewis, C. S. *The Screwtape Letters*. Macmillan, 1971. Originally published in 1942.

Macdonald, Dwight. "A Theory of Mass Culture." *Diogenes* 3 (1953): 1–17.

Merrell, Robert E. "Semi-Annual History for the Command Chaplain Function, 1 January 1988–30 June 1988," no date. In *History of the United States Air Force Academy, 1 July 1987–30 June 1988*, edited by Elizabeth A. Muenger. Historical Division, 1989.

Meyer, Natalie. "State of Colorado: Abstract of Votes Cast, 1992." Elections and Licensing Division, Office of the Secretary of State of Colorado, no date.

Miller, Ed Mack. *Wild Blue U*. Macmillan, 1972.

Moore, Thermon E. "Semiannual Chaplain Historical Reports, 1 January–30 June 1990," October 10, 1990. In *History of the United States Air Force Academy, 1 July 1989–30 June 1990*, vol. 6, edited by Elizabeth A. Muenger. Historical Division, 1991.

Moore, Thermon E. "Semiannual Chaplain Reports, 1 July–31 December 1990," no date. In *History of the United States Air Force Academy, 1 July 1990–30 June 1991*, edited by Elizabeth A. Muenger. Historical Division, 1992.

Moore, Thermon E. "Semiannual History for the Office of Cadet Chaplain Activities, 1 January–30 June 1989," no date. In *History of the United States Air Force Academy, 1 July 1988–30 June 1989*, edited by Elizabeth A. Muenger. Historical Division, 1990.

Muenger, Elizabeth A., ed. *History of the United States Air Force Academy, 1 July 1989–30 June 1990*. Historical Division, 1991.

Muenger, Elizabeth A., ed. *History of the United States Air Force Academy, 1 July 1992–30 June 1993*. Historical Division, 1994.

Muenger, Elizabeth A., ed. *History of the United States Air Force Academy, 1 July 1997–30 June 1998*. Historical Division, 1999.

Muenger, Elizabeth A., ed. *History of the United States Air Force Academy, 1 July 1999–30 June 2000*. Historical Division, 2001.

Muenger, Elizabeth A., ed. *History of the United States Air Force Command, 1 July 2002–30 June 2003*. Historical Division, 2004.

Noebel, David A. *Communism, Hypnotism and the Beatles*. Christian Crusade Publications, 1965.

Noebel, David A. *The Homosexual Revolution*. American Christian College Press, 1977.

Noebel, David A. *Slaughter of the Innocent*. American Christian College Press, 1973.

Noebel, David A. *Understanding the Times: The Story of the Biblical Christian, Marxist-Leninist, and Secular Humanist Worldviews*. Summit Press, 1991.

Noebel, David A., Wayne C. Lutton, and Paul Cameron. *AIDS: Acquired Immune Deficiency Syndrome, Special Report*. Summit Research Institute, 1986.

Olsen, Mark. *Refuge*. Cascade Press, 1996.

Otis, George, Jr. *The Last of the Giants: Lifting the Veil on Islam and the End Times*. Chosen Books, 1991.

Penabaz, Fernando. *Crusading Preacher from the West*. Christian Crusade, 1965.

Penn-Lewis, Jessie, with Evan Roberts. *War on the Saints*. The Overcomer Office, 1912.

Peretti, Frank. *Piercing the Darkness*. Crossway Books, 1989.

Peretti, Frank. *This Present Darkness*. Crossway Books, 1986.

Price, James E. "Annual History for the Staff Chaplain's Office, 1 July 1993–30 June 1994," no date. In *History of the United States Air Force Academy, 1 July 1993–30 June 1994*, vol. 8, edited by Elizabeth A. Muenger. Historical Division, 1995.

Rayburn, Jim. *The Diaries of Jim Rayburn.* Edited by Kit Sublett. Whitecaps Media, 2008.

Rayburn, Jim, III. *Dance, Children, Dance: The Story of Jim Rayburn, Founder of Young Life.* Tyndale House, 1984.

"The Religious Climate at the U.S. Air Force Academy: Hearings before the Military Personnel Subcommittee of the U.S. House Committee on Armed Services." 109th Congress, 2005.

Report of the Headquarters Review Group concerning the Religious Climate at the U.S. Air Force Academy. United States Air Force, 2005.

Report of the Panel to Review Sexual Misconduct Allegations at the U.S. Air Force Academy. September 22, 2003. Accessed February 5, 2013. www.defense.gov/news/Sep2003/d20030922usafareport.pdf (site discontinued).

Rueda, Enrique. *The Homosexual Network: Private Lives and Public Policy.* Devin Adair, 1982.

Rueda, Enrique, and Michael Schwartz. *Gays, AIDS, and You.* Devin-Adair, 1987.

"Semi-Annual History Report of the Command Chaplain Function, for the Period 1 January 1983 through 30 June 1983." In *History of the United States Air Force Academy, 1 January 1983–31 December 1984*, edited by Elizabeth A. Muenger. Historical Division, 1985.

Sheets, Dutch. *Intercessory Prayer.* Regal Books, 1996.

Shoemaker, Harold D. Memo to the superintendent, November 28, 1966. In *History of the United States Air Force Academy, 1 July 1966–30 June 1967*, vol. 7, edited by M. Hamlin Cannon and Henry S. Fellerman. Historical Division, 1968.

Skinner, Betty Lee. *Daws: The Story of Dawson Trotman, Founder of the Navigators.* Zondervan, 1977.

United States Air Force Academy 1954–2004: 50th Anniversary Oral History. Friends of the Air Force Academy, 2004.

Wagner, C. Peter, ed. *Breaking Strongholds in Your City: How to Use Spiritual Mapping to Make Your Prayers More Strategic, Effective, and Targeted.* Regal Books, 1993.

Wagner, C. Peter, ed. *Territorial Spirits: Insights on Strategic-Level Spiritual Warfare from Nineteen Christian Leaders.* Sovereign World, 1991.

Wagner, C. Peter. *Warfare Prayer: How to Seek God's Power and Protection in the Battle to Build His Kingdom.* Regal Books, 1992.

Wagner, C. Peter, ed. *Wrestling with Dark Angels: Toward a Deeper Understanding of the Supernatural Forces in Spiritual Warfare.* Regal Books, 1990.

Warfield, B. B. *Counterfeit Miracles.* Scribner, 1918.

Weinstein, Michael L., and Davin Seay. *With God on Our Side: One Man's War against an Evangelical Coup in America's Military.* Thomas Dunne Books, 2006.

Williamson, Jack D. "National Conference on Ministry to the Armed Forces Team Assessment Report on Religious Climate at the United States Air Force Academy," June 16, 2005. Included as an appendix to the "Report of the Headquarters Review Group concerning the Religious Climate at the U.S. Air Force Academy," United States Air Force, 2005.

Willmer, Wesley Kenneth. *The Prospering Parachurch: Enlarging the Boundaries of God's Kingdom.* Jossey-Bass, 1998.

Wright, J. Elwin. *The Old Fashioned Revival Hour and the Broadcasters.* Garland, 1988.

INTERVIEWS BY THE AUTHOR

Alyn, Jody. Colorado Springs, CO. June 4, 2015.
Cathey, Carolyn. Colorado Springs, CO (by phone). July 1, 2015
Dodd, Patton. San Antonio, TX (by Zoom). February 2, 2024.
Finley, Dave, and Judy Finley. Colorado Springs, CO. August 15, 2013.
Hazlehurst, John. Colorado Springs, CO (by phone). October 14, 2013.
Krohnfeldt, Les. Colorado Springs, CO. October 14, 2013.
Link, Dan. Colorado Springs, CO (by phone). June 27, 2019.
Loeffler, Bruce. Colorado Springs, CO. June 9, 2015.
McCaffrey, Ray. Colorado Springs, CO (by phone). March 14, 2018.
Miller, John. Colorado Springs, CO (by phone). August 26, 2016.
Paauw, Glenn. Colorado Springs, CO (by phone). February 5, 2018.
Rost, Nori. Colorado Springs, CO. June 9, 2015.
Schriner, Nolan. Colorado Springs, CO. August 19, 2013.
Scott, Robert "Rocky." Colorado Springs, CO (by phone). September 12, 2019.
Shaver, Mike. Colorado Springs, CO (by phone). August 29, 2019.
Skorman, Richard. Colorado Springs, CO. June 9, 2015.
Stoller-Lee, Will. Colorado Springs, CO. June 4, 2015.
Weiss, John. Colorado Springs, CO (by phone). April 3, 2018.
White, James W. Colorado Springs, CO. August 19, 2013.

Secondary Sources

BOOKS AND DISSERTATIONS

Abbott, Carl, Stephen J. Leonard, and Thomas J. Noel. *Colorado: A History of the Centennial State*. 4th ed. University Press of Colorado, 2005.
Adelakun, Abimbola. *Powerful Devices: Prayer and the Political Praxis of Spiritual Warfare*. Rutgers University Press, 2023.
Aho, James. *The Politics of Righteousness: Idaho Christian Patriotism*. University of Washington Press, 1990.
Andrews, Thomas G. *Killing for Coal: America's Deadliest Labor War*. Harvard University Press, 2008.
Atkins, Gregory James. "America's Theopolis: Boosters, Businesses, and Christian Nonprofits in Colorado Springs, 1871–2000." PhD diss., Washington State University, 2019.
Beaman, Lori G. *The Transition of Religion to Culture in Law and Public Discourse*. Routledge, 2020.
Bebbington, David W. *Evangelicalism in Modern Britain: A History from the 1730s to the 1980s*. Unwin Hyman, 1989.
Bennett, Daniel. *Defending Faith: The Politics of the Christian Conservative Legal Movement*. University Press of Kansas, 2017.
Berry, Damon T. *The New Apostolic Reformation, Trump, and Evangelical Politics: The Prophecy Voter*. Bloomsbury Academic, 2023.

Bowler, Kate. *Blessed: A History of the American Prosperity Gospel*. Oxford University Press, 2013.

Braden, Charles Samuel. *These Also Believe: A Study of Modern American Cults and Minority Religious Movements*. Macmillan, 1949.

Bruce, Steve. *The Rise and Fall of the New Christian Right: Conservative Protestant Politics in America, 1977–1988*. Oxford University Press, 1988.

Bruce, Steve. *Secularization: In Defence of an Unfashionable Theory*. Oxford University Press, 2015.

Bull, Chris, and John Gallagher. *Perfect Enemies: The Religious Right, the Gay Movement, and the Politics of the 1990s*. Crown, 1996.

Burlein, Ann. *Lift High the Cross: Where White Supremacy and the Christian Right Converge*. Duke University Press, 2002.

Butler, Anthea. *White Evangelical Racism: The Politics of Morality in America*. University of North Carolina Press, 2021.

Carleton, Don E. *Red Scare! Right-Wing Hysteria, Fifties Fanaticism, and Their Legacy in Texas*. University of Texas Press, 1985.

Carpenter, Joel A. *Revive Us Again: The Reawakening of American Fundamentalism*. Oxford University Press, 1997.

Cohen, Lizabeth. *A Consumers' Republic: The Politics of Mass Consumption in Postwar America*. Random House, 2003.

Cohen, Marty. *Moral Victories in the Battle for Congress: Cultural Conservatism and the House GOP*. University of Pennsylvania Press, 2019.

Congdon, David W. *Who Is a True Christian? Contesting Religious Identity in American Culture*. Cambridge University Press, 2024.

Cooper, Melinda. *Family Values: Between Neoliberalism and the New Social Conservatism*. Zone Books, 2017.

Cox, Harvey. *Fire from Heaven: The Rise of Pentecostal Spirituality and the Reshaping of Religion in the Twenty-First Century*. Addison-Wesley, 1995.

Cronin, Thomas E., and Robert D. Loevy. *Colorado Politics and Policy: Governing a Purple State*. University of Nebraska Press, 2012.

Curtis, Jesse. *The Myth of Colorblind Christians: Evangelicals and White Supremacy in the Civil Rights Era*. New York University Press, 2021.

Diamond, Sara. *Spiritual Warfare: The Politics of the Christian Right*. South End Press, 1989.

Dochuk, Darren. *Anointed with Oil: How Christianity and Crude Made Modern America*. Basic Books, 2019.

Dochuk, Darren. *From Bible Belt to Sunbelt: Plain-Folk Religion, Grassroots Politics, and the Rise of Evangelical Conservatism*. W. W. Norton, 2011.

Dowland, Seth. *Family Values and the Rise of the Christian Right*. University of Pennsylvania Press, 2015.

Dugan, Kimberly B. *The Struggle over Gay, Lesbian, and Bisexual Rights: Facing Off in Cincinnati*. Routledge, 2005.

Du Mez, Kristin Kobes. *Jesus and John Wayne: How White Evangelicals Corrupted a Faith and Fractured a Nation*. Liveright, 2020.

Ellis, Christopher, and James A. Stimson. *Ideology in America*. Cambridge University Press, 2012.

Ellis, Richard. *Democratic Delusions: The Initiative Process in America*. University Press of Kansas, 2002.

Eskridge, William N. *Dishonorable Passions: Sodomy Laws in America, 1861–2003*. Viking, 2008.

Fejes, Fred. *Gay Rights and Moral Panic: The Origins of America's Debate on Homosexuality*. Palgrave Macmillan, 2008.

Fetner, Tina. *How the Religious Right Shaped Lesbian and Gay Activism*. University of Minnesota Press, 2008.

Fiorina, Morris P., with Samuel J. Abrams and Jeremy C. Pope. *Culture War? The Myth of a Polarized America*. Pearson Longman, 2005.

Frank, Gillian. "Save Our Children: The Sexual Politics of Child Protection in the United States, 1965–1990." PhD diss., Brown University, 2009.

Gagné, André. *American Evangelicals for Trump*. Routledge, 2023.

Gaston, K. Healan. *Imagining Judeo-Christian America: Religion, Secularism, and the Redefinition of Democracy*. University of Chicago Press, 2019.

Gelman, Andrew. *Red State, Blue State, Rich State, Poor State: Why Americans Vote the Way They Do*. Princeton University Press, 2010.

Gilgoff, Dan. *The Jesus Machine: How James Dobson, Focus on the Family, and Evangelical America Are Winning the Culture War*. St. Martin's Press, 2007.

Gloege, Timothy E. W. *Guaranteed Pure: The Moody Bible Institute, Business, and the Making of Modern Evangelicalism*. University of North Carolina Press, 2015.

Goldberg, Robert Alan. *Hooded Empire: The Ku Klux Klan in Colorado*. University of Illinois Press, 1981.

Goldman, Peter, Thomas M. DeFrank, Mark Miller, Andrew Murr, and Tom Mathews. *Quest for the Presidency 1992*. Texas A&M University Press, 1994.

Gorski, Philip S., and Samuel L. Perry. *The Flag and the Cross: White Christian Nationalism and the Threat to American Democracy*. Oxford University Press, 2022.

Graziano, Michael. *Errand into the Wilderness of Mirrors: Religion and the History of the CIA*. University of Chicago Press, 2021.

Green, John C., James L. Guth, Corwin E. Smidt, and Lyman A. Kellstedt. *Religion and the Culture Wars: Dispatches from the Front*. Rowman and Littlefield, 1996.

Green, John C., Mark J. Rozell, and Clyde Wilcox, eds. *The Christian Right in American Politics: Marching to the Millennium*. Georgetown University Press, 2003.

Grem, Darren E. *The Blessings of Business: How Corporations Shaped Conservative Christianity*. Oxford University Press, 2016.

Griffith, Aaron. *God's Law and Order: The Politics of Punishment in Evangelical America*. Harvard University Press, 2020.

Griffith, R. Marie. *Moral Combat: How Sex Divided American Christians and Fractured American Politics*. Basic Books, 2017.

Gunn, T. Jeremy. *Spiritual Weapons: The Cold War and the Forging of an American National Religion*. Praeger, 2009.

Hamilton, Michael S. "The Fundamentalist Harvard: Wheaton College and the Continuing Vitality of American Evangelicalism, 1919–1965." PhD diss., University of Notre Dame, 1994.

Hammond, Sarah Ruth. *God's Businessmen: Entrepreneurial Evangelicals in Depression and War*. University of Chicago Press, 2017.

Hart, D. G. *Deconstructing Evangelicalism: Conservative Protestantism in the Age of Billy Graham*. Baker Academic, 2004.

Hartman, Andrew. *A War for the Soul of America: A History of the Culture Wars*. University of Chicago Press, 2015.

Hendershot, Heather. *Shaking the World for Jesus: Media and Conservative Evangelical Culture*. University of Chicago Press, 2004.

Henry, Daryn. *A. B. Simpson and the Making of Modern Evangelicalism*. McGill-Queen's University Press, 2019.

Herman, Didi. *The Antigay Agenda: Orthodox Vision and the Christian Right*. University of Chicago Press, 1997.

Herzog, Jonathan P. *The Spiritual-Industrial Complex: America's Religious Battle against Communism in the Early Cold War*. Oxford University Press, 2011.

Heyrman, Christine. *American Apostles: When Evangelicals Entered the World of Islam*. Hill and Wang, 2015.

Hixson, William B. *Search for the American Right Wing: An Analysis of the Social Science Record, 1955–1987*. Princeton University Press, 1992.

Holland, Jennifer L. *Tiny You: A Western History of the Anti-Abortion Movement*. University of California Press, 2020.

Hollinger, David A. *Christianity's American Fate: How Religion Became More Conservative and Society More Secular*. Princeton University Press, 2022.

Holvast, Rene. *Spiritual Mapping in the United States and Argentina, 1989–2005: A Geography of Fear*. Brill, 2009.

HoSang, Daniel Martinez. *Racial Propositions: Ballot Initiatives and the Making of Postwar California*. University of California Press, 2010.

Howard, Clayton. *The Closet and the Cul-de-Sac: The Politics of Sexual Privacy in Northern California*. University of Pennsylvania Press, 2019.

Howard, Jay R., and John M. Streck. *Apostles of Rock: The Splintered World of Contemporary Christian Music*. University Press of Kentucky, 1999.

Hudnut-Beumler, James. *In Pursuit of the Almighty's Dollar: A History of Money and American Protestantism*. University of North Carolina Press, 2007.

Hunter, James Davison. *American Evangelicalism: Conservative Religion and the Quandary of Modernity*. Rutgers University Press, 1983.

Hunter, James Davison. *Culture Wars: The Struggle to Define America*. Basic Books, 1991.

Hunter, James Davison, and Alan Wolfe, eds. *Is There a Culture War? A Dialogue on Values and American Public Life*. Brookings Institution Press, 2006.

Hutchison, William. *Religious Pluralism in America: The Contentious History of a Founding Ideal*. Yale University Press, 2003.

Inboden, William. *Religion and American Foreign Policy, 1945–1960: The Soul of Containment*. Cambridge University Press, 2008.

Jenkins, Philip. *Mystics and Messiahs: Cults and New Religions in American History.* Oxford University Press, 2000.

Jones, Robert P. *The End of White Christian America.* Simon and Schuster, 2016.

Kasselstrand, Isabella, Phil Zuckerman, and Ryan T. Cragun. *Beyond Doubt: The Secularization of Society.* New York University Press, 2023.

Keen, Lisa, and Suzanne B. Goldberg. *Strangers to the Law: Gay People on Trial.* University of Michigan Press, 1998.

King, David P. *God's Internationalists: World Vision and the Age of Evangelical Humanitarianism.* University of Pennsylvania Press, 2019.

Klarman, Michael J. *From the Closet to the Altar: Courts, Backlash, and the Struggle for Same-Sex Marriage.* Oxford University Press, 2013.

Kruse, Kevin Michael. *One Nation under God: How Corporate America Invented Christian America.* Basic Books, 2015.

Lichtman, Allan J. *White Protestant Nation: The Rise of the American Conservative Movement.* Publishers Group West, 2008.

Lienesch, Michael. *Redeeming America: Piety and Politics in the New Christian Right.* University of North Carolina Press, 1993.

Loevy, Robert D. *Colorado College: A Place of Learning.* Colorado College, 1999.

Loveland, Anne C. *American Evangelicals and the U.S. Military, 1942–1993.* Louisiana State University Press, 1996.

Luhrmann, T. M. *When God Talks Back: Understanding the American Evangelical Relationship with God.* Vintage Books, 2012.

Markusen, Ann R., Peter Hall, Scott Campbell, and Sabina Deitrick. *The Rise of the Gunbelt: The Military Remapping of Industrial America.* Oxford University Press, 1991.

Marsden, George M. *Fundamentalism and American Culture.* Oxford University Press, 2006. Originally published in 1980.

Marsden, George M. *Reforming Fundamentalism: Fuller Seminary and the New Evangelicalism.* William B. Eerdmans, 1987.

Martin, Lerone A. *The Gospel of J. Edgar Hoover: How the FBI Aided and Abetted the Rise of White Christian Nationalism.* Princeton University Press, 2023.

Mayer, Jane. *Dark Money: The Hidden History of the Billionaires behind the Rise of the Radical Right.* Doubleday, 2016.

McAlister, Melani. *The Kingdom of God Has No Borders: A Global History of American Evangelicals.* Oxford University Press, 2018.

McCloud, Sean. *American Possessions: Fighting Demons in the Contemporary United States.* Oxford University Press, 2015.

McGirr, Lisa. *Suburban Warriors: The Origins of the New American Right.* Princeton University Press, 2001.

Mead, Frank S., with Samuel S. Hill. *Handbook of Denominations in the United States.* Abingdon Press, 1995. Originally published in 1951.

Miller, Steven P. *The Age of Evangelicalism: America's Born-Again Years.* Oxford University Press, 2014.

Moore, R. Laurence. *Selling God: American Religion in the Marketplace of Culture.* Oxford University Press, 1994.

Moreton, Bethany. *To Serve God and Wal-Mart: The Making of Christian Free Enterprise.* Harvard University Press, 2009.

Mulloy, D. J. *The World of the John Birch Society: Conspiracy, Conservatism, and the Cold War.* Vanderbilt University Press, 2014.

Nash, Gerald D. *The Federal Landscape: An Economic History of the Twentieth-Century West.* University of Arizona Press, 1999.

Nauman, Robert Allen. *On the Wings of Modernism: The United States Air Force Academy.* University of Illinois Press, 2004.

Noel, Thomas J., and Cathleen M. Norman. *A Pikes Peak Partnership: The Penroses and the Tutts.* University Press of Colorado, 2000.

Noll, Mark A., David W. Bebbington, and George M. Marsden, eds. *Evangelicals: Who They Have Been, Are Now, and Could Be.* William B. Eerdmans, 2019.

Oliver, Kendrick. *To Touch the Face of God: The Sacred, the Profane, and the American Space Program.* Johns Hopkins University Press, 2013.

Peirce, Neal R. *The Mountain States of America: People, Politics, and Power in the Eight Rocky Mountain States.* W. W. Norton, 1972.

Petro, Anthony. *After the Wrath of God: AIDS, Sexuality, and American Religion.* Oxford University Press, 2015.

Phillips-Fein, Kim. *Invisible Hands: The Making of the Conservative Movement from the New Deal to Reagan.* W. W. Norton, 2009.

Pietsch, B. M. *Dispensational Modernism.* Oxford University Press, 2015.

Porterfield, Amanda, John Corrigan, and Darren E. Grem, eds. *The Business Turn in American Religious History.* Oxford University Press, 2017.

Posner, Sarah. *Unholy: Why White Evangelicals Worship at the Altar of Donald Trump.* Random House, 2020.

Preston, Andrew. *Sword of the Spirit, Shield of Faith: Religion in American War and Diplomacy.* Alfred A. Knopf, 2012.

Redekop, John H. *The American Far Right: A Case Study of Billy James Hargis and Christian Crusade.* William B. Eerdmans, 1968.

Ribuffo, Leo P. *The Old Christian Right: The Protestant Far Right from the Great Depression to the Cold War.* Temple University Press, 1983.

Rieder, Jonathan, ed. *The Fractious Nation? Unity and Division in Contemporary American Life.* University of California Press, 2003.

Riesebrodt, Martin. *Pious Passion: The Emergence of Modern Fundamentalism in the United States and Iran.* University of California Press, 1993.

Rimmerman, Craig A. *From Identity to Politics: The Lesbian and Gay Movements in the United States.* Temple University Press, 2001.

Rimmerman, Craig A., Kenneth D. Wald, and Clyde Wilcox, eds. *The Politics of Gay Rights.* University of Chicago Press, 2000.

Rogin, Michael Paul. *The Intellectuals and McCarthy: The Radical Specter.* MIT Press, 1967.

Rogin, Michael Paul. *Ronald Reagan, the Movie: And Other Episodes in Political Demonology.* University of California Press, 1987.

Ronsvalle, John, and Sylvia Ronsvalle. *Behind the Stained Glass Windows: Money Dynamics in the Church.* Baker Books, 1996.

Schäfer, Axel R. *Piety and Public Funding: Evangelicals and the State in Modern America*. University of Pennsylvania Press, 2012.

Scheitle, Christopher P. *Beyond the Congregation: The World of Christian Nonprofits*. Oxford University Press, 2010.

Schemo, Diana. *Skies to Conquer: A Year inside the Air Force Academy*. John Wiley and Sons, 2010.

Schrecker, Ellen. *Many Are the Crimes: McCarthyism in America*. Princeton University Press, 1998.

Schultz, Kevin Michael. *Tri-Faith America: How Catholics and Jews Held Postwar America to Its Protestant Promise*. Oxford University Press, 2011.

Scott, Amy L. "Remaking Urban in the American West: Lifestyle Politics, Micropolitan Urbanism, and Hip Capitalism in Boulder, Colorado, 1958–1978." PhD diss., University of New Mexico, 2007.

Self, Robert O. *All in the Family: The Realignment of American Democracy since the 1960s*. Hill and Wang, 2012.

Shearer, Tobin Miller. *Two Weeks Every Summer: Fresh Air Children and the Problem of Race in America*. Cornell University Press, 2017.

Shermer, Elizabeth Tandy. *Sunbelt Capitalism: Phoenix and the Transformation of American Politics*. University of Pennsylvania Press, 2013.

Sherry, Michael S. *In the Shadow of War: The United States since the 1930s*. Yale University Press, 1995.

Shipps, Jan, and Mark Silk, eds. *Religion and Public Life in the Mountain West: Sacred Landscapes in Transition*. AltaMira Press, 2004.

Silliman, Daniel. *Reading Evangelicals: How Christian Fiction Shaped a Culture and a Faith*. William B. Eerdmans, 2021.

Smith, Christian. *American Evangelicalism: Embattled and Thriving*. University of Chicago Press, 1998.

Smith, Mark A. *Secular Faith: How Culture Has Trumped Religion in American Politics*. University of Chicago Press, 2015.

Spoede, Robert W. *More Than Conquerors: A History of the Officers' Christian Fellowship of the U.S.A., 1943–1983*. OCF Books, 1993.

Sprague, Marshall. *Newport in the Rockies: The Life and Good Times of Colorado Springs*. Swallow Press/Ohio University Press, 1987. Originally published in 1961.

Stahl, Ronit Y. *Enlisting Faith: How the Military Chaplaincy Shaped Religion and State in Modern America*. Harvard University Press, 2017.

Stephens, Hilde Løvdal. *Family Matters: James Dobson and Focus on the Family's Crusade for the Christian Home*. University of Alabama Press, 2019.

Stephens, Randall J. *The Devil's Music: How Christians Inspired, Condemned, and Embraced Rock 'n' Roll*. Harvard University Press, 2018.

Stephens, Randall J. *The Fire Spreads: Holiness and Pentecostalism in the American South*. Harvard University Press, 2010.

Stephens, Randall J., and Karl Giberson. *The Anointed: Evangelical Truth in a Secular Age*. Belknap Press of Harvard University Press, 2011.

Stewart, Katherine. *Money, Lies, and God: Inside the Movement to Destroy American Democracy*. Bloomsbury Publishing, 2025.

Stewart, Katherine. *The Power Worshippers: Inside the Dangerous Rise of Religious Nationalism*. Bloomsbury Publishing, 2019.

Stone, Amy L. *Gay Rights at the Ballot Box*. University of Minnesota Press, 2012.

Sullivan, Winnifred Fallers. *Prison Religion: Faith-Based Reform and the Constitution*. Princeton University Press, 2009.

Sutton, Matthew Avery. *Aimee Semple McPherson and the Resurrection of Christian America*. Harvard University Press, 2007.

Sutton, Matthew Avery. *American Apocalypse: A History of Modern Evangelicalism*. Belknap Press of Harvard University Press, 2014.

Sutton, Matthew Avery. *Double Crossed: The Missionaries Who Spied for the United States during the Second World War*. Basic Books, 2019.

Swartz, David R. *Moral Minority: The Evangelical Left in an Age of Conservatism*. University of Pennsylvania Press, 2012.

Szasz, Ferenc Morton. *Religion in the Modern American West*. University of Arizona Press, 2000.

Turner, John G. *Bill Bright and Campus Crusade for Christ: The Renewal of Evangelicalism in Postwar America*. University of North Carolina Press, 2008.

Vaca, Daniel. *Evangelicals Incorporated: Books and the Business of Religion in America*. Harvard University Press, 2019.

Wacker, Grant. *America's Pastor: Billy Graham and the Shaping of a Nation*. Belknap Press of Harvard University Press, 2014.

Wacker, Grant. *Heaven Below: Early Pentecostals and American Culture*. Harvard University Press, 2001.

Wall, Wendy. *Inventing the American Way: The Politics of Consensus from the New Deal to the Civil Rights Movement*. Oxford University Press, 2008.

Weaver, John. *The New Apostolic Reformation: History of a Modern Charismatic Movement*. McFarland and Company, 2016.

White, Heather Rachelle. *Reforming Sodom: Protestants and the Rise of Gay Rights*. University of North Carolina Press, 2015.

Whitehead, Andrew L., and Samuel L. Perry. *Taking America Back for God: Christian Nationalism in the United States*. Oxford University Press, 2020.

Wilcox, Clyde A. *God's Warriors: The Christian Right in Twentieth-Century America*. Johns Hopkins University Press, 1992.

Williams, Daniel K. *God's Own Party: The Making of the Christian Right*. Oxford University Press, 2010.

Williams, Rhys H., ed. *Cultural Wars in American Politics: Critical Reviews of a Popular Myth*. Aldine de Gruyter, 1997.

Witt, Stephanie L., and Suzanne McCorkle. *Anti-Gay Rights: Assessing Voter Initiatives*. Praeger, 1997.

Worthen, Molly. *Apostles of Reason: The Crisis of Authority in American Evangelicalism*. Oxford University Press, 2013.

Wuthnow, Robert. *The Crisis in the Churches: Spiritual Malaise, Fiscal Woe*. Oxford University Press, 1997.

Wuthnow, Robert. *The Restructuring of American Religion: Society and Faith since World War II*. Princeton University Press, 1988.

Young, Neil J. *We Gather Together: The Religious Right and the Problem of Interfaith Politics.* Oxford University Press, 2016.

Zubovich, Gene. *Before the Religious Right: Liberal Protestants, Human Rights, and the Polarization of the United States.* University of Pennsylvania Press, 2022.

JOURNAL ARTICLES AND BOOK CHAPTERS

Altman, Michael J. "'Religion, Religions, Religious' in America: Toward a Smithian Account of 'Evangelicalism.'" *Method and Theory in the Study of Religion* 31, no. 1 (2019): 71–82.

Atkins, Gregory. "'Business Sense If Not Souls': Boosters and Religion in Colorado Springs, 1871–1909." *Journal of the Gilded Age and Progressive Era* 17, no. 1 (2018): 77–97.

Bederman, Gail. "'The Women Have Had Charge of the Church Work Long Enough': The Men and Religion Forward Movement of 1911–1912 and the Masculinization of Middle-Class Protestantism." *American Quarterly* 41, no. 3 (1989): 432–65.

Blee, Kathleen M., and Kimberly A. Creasap. "Conservative and Right-Wing Movements." *Annual Review of Sociology* 36 (2010): 269–86.

Brint, Steven. "What If They Gave a War . . . ?" *Contemporary Sociology* 21, no. 4 (1992): 438–40.

Brint, Steven, and Seth Abrutyn. "Who's Right about the Right? Comparing Competing Explanations of the Link between White Evangelicals and Conservative Politics in the United States." *Journal for the Scientific Study of Religion* 49, no. 2 (2010): 328–50.

Burris, Val. "Small Business, Status Politics, and the Social Base of New Christian Right Activism." *Critical Sociology* 27, no. 1 (2001): 29–55.

Chaves, Mark. "All Creatures Great and Small: Megachurches in Context." *Review of Religious Research* 47, no. 4 (2006): 329–46.

Chaves, Mark. "Rain Dances in the Dry Season: Overcoming the Religious Congruence Fallacy." *Journal for the Scientific Study of Religion* 49, no. 1 (2010): 1–14.

Chaves, Mark, and Philip Gorski. "Religious Pluralism and Religious Participation." *Annual Review of Sociology* 27 (2001): 261–81.

Comiskey, Joel. "Rev. Cho's Cell Groups and Dynamics of Church Growth." In *Charis and Charisma: David Yonggi Cho and the Growth of Yoido Full Gospel Church*, edited by Myung Sung-Hoon and Hong Young-Go. Regnum, 2003.

Connolly, Andrew. "Masculinity, Political Action, and Spiritual Warfare in the Fictional Ministry of Frank E. Peretti." *Christianity and Literature* 69, no. 1 (2020): 53–72.

Corwin, Gary. "This Present Nervousness." *Evangelical Missions Quarterly* 31, no. 2 (1995): 148–49.

Crockett, E. C. "The Problem of Tax Exempt Property in Colorado." *Rocky Mountain Law Review* 19 (December 1946): 22–48.

Curtis, Jesse. "White Evangelicals as a 'People': The Church Growth Movement from India to the United States." *Religion and American Culture* 30, no. 1 (2020): 108–46.

Davis, David Brion. "Some Themes of Counter-Subversion: An Analysis of Anti-Masonic, Anti-Catholic, and Anti-Mormon Literature." *Mississippi Valley Historical Review* 47, no. 2 (1960): 205–24.

Dayton, Donald W. "'The Search for the Historical Evangelicalism,' George Marsden's History of Fuller Seminary as a Case Study." *Christian Scholar's Review* 23, no. 1 (1993): 12–33.

Dayton, Donald W. "Theological Roots of Pentecostalism." *Pneuma* 2, no. 1 (1980): 3–21.

DeBernardi, Jean. "Spiritual Warfare and Territorial Spirits: The Globalization and Localisation of a 'Practical Theology.'" *Religious Studies and Theology* 18, no. 2 (1999): 66–96.

Dias, Ric. "The Great Cantonment: Cold War Cities in the American West." In *The Cold War American West, 1945–1989*, edited by Kevin J. Fernlund. University of New Mexico Press, 1998.

Dochuk, Darren. "'Heavenly Houston': Billy Graham and Corporate Civil Rights in Sunbelt Evangelicalism's 'Golden Buckle.'" In *Billy Graham: American Pilgrim*, edited by Andrew Finstuen, Grant Wacker, and Anne Blue Wills. Oxford University Press, 2017.

Dudas, Jeffrey R. "In the Name of Equal Rights: 'Special' Rights and the Politics of Resentment in Post–Civil Rights America." *Law and Society Review* 39, no. 4 (2005): 723–57.

Dunn, Joshua. "Who Governs in God's City?" *Society* 49, no. 1 (2012): 24–32.

Eskridge, Larry K. "Barnhouse, Donald Grey." In *American National Biography*. Oxford University Press, 2002.

Eskridge, Larry. "Money Matters: The Phenomenon of Financial Counselor Larry Burkett and Christian Financial Concepts." In *More Money, More Ministry: Money and Evangelicals in Recent North American History*, edited by Larry Eskridge and Mark A. Noll. William B. Eerdmans, 2000.

Evans, John H. "'Culture Wars' or Status Group Ideology as the Basis of US Moral Politics." *International Journal of Sociology and Social Policy* 16, no. 1/2 (1996): 15–34.

Failinger, Marie. "*United States v. Ballard*: Government Prohibited from Declaring Religious Truth." In *Law and Religion: Cases in Context*, edited by Leslie C. Griffin. Wolters Kluwer Law and Business, 2010.

Fisher, Linford D. "Evangelicals and Unevangelicals: The Contested History of a Word, 1500–1950." *Religion and American Culture* 26, no. 2 (2016): 184–226.

Frank, Gillian A. "'The Civil Rights of Parents': Race and Conservative Politics in Anita Bryant's Campaign against Gay Rights in 1970s Florida." *Journal of the History of Sexuality* 22, no. 1 (2012): 126–60.

Gardella, Peter. "Spiritual Warfare in the Fiction of Frank Peretti." In *Religions of the United States in Practice*, vol. 2, edited by Colleen McDannell. Princeton University Press, 2018.

Gilbert, James B. "Cultural Skirmishes." *Reviews in American History* 21, no. 2 (1993): 346–51.

Gorski, Philip. "The Long Withdrawing Roar: From Culture Wars to Culture Clashes." *Hedgehog Review* (Summer 2021). https://hedgehogreview.com/issues/distinctions-that-define-and-divide/articles/the-long-withdrawing-roar.

Gray, Mia, and Ann R. Markusen. "Colorado Springs: A Military-Anchored City in Transition." In *Second Tier Cities: Rapid Growth beyond the Metropolis*, edited by

Ann R. Markusen, Yong-Sook Lee, and Sean DiGiovanna. University of Minnesota Press, 1999.

Greenberg, David. "The Reorientation of Liberalism in the 1980s." In *Living in the Eighties*, edited by Gil Troy and Vincent A. Cannato. Oxford University Press, 2009.

Grem, Darren E. "*Christianity Today*, J. Howard Pew, and the Business of Conservative Evangelicalism." *Enterprise and Society* 15, no. 2 (2014): 337–79.

Guberman, Rachel. "'No Discrimination and No Special Rights': Gay Rights, Family Values, and the Politics of Moderation in the 1992 Election." In *Beyond the Politics of the Closet: Gay Rights and the American State since the 1970s*, edited by Jonathan Bell. University of Pennsylvania Press, 2020.

Guelich, Robert A. "Spiritual Warfare: Jesus, Paul and Peretti." *Pneuma* 13, no. 1 (1991): 33–64.

Hamilton, Michael S. "The Interdenominational Evangelicalism of D. L. Moody and the Problem of Fundamentalism." In *American Evangelicalism: George Marsden and the State of American Religious History*, edited by Darren Dochuk, Thomas Kidd, and Kurt W. Peterson. University of Notre Dame Press, 2014.

Handy, Robert T. "The Protestant Quest for a Christian America, 1830–1930." *Church History* 22, no. 1 (1953): 8–20.

Hardy, Rebeka, and Mark E. Roberts. "Youth with a Mission." In *The Essential Handbook of Denominations and Ministries*, edited by George Thomas Kurian and Sarah Claudine Day. Baker Books, 2017.

Hayward, Rhodri. "Lewis, Jessie Elizabeth Penn-." In *The Oxford Dictionary of National Biography*. Oxford University Press, 2004.

Hedges, Daniel. "Wagner, Charles Peter." In *Biographical Dictionary of Evangelicals*, edited by Timothy Larsen, Mark Noll, and David Bebbington. InterVarsity Press, 2003.

Hollinger, David A. "The Religious Tide's Withdrawing Roar: Heard on American Shores?" *Reviews in American History* 51, no. 3 (2023): 271–77.

Hollinger, David A. "The 'Secularization' Question and the United States in the Twentieth Century." *Church History* 70, no. 1 (2001): 132–43.

Horowitz, David A. "The Normality of Extremism: The Ku Klux Klan Revisited." *Society* 35, no. 6 (1998): 71–77.

Hout, Michael, and Claude S. Fischer. "Why More Americans Have No Religious Preference: Politics and Generations." *American Sociological Review* 67, no. 2 (2002): 165–90.

Howard, Jay R. "Vilifying the Enemy: The Christian Right and the Novels of Frank Peretti." *Journal of Popular Culture* 28, no. 3 (1994): 193–206.

Koppelman, Andrew. "*Romer v. Evans* and Invidious Intent." *William and Mary Bill of Rights Journal* 6, no. 1 (1997): 89–146.

Kruse, Kevin. "Compassionate Conservatism: Religion in the Age of George W. Bush." In *The Presidency of George W. Bush: A First Historical Assessment*, edited by Julian Zelizer. Princeton University Press, 2010.

Lassiter, Matthew D. "Big Government and Family Values: Political Culture in the Metropolitan Sunbelt." In *Sunbelt Rising: The Politics of Place, Space, and Region*, edited by Michelle Nickerson and Darren Dochuk. University of Pennsylvania Press, 2011.

Lassiter, Matthew D. "Inventing Family Values." In *Rightward Bound: Making America Conservative in the 1970s*, edited by Bruce J. Schulman and Julian E. Zelizer. Harvard University Press, 2008.

Lassiter, Matthew D. "Political History beyond the Red-Blue Divide." *Journal of American History* 98, no. 3 (2011): 760–64.

Layman, Geoffrey C., and John C. Green. "Wars and Rumours of Wars: The Contexts of Cultural Conflict in American Political Behavior." *British Journal of Political Science* 36, no. 1 (2006): 61–89.

Lehman, Derek, and Darren E. Sherkat. "Measuring Religious Identification in the United States." *Journal for the Scientific Study of Religion* 57, no. 4 (2018): 779–94.

Lewis, Andrew R. "Christian Nationalism and the Remaking of Religion and Politics." *Sociology of Religion* 82, no. 1 (2021): 111–15.

Lewis, James R. "Works of Darkness: Occult Fascination in the Novels of Frank Peretti." In *Magical Religion and Modern Witchcraft*, edited by James R. Lewis. SUNY Press, 1996.

Lipin, Lawrence M., and William Lunch. "Moralistic Direct Democracy: Political Insurgents, Religion, and the State in Twentieth-Century Oregon." *Oregon Historical Quarterly* 110, no. 4 (2009): 514–45.

Lunch, William M. "The Christian Right in the Northwest: Two Decades of Frustration in Oregon and Washington." In *The Christian Right in American Politics: Marching to the Millennium*, edited by John C. Green, Mark J. Rozell, and Clyde Wilcox. Georgetown University Press, 2003.

Margolis, Michele F. "Who Wants to Make America Great Again? Understanding Evangelical Support for Donald Trump." *Religion and Politics* 13 (July 2019): 1–30.

Marti, Gerardo, and Mark Mulder. "Capital and the Cathedral: Robert H. Schuller's Continual Fundraising for Church Growth." *Religion and American Culture* 30, no. 1 (2020): 63–107.

McCloud, Sean. "Mapping the Spatial Limbos of Spiritual Warfare: Haunted Houses, Defiled Land and the Horrors of History." *Material Religion* 9, no. 2 (2013): 166–85.

McConkey, Dale. "Whither Hunter's Culture War? Shifts in Evangelical Morality, 1988–1998." *Sociology of Religion* 62, no. 2 (2001): 149–74.

McDannell, Colleen. "Beyond Dr. Dobson: Women, Girls, and Focus on the Family." In *Women and Twentieth-Century Protestantism*, edited by Margaret Lamberts Bendroth and Virginia Lieson Brereton. University of Illinois Press, 2002.

Miller-Davenport, Sarah. "'Their Blood Shall Not Be Shed in Vain': American Evangelical Missionaries and the Search for God and Country in Post–World War II Asia." *Journal of American History* 99, no. 4 (2013): 1109–32.

Moore, Leonard J. "Good Old-Fashioned New Social History and the Twentieth-Century American Right." *Reviews in American History* 24, no. 4 (1996): 555–73.

Moreton, Bethany. "Why Is There So Much Sex in Christian Conservatism and Why Do So Few Historians Care Anything about It?" *Journal of Southern History* 75, no. 3 (2009): 717–38.

Mumford, Kevin. "The Trouble with Gay Rights: Race and the Politics of Sexual Orientation in Philadelphia, 1969–1982." *Journal of American History* 98, no. 1 (2011): 49–72.

Phillips-Fein, Kim. "Conservatism: A State of the Field." *Journal of American History* 98, no. 3 (2011): 723–43.

Pierard, Richard V. "*Pax Americana* and the Evangelical Missionary Advance." In *Earthen Vessels: American Evangelicals and Foreign Missions, 1880–1980*, edited by Joel A. Carpenter and Wilbert R. Shenk. Wipf and Stock Publishers, 2012.

Rabkin, Jeremy. "The Culture War That Isn't." *Policy Review*, no. 96 (September 1999): 3–19.

Reynolds, Amber Thomas. "Robert Walker's *Christian Life* Magazine: A Missing Link between Mainstream American Evangelicalism and Charismatic Renewal." In *Transatlantic Charismatic Renewal, c. 1950–2000*, edited by Andrew Atherstone, John Maiden, and Mark P. Hutchinson. Brill, 2021.

Ribuffo, Leo P. "Conservatism and American Politics." *Journal of the Historical Society* 3, no. 2 (2003): 163–75.

Ribuffo, Leo P. "George W. Bush and the Latest Evangelical Menace." *Dissent* 53, no. 4 (2011): 42–49.

Ribuffo, Leo P. "Religion in the History of U.S. Foreign Policy." In *The Influence of Faith: Religious Groups and U.S. Foreign Policy*, edited by Elliott Abrams. Rowman and Littlefield, 2001.

Ribuffo, Leo P. "Why Is There So Much Conservatism in the United States and Why Do So Few Historians Know Anything about It?" *American Historical Review* 99, no. 2 (1994): 438–49.

Ridgely, Susan B. "Conservative Christianity and the Creation of Alternative News: An Analysis of Focus on the Family's Multimedia Empire." *Religion and American Culture* 30, no. 1 (2020): 1–25.

Riesebrodt, Martin. "Fundamentalism and the Resurgence of Religion." *Numen* 47, no. 3 (2000): 266–87.

Russell, C. Allyn. "Donald Grey Barnhouse: Fundamentalist Who Changed." *Journal of Presbyterian History* 59, no. 1 (1981): 33–57.

Schultz, William. "The Rise and Fall of 'No Special Rights.'" *Oregon Historical Quarterly* 122, no. 1 (2021): 6–37.

Schwarz, Stephen. "Limiting Religious Tax Exemptions: When Should the Church Render unto Caesar?" *University of Florida Law Review* 29, no. 1 (1976): 50–105.

Senter, Mark H. "Mother of the Parachurch High School Movement in America: A Look at the Miracle Book Club at Evelyn McClusky." *Christian Education Journal* 11, no. 3 (1991): 73–85.

Shelley, Bruce L. "Parachurch Groups (Voluntary Societies)." In *Dictionary of Christianity in America*, edited by Daniel G. Reid, Robert Dean Linder, Bruce L. Shelley, and Harry S. Stout. InterVarsity Press, 1990.

Shelley, Bruce L. "The Rise of Evangelical Youth Movements." *Fides et Historia* 18, no. 1 (1986): 45–63.

Sherkat, Darren E., Derek Lehman, and Nabil Bill Julkif. "Mooring Christian Nationalism: How Religious Institutions, Participation, and Beliefs Inform Christian Nationalism." *Sociological Quarterly* 65, no. 2 (2023): 1–20.

Shields, Jon A. "Fighting Liberalism's Excesses: Moral Crusades during the Reagan Revolution." *Journal of Policy History* 26, no. 1 (2014): 103–20.

Silliman, Daniel. "An Evangelical Is Anyone Who Likes Billy Graham: Defining Evangelicalism with Carl Henry and Networks of Trust." *Church History* 90, no. 3 (2021): 621–43.

Smith, Jesse, and Gary J. Adler. "What Isn't Christian Nationalism? A Call for Conceptual and Empirical Splitting." *Socius* 8 (January 2022): 1–14.

Smith, Mark A. "Religion, Divorce, and the Missing Culture War in America." *Political Science Quarterly* 125, no. 1 (2010): 57–85.

Sutton, Matthew Avery. "Redefining the History and Historiography on American Evangelicalism in the Era of the Religious Right." *Journal of the American Academy of Religion*, August 2024, 1–24.

Sutton, Matthew Avery. "Was FDR the Antichrist? The Birth of Fundamentalist Antiliberalism in a Global Age." *Journal of American History* 98, no. 4 (2012): 1052–74.

Sweet, Leonard I. "The Evangelical Tradition in America." In *The Evangelical Tradition in America*, edited by Leonard I. Sweet. Mercer University Press, 1984.

Verter, Bradford. "Spiritual Capital: Theorizing Religion with Bourdieu against Bourdieu." *Sociological Theory* 21, no. 2 (2003): 150–74.

Voas, David, and Mark Chaves. "Is the United States a Counterexample to the Secularization Thesis?" *American Journal of Sociology* 121, no. 5 (2016): 1517–56.

Wacker, Grant. "The Holy Spirit and the Spirit of the Age in American Protestantism, 1880–1910." *Journal of American History* 72, no. 1 (1985): 45–62.

Wacker, Grant. "Searching for Norman Rockwell: Popular Evangelicalism in Contemporary America." In *The Evangelical Tradition in America*, edited by Leonard I. Sweet. Mercer University Press, 1984.

Wacker, Grant. "Wimber and Wonders—What about Miracles Today?" *Reformed Journal* 37, no. 4 (1987): 16–19.

Walsh, David Austin. "The Right-Wing Popular Front: The Far Right and American Conservatism in the 1950s." *Journal of American History* 107, no. 2 (2020): 411–32.

Williams, Rhys. "Review of Michael O. Emerson and Christian Smith, *Divided by Faith: Evangelical Religion and the Problem of Race in America*." *Sociology of Religion* 65, no. 2 (2004): 178–79.

Wilson, D. J. "Cho, David (Paul) Yonggi (Yong-gi)." In *The New International Dictionary of the Pentecostal and Charismatic Movements*, edited by Stanley M. Burgess and Eduard M. van der Maas. Zondervan, 2002.

Witwer, David. "Westbrook Pegler and the Anti-Union Movement." *Journal of American History* 92, no. 2 (2005): 527–52.

Zeller, Benjamin E. "American Postwar 'Big Religion': Reconceptualizing Twentieth-Century American Religion Using Big Science as a Model." *Church History* 80, no. 2 (2011): 321–51.

Index

Page numbers in italics indicate illustrations.

Abolition of Man, The (Lewis), 81
abortion, 63, 64, 131
Ackerman, Jasper, 28
AD2000 Movement, 133
African Americans used by antigay campaign, 69–71, 87
AIDS (pamphlet by Noebel et al.), 64
AIDS pandemic, 64, 83
AIDS: What the Government Isn't Telling You (Day), 82
Air Force Academy, 6, 9, 21–22, 31; Basic Cadet Training (BCT), 105–6; Cadet Chapel, 95–99, *97*; Cadet Social Climate Surveys, 111; Center for Character Development, 105–7, 108; chapel attendance, mandatory, 100–103; chaplains, 94; Christian Leadership Ministries, 107; history of, 92–95; religious atmosphere, 91–92; religious control of cadets, relaxation of, 98–100; religious diversity within, 94; religious practices, under investigation, 110–13; revivals, annual, 104; sexual assault scandal, 108–9; SPIRE (Special Programs in Religious Education), 104, 108; Wings of Blue skydiving team, 36
Amendment 2 (Colorado, 1992), 60, 69–71; Boycott Colorado movement, 73–74, 77; election results, 71–72; *Evans v. Romer*, 85–90; impact of, 72–74, 84–85; media coverage of, 72–73; opposition to, 70–71, 72, 75–76
American Christian College, 63
American Civil Liberties Union (ACLU), 73; and religious requirements at military academies, 101–3
American Evangelicalism (Hunter), 65
American Family Association, 82
Americans United for Separation of Church and State, 110
Andrew Wommack Ministries, 139–41
Annacondia, Carlos, 122

199

anti-Communism, 31, 61; Christian Anti-Communism Summer College, 62
antigay activism: Amendment 2, 69–71; antigay science, 83–84; Colorado Model (CFV), 79–90; "family values" vs. tolerance, 85; Glen Eyrie conferences, 83–84
antisemitism, 29
apocalypticism, 13–14
Apple (technology company), 55
Are Gay Rights Right? (Magnuson), 82
Aries, Frank, 44
Aries Properties, 44
Armstrong, Bill, 35, 68
Arnold, Clinton, 125
Art of Family Living, 54
Asay, Chuck, 74
Association of Christian Schools International, 51
autarchy, 30

Ballard, Edna, 28–29
Ballard, Guy, 28–29
Baptist Student Union, 104
Barnhouse, Donald Grey, 117, 121
Basic Rights Oregon, 85
Bauer, Gary, 64, 89
Bayless, Jeffrey, 86, 88
Beatles (musical group), 63
Bebbington, David W., 4
Bennett, John S., 94–96, 98
Berger, Peter, 65
Berneking, Gerald, 2
Bethel College, 46
Billy Graham Evangelistic Association, 20–21
Black Americans used by antigay campaign, 69–71, 87
Blunt, Wilfred, 2
Bowers v. Hardwick, 88, 89
Boycott Colorado movement, 73–74, 77
boycotts, impact of, 73
Boyd, Brady, 138
Brady, Roger A., 111, 112
"Brady Report," 111

Bransford, Stephen, 79
Briargate (planned community), 50
Bright, Bill, 14, 49, 118–19, 126
Broadmoor Hotel, 8
Brown, Fred, 73
Buchanan, Pat, 70, 79
Burton College, 62
Bush, George H. W., 36, 70
Bush, George W., 92, 111–12, 131–32, 136, 140
Bush, Luis, 133
Butler, Jay, 67

Cadet Chapel, Air Force Academy, 95–99, 97. *See also* Air Force Academy
California: criticized for moral decay, 50–51; Focus on the Family relocation from, 50–51; tax exemptions for religious institutions, 39–40; Traditional Values Coalition, 69
Cameron, Paul, 64, 69, 70, 83, 87
Camp Carson, 21
Campus Crusade for Christ, 13–15, 48–49; Christian Leadership Ministries, 107
capitalism: consumer capitalism, 4; free market capitalism, 34, 116
Carpenter, Joel, 24
Carto, Willis, 29
Cary, North Carolina, 47
Catholic Newman Club, 104
cell groups, 129
Center for Character Development (Air Force Academy), 105–7
Chaplain, The, 100
chaplains: character, emphasis on, 105–7; and mandatory chapel attendance in military academies, 101–2
Chappell, Wallace, 16
Charis Bible College, 139, 141
charismatic traditions, 116; and charismatic renewal, 116–17; worship style, 127
Chauncey, George, 87
Child Molestation and Homosexuality (Cameron), 83

200   Index

child-rearing practices, 35–36
Children at Risk (Dobson), 64
Cho, David Yonggi, 129
Christian and Missionary Alliance, 47, 48
Christian Booksellers Association, 34
Christian Camping International, 39
Christian Camps Foundation, 23
Christian Century (periodical), 100–101
Christian Coalition, 68, 82
Christian Crusade ministry, 62; Christian Anti-Communism Summer College, 62
Christianity Today (periodical), 13, 53–54; "Culture War Casualties" (Woodbridge), 64
Christian nationalism, 4, 6–7
Christian Workers Foundation, 19
Cincinnati, Ohio, 84, 90
Citizens Project, 57–58, 76, 140
Clark, Albert P., 102
Clinton, Bill, 70
Cold War, 4; ideology of, and Christian nationalism, 7, 38; impact on Colorado Springs, 6
Colorado: HB1059, 66–67; home rule, 66; Initiative 43, 137; Referendum I, 137; Republican-Democratic dynamics, 140; state constitution amendments, 67; tax code, 36–42. *See also* Amendment 2
Colorado College, 8
Colorado for Family Values (CFV), 60, 67–78; *CFV Report*, 80; Colorado Model, 79–90; Community Watch Seminars, 77; Glen Eyrie conferences, 81–83
Colorado Legal Initiatives Project, 85
Colorado Model (CFV), 79–90
Colorado Springs, Colorado: Camp Carson, 21–22; Chamber of Commerce, 21–22, 36; Christian Crusade's ties to area, 62; early history of, 7–9; economic frameworks, 21, 42–53; evangelical migration to, 36–37; as "Evangelical Vatican," 53–58; Garden of the Gods, 1–3, *3*; harassment campaigns targeting "un-Christian" elements, 56–57; high-tech companies, 42, 44; local workforce, 54–55; mayoral race (1999), 77–78; military impact on local economy, 5–6; military presence, 42–43; progressive strategy against culture war model, 60–61; property values and home foreclosures, 43–44; public schools, 56–57. *See also* Air Force Academy
Colorado Springs Association of Evangelicals, 3, 126, 131
Colorado Springs Business Journal, 55
Colorado Springs Men's Council, 56
Colorado Springs Ministerial Alliance, 1–3
Colson, Charles, 35
"Come Together Colorado" proposal, 75–76
Compassion International, 5, 34, 47, 58
Concerned Women for America, 68, 82
Congress of Freedom, 29
Considine, Terry, 41
Consolidated Space Operations Center, 43
Cook, Colin, 77
Cook, David C., 52
Cook, Martin, 108
Copeland, Kenneth, 141
COVID-19 pandemic, 140
Cowboy Church of the Rockies, 56
creationism, 52
Cripple Creek, 8
crusades: Billy Graham, 20–21
"Culture War Casualties" (Woodbridge), 64
culture war issues, 6; history of in US, 60. *See also* gay rights
Culture Wars (Hunter), 65–66, 87–88

Dallas Theological Seminary, 15
Daly, Jim, 140
Dare to Discipline (Dobson), 49
Dave Dravecky Foundation, 54
Dawson, John, 121
Day, Lorraine, 82
DeBerry, Fisher, 107–8, 110

Defense of Marriage Act, 89–90
Democratic Leadership Conference, 70
demonic power, emphasis on, 117–22
Dempsey, Jack, 8
Department of Defense Appropriations Act (2006), 112
Dialogue Dinners (Citizens Project), 76
Divine, Amy, 57, 76
Dobson, James, 35–36, 49–51, 51, 90, 131; Air Force Academy guest speaker, 104; defense of Haggard, 138; local politics in Colorado, 68; removed from Focus on the Family, 140; on secular humanism, 64
Dog Training, Fly Fishing, and Sharing Christ in the 21st Century (Haggard), 127
Donner, Robert, 30
Douglas, James, 96
Dubofsky, Jean, 89

Eagle Forum, 68, 82
Eastman, Dick, 2, 52, 124, 134–35
Economic Development Corporation (EDC), 45, 77
Economic Development Group, 46
Eisenhower, Dwight, 14
Eldredge, John, 82–83
Elliston, Edgar, 133–34
El Paso County, Colorado, 22; employment statistics, 55; religious demographics, 54; tax structures, 42. *See also* Colorado Springs, Colorado
El Pomar Foundation, 45–46, 50
Engel v. Vitale, 100
Episcopal Church, 98
Equality Colorado, 71
Equal Protection Clause, 88, 89
Equal Rights, Not Special Rights (ERNSR), 84
Eskridge, Larry, 141
Establishment Clause, 65, 101, 108, 110
Evangelical Christian Publishers Association, 119
evangelical movement: businesslike aspects of, 36–37; centrality and impact of, 17–18; Christianity fused with military power, 96–97; and Cold War, impact of, 6; Colorado Springs as center of, 3–4, 53–58; conversion, religious, as goal, 14–15; definitions, 4–5; emergence and early history (mid-twentieth century), 4; and militaristic language, 122–23; missionary work and global vision, 130; neo-evangelical version of fundamentalism (1930s/40s), 13–21; The Net coalition, 130–31; and Northeastern and Midwestern cities, 12–13; person-to-person, 20–21; structure of movement, 5–6; Trump, support for, 140–41. *See also* neo-evangelical movement
"Evangelical Vatican," 53–58
Evans, Richard, 86–87
Evans v. Romer, 85–90
Every Home for Christ, 2, 51, 52, 124, 134–35

faith financing, 18–19
Falcon Lair Foundation, 29
Family Research Council, 89–90
Family Research Institute, 83
Fantus Company (consulting firm), 44–45
Fellowship of Christian Athletes, 5, 13, 103
First Amendment: Establishment Clause, 65, 101, 108, 110
First Christian Church, Colorado Springs, 2, 3
First Congregational Church of Fort Collins v. Wright, 37
First Things (conservative journal), 73
Focus on the Family, 35–36, 49–51, 82, 83; and culture wars, 60
forest fires (1948), 11–12
Formosa Crusades, 48
Foursquare Gospel Church, 91
Freedom Schools, 13, 30–34
Freedom Watch (Citizens Project newsletter), 57
Free Press (newspaper), 33
Frey, William, 41

friendship, and fundraising, 18–19
Friendship International, 52
Fuller, Charles, 18–19, 24, 61
Fuller, Grace, 18–19
Fuller Theological Seminary, 13, 19, 116; Academic Symposium on Power Evangelicalism, 126; Institute of Youth Ministries, 133; MC510: Signs & Wonders course, 118; School of World Missions, 118
fundamentalism, 13–21. *See also* evangelical movement
fundraising: faith financing, 18–19; shift from faith-based to strategy, 19–20

Garden of the Gods, 1–3, *3*
Gay and Lesbian Alliance Against Defamation, 73
Gay Politics vs. Colorado (Bransford), 79, 81
gay rights: campaign against, 59–90; Glen Eyrie meeting (1994), 59; and home rule in Colorado, 66, 67; "No Special Rights/Privileges" slogan, 68, 69, 71–72, 84–85, 89
Gazette Telegraph (newspaper), 29, 33, 53–54
General Conference of the Church of God (Seventh Day), 39
General Conference of the Church of God v. Carper, 39, 40
Generals of Intercession ministry, 119, 135
George, Robert, 87
Girl Scouts of America, 29
Glen Eyrie, 23, 25–27, *26*; campaign against gay rights, 1994 meeting, 59; CFV conferences, 81–83; and fundraising, 27; funds for purchase, 28
Global Harvest Ministries, 133
Global Mapping International, 51–52
Goldwater, Barry, 30
Goldwater Republicans, 62
Gospel Truth (television program), 140
Graham, Billy, 13–14, 20–21, 23–24, 116, 141, 142; Glen Eyrie, 26

Graham, Ruth, 26
Grand View Hotel, 62
Grant, Amy, 119, 120
Greater Europe Mission, 13
Green, Richard, 87
Ground Zero (gay rights organization), 73

Haggard, Gayle, 127
Haggard, Ted, 10, 55, 115–16, 126–33, *128*, 141–42; and antigay movement, 136–37; exposure of illicit activity of, 137–38; as leader of spiritual warfare movement, 136–37; media coverage of, 131; political involvement, 131–32; public confession of, 138; and World Prayer Center, 132–33
Hand, William Brevard, 65
Hands Off Washington, 85
Hanifen, Richard, 131
Hankamer, Earl, 24
Hardy, Porter, 96
Hargis, Billy James, 61–63; sexual misconduct allegations against, 62–63
Harmon, Hubert, 94
Hawaii, and same-sex marriage, 89
Hayek, Friedrich, 30
Hayford, Jack, 119
HCJB (missionary radio station), 14, 24, 52
Hefley, Joel, 133
Helmers & Howard, 53
Henderson, William C., 33
Hill, Guss, 23, 27
Hoiles, R. C., 29–33
Homosexual Network, The (Rueda), 63–64, 81
Homosexual Revolution (Noebel), 63
Hoover, J. Edgar, 28
Hope College, 61
Hosmer, Bradley, 105–6, 108
Hostetler, John, 113
House Committee on Armed Services, 112
Huckabay, Gary, 104
Human Rights Campaign Fund, 84

Index   203

Hunter, James Davison, 65–66, 87–88
Hybl, Bill, 45–46

I AM movement, 28–29
Idaho: Proposition 1 (1994), 85
International Bible Society, 2, 48, 52
International Ministries Fellowship, 53
International Students Inc., 34
Inter-Varsity Christian Fellowship, 15
Invisible War, The (Barnhouse), 117, 121
Iranian Revolution, 130
Irwin, Jim, 104
Isaac, Robert, 35
Islam, 130

Jacobs, Cindy, 119, 124–25, 135, 138
Jericho Center for Global Evangelism, 135
Jericho Hour, The (Eastman), 135
Jessen, Paul, 77
John Birch Society, 31, 62
Jones, Clarence, 14, 24
Jones, Mike, 137–38
Jones, Walter, 113
Junior Achievement, 45

Kay, Douglas, 81
Kemp v. Pillar of Fire, 37
Kennedy, Anthony, 89
Kerry, John, 136
Keswick Conferences, 117
King's Business, The (periodical), 17
Koch, Charles, 31
Koop, C. Everett, 83
Kraft, Charles, 119
Kuiper, Bernie, 134
Ku Klux Klan, 9

LaHaye, Tim, 6
Last of the Giants, The (Otis), 123, 130
Lausanne Congress on World
    Evangelization, 118–19
LeFevre, Lois, 30
LeFevre, Robert, 28–34
Leslie, Kristen, 91–92, 105, 109, 112
Lewis, C. S., 62, 81, 117

Lewis, Michael, 73
liberalism, stereotype of, 46–47
libertarianism, 30, 33
Liberty Park (proposed theme park), 44
List, Martin, 43
Los Angeles riots (1992), 130–31
Love, Robert D., 31
Luce, Albert W., 1
Lutton, Wayne C., 64

MacArthur, Douglas, 14
Magnuson, Roger, 82
Maguire, Russell, 24
Mahon, George, 96
Makepeace, Mary Lou, 78, 133
Mansfield, Harvey, 87
Marco, Tony, 66–69, 86
Marmor, Judd, 87
Martin, Edward, 14
Martinez, Shirley, 109–10
Master Books, 52
Maurer, Mary Anne, 41
Maurer v. Young Life, 41
McCarthy, Joseph, 62
McCartney, Bill, 68, 83
McCormick, Brian, 67–68
McGavran, Donald, 118
McGlone v. First Baptist Church, 37
MCI (telecommunications company), 55
McPherson, Aimee Semple, 15, 141
Melodyland Christian Center, 126
Merrill, John O., 95
Methodist Cadet Fellowship, 104
Mighty I AM movement, 28–29
military forces: Navigators ties to, 17;
    presence in Colorado Springs, 42–43.
    See also Air Force Academy
Military Religious Freedom Foundation,
    113
Miller, John, 86
Miller, Steven, 111
Milliken, Roger, 31
Milwaukee Bible College, 61
Ministries Today (magazine), 126
Miracle Book Club, 15

miracles, 24–25. *See also* providence
Missionary Church, 46
Missionary Training International, 52
missionary work and global vision, 130
Mitchell, John, 19
Moorman, Thomas S., 101
moral decline, United States, 17–18
Morton, MeLinda, 92, 112, 113
Moyers, Bill, 131
Müller, George, 18, 19
Murder, Violence, and Homosexuality (Cameron), 83
mythology, classical, in school curricula, 56–57

National Association of Evangelicals, 19, 115, 116, 136
National Conference on Ministry to the Armed Forces (NCMAF), 110–11
National Day of Prayer, 14, 109
National Endowment for the Arts, 131
National Gay and Lesbian Task Force, 73
nationalism, 4, 6–7
National Legal Foundation, 65, 68
National Opinion Research Center polls, 87
National Prayer Breakfast, 104
National Test Facility (supercomputer simulations), 43
Navigators, 15–17; Air Force Academy fellowship, 104; and Billy Graham crusades, 21; evangelism, centrality of, 17–18; and fundraising, 19–20; Glen Eyrie purchase, 25–27, 26; language of providence, 25; move to Colorado Springs, 23; person-to-person evangelization, 20–21; property, need for, 20–21; and Young Life, cooperation with, 18
neo-evangelical movement, 13–21; business leaders, partnerships with, 27–28; government, opposition to, 32–34; patriotism, as tool, 18; Summit Ministries, 61–62. *See also* evangelical movement

The Net (evangelical coalition), 130–31
Netsch, Walter, 95
New Apostolic Reformation, 138
New Holy War, The (PBS special), 73
New Life (megachurch), 3–4, 55, 104, 115, 126, 127; and warfare prayer, 129; worship center construction (2004), 136, 137
Noebel, David, 61–64, 66–67, 82
North American Aerospace Defense Command (NORAD), 133
North American Conference on Strategic-Level Prayer, 126
Norton, Gale, 86, 87
"No Special Rights/Privileges" slogan, 68, 69, 71–72, 84–85, 89
Nyack, New York, 47

Obergefell v. Hodges, 141
Obey, David, 112–13
OC International, 48
Officers' Christian Fellowship, 104
Old Fashioned Revival Hour (radio program), 18, 24, 61
Olsen, Mark, 79–81
Operation Rescue, 131
Oral Roberts University, 126
Oregon: Measure 9 (1992), 70–71, 85; Measure 13 (1994), 85
Oregon Citizens Alliance (OCA), 69, 71, 88
Orlando, Florida, 49
Orsi, Robert, 125
Otis, George, 123, 130, 138
Overseas Crusades, 13

Palmer, William Jackson, 7–8, 23
parachurch ministries, 5; place as factor in fundraising, 12–13
Pasadena, California, 126
Path Levelers, 53
patriotism, 7. *See also* Christian nationalism
Pegler, Westbrook, 29
Penn-Lewis, Jessie, 117

Penrose, Spencer, 8–9, 45
Pentecostalism, 116–17
People for the American Way, 57
Peretti, Frank, 119–21, 128
Perkins, Will, 67, 69, 76–78, 81, 84, 86
Perry, Samuel, 6–7
Piercing the Darkness (Peretti), 119–21, 132
Pikes Peak region, 22. *See also* El Paso County, Colorado
Polis, Jared, 140
Powell, Jim, 2
prayer: mass prayer, 133; prayer chains, 132; in public schools, 100; and spiritual warfare movement, 123–24; warfare prayer, 128–29
Prayer Corps, 134
Presbyterian Cadet Fellowship, 104
Price, James E., 106
Primary Purpose (Haggard), 127
Prison Fellowship Ministries, 35
prosperity gospel, 141
providence, 24–25
publishing companies, 52–53
Pueblo, Colorado, 28

Rabey, Steve, 53–54
racism and segregation, 32
railroad construction, 8
Rampart College, 32–33
Rayburn, Jim, 11–12, 15–17, 19–20, 22–23, 25, 27, 141–42
Reagan, Ronald, 43–44
Refuge (Olsen), 79–81
religion, as term for tax purposes, 39
Rendell, Edward, 73
Republican Party, 60; evangelical ties in twenty-first century, 142; Republican National Convention (1992), 79; use of culture wars issues, 70
Restoration Fellowship Foursquare Gospel Church, 77
Revenue Act (1894), 37
revivalism, 5, 13
Robb, John, 119
Roberts, Evan, 117

Robertson, A. Willis, 95
Robertson, Pat, 6, 65, 68
Rockefeller, John D., Jr., 8
Roe v. Wade, 63
Romer, Roy, 41, 86
Romero, Angela, 86
Romney, Mitt, 142
Roosevelt, Franklin D., 29
Rueda, Enrique, 63–64, 81
Ryle, James, 81

same-sex marriage/partnerships, 89, 137, 141
San Diego, California, 6
Sanny, Lorne, 47
Scalia, Antonin, 89
Schemo, Diana, 113
Scott, Robert "Rocky," 46
Screwtape Letters, The (Lewis), 117
Scrivner, Errett, 95
secular humanism: in Alabama textbook case, 65; portrayed as in conflict with Christianity, 64–65; used as label for opposition, 60, 63
Sentinel Group, 123
Sharlet, Jeff, 136
Sheets, Dutch, 123–24, 135, 138
Shoemaker, Harold D., 101
Shuttle Operations Planning Complex, 43
Sieminski, Alfred, 96
Silvoso, Edgardo, 122
SIM (Sudan Interior Mission), 47
Simpson, A. B., 47
Singin' River Ranch, 39
Skidmore, Owings & Merrill (architectural firm), 95
Skinner, Betty Lee, 17, 20
Skipworth, David, 56–57
Skorman, Richard, 76
Slaughter of the Innocent (Noebel), 63
Smith, Michael W., 119
Smith v. Board of School Commissioners of Mobile County, 65, 87
Snyder, Greg, 56
Souter, David, 89

Southern Baptist Theological Seminary, 104
SPIRE (Special Programs in Religious Education), 104, 108
spiritual warfare movement: Colorado Springs as capital, 136; criticism of, 125–26; demonic power, emphasis on, 117–22; history of and growing influence, 116–26; language of, 115–16; militaristic language, 122–23; and prayer, 123–24; and territoriality, 121; therapeutic elements of, 124; and unity, 125; Wagner's leadership, 116; warfare prayer, 128–29; and worldview, 123–24
Spiritual Warfare Network, 119, 121
Stahl, Ronit, 100
Stalin, Joseph, 29
Star Ranch, 11–12, 23–27; and fundraising, 27; Star Ranch Committee, 27
Stevens, John (pastor), 134
Stevens, John Paul (Supreme Court justice), 88–89
Stone, H. Chase, 31
Strategic Defense Initiative, 43
Summit Ministries, 60–64
Sutton, Matthew, 5

Taft, Robert, 29
Taking America Back for God (Whitehead and Perry), 6–7
Taking Our Cities for God (Wagner), 121
Tarkenton, Fran, 103
tax exemptions for religious institutions, 37–42
Tax Reform Act (1969), 45
Taylor, Herbert J., 19, 23, 25, 27
Taylor, Hudson, 18, 19
Tebedo, Kevin, 67, 69, 70, 76, 77, 81, 86–87
Temko, Allan, 97–98
10/40 window, 133, 135
territoriality, concept of, 121
This Present Darkness (Peretti), 119–20
Tiahrt, Todd, 112
Tomberlin, Jim, 134

Traditional Values Coalition (Anaheim, California), 69, 82
Trans World Radio, 47
Tribe, Laurence, 88, 89
Triggs, Doug, 57, 76
Trotman, Dawson, 15–21, 141, 142; Glen Eyrie purchase, 25–26, *26*
Truman, Harry, 14
Trump, Donald, 140, 142
tuberculosis sanatoriums, 8–9
Twilight Labyrinth, The (Otis), 123
Tymkovich, Timothy, 88–89

Understanding the Times (Noebel), 82
unemployment taxes, religious exemptions, 40
United Methodist Church: Youth Department, 16
United Nations, opposition to, 29
United States: American culture, centrality of religion, 14; Christianization efforts, 13–14; as "Christian nation," 6–7; religious revival post–World War II, 93
United States Day Committee, 29
US Air Force Academy. *See* Air Force Academy
US Space Foundation, 45

Village Seven Presbyterian Church, 67, 134
Virginia Beach, 6

Wagner, C. Peter, 10, 116, 118–19, 121–22; and AD2000 Movement, 133; and militaristic language, 122–23; *Ministries Today* magazine, 126; New Apostolic Reformation, 138; on prayer, 124; survey of Colorado Springs, 134
Wagner Leadership Institute, 133
Walta, Greg, 75–76
War on the Saints (Penn-Lewis and Roberts), 117
Warren, Robert H., 99–101
Warriors Not Wimps for Jesus, 82

Watties, Warren, 91
Wayerhaeuser, C. Davis, 19
Webb, Wilma, 66
Weida, Johnny, 109, 110, 112, 113
Weinstein, Mikey, 92, 109
Welch, Robert, 62
West-Brandt Foundation, 39
West-Brandt Foundation, Inc. v. Carper, 39
Wheaton, Illinois, 135
Wheaton College, 47
White, James W., 131
White, Jerry, 104
Whitehead, Andrew, 6–7
"Why I Use 'Fighting Words'" (Dobson), 64
Williamson, Jack D., 112
Wimber, John, 118
Wommack, Andrew, 139–42
Woodbridge, John D., 64
Woodland Park, Colorado, 139–40
Woodmen Valley Chapel, 104, 134
World Missions for Jesus, 127
World Prayer Center, 115–16, 132–33
World Vision, 5, 13, 119
World War II: patriotism tied to Christianity, 2, 5–6
Worrell, Alice Neddo, 46–49, 52, 54–55

Yoido Full Gospel Church, 129
Young Life Campaign v. Patino, 40
Young Life ministry, 11–12, 15–16; evangelism, centrality of, 17–18; exemption from Colorado unemployment tax, 40; fundraising, 19–20, 27; language of providence, 25; move to Colorado Springs, 22–23; and Navigators, cooperation with, 18; relocation to Colorado Springs, 27; sleepaway camps, 20–21; Star Ranch purchase, 23–27; tax exemption for religious purposes, 38–41
youth evangelization: popular youth as targets, 15–16
Youth for Christ (YFC), 5, 13, 48

Zielinski, Constantine, 94
Zuckert, Eugene, 97

www.ingramcontent.com/pod-product-compliance
Lightning Source LLC
Chambersburg PA
CBHW032023230426
43671CB00005B/188